Salvage

Salvage

*Cultural Resilience among
the Jorai of Northeast Cambodia*

Krisna Uk

Cornell University Press
Ithaca and London

Copyright © 2016 by Cornell University

All rights reserved. Except for brief quotations in a review, this book, or parts thereof, must not be reproduced in any form without permission in writing from the publisher. For information, address Cornell University Press, Sage House, 512 East State Street, Ithaca, New York 14850.

First published 2016 by Cornell University Press

First printing, Cornell Paperbacks, 2016

Printed in the United States of America

Library of Congress Cataloging-in-Publication Data

Names: Uk, Krisna, 1975– author.
Title: Salvage : cultural resilience among the Jorai of northeast
    Cambodia / Krisna Uk.
Description: Ithaca : Cornell University Press, 2016. | Includes
    bibliographical references and index.
Identifiers: LCCN 2016019499 | ISBN 9781501703027 (cloth : alk. paper) |
    ISBN 9781501703034 (pbk. : alk. paper)
Subjects: LCSH: Jarai (Southeast Asian people)—Cambodia—Rôtânôkiri
    (Province) | Ethnology—Cambodia—Rôtânôkiri (Province)
Classification: LCC DS554.46.J37 S25 2016 | DDC 305.899/22—dc23
LC record available at https://lccn.loc.gov/2016019499

Cornell University Press strives to use environmentally responsible suppliers and materials to the fullest extent possible in the publishing of its books. Such materials include vegetable-based, low-VOC inks and acid-free papers that are recycled, totally chlorine-free, or partly composed of nonwood fibers. For further information, visit our website at www.cornellpress.cornell.edu.

Cloth printing   10 9 8 7 6 5 4 3 2 1

Paperback printing 10 9 8 7 6 5 4 3 2 1

To Dr. Someth Uk

Contents

List of Figures — ix
List of Text Boxes — x
Preface — xi
Acknowledgments — xxx

1. Ways of Being Jorai — 1
2. Local Lives Caught in the Storm of Global History — 34
3. Postconflict Strategies of the Jorai *Homo Faber* — 74
4. Adjusting Rituals — 110
5. Aesthetic Forms of Memory — 145

6. Leu, Present and Future	175
Conclusion	206
References	211
Index	219

Figures

1. Leu villagers	xxi
2. Bombing map of Ratanakiri	83
3. Hunting for the bombs	86
4. Plane flying for Veam's funeral, Leu village	112
5. Author's reproduction of carved motifs on Siu's bamboo pipe	152
6. Beuragn reproducing a *pósat atâo* on paper	154
7. Author's reproduction of Beuragn's illustration of a *pósat atâo*, Plói Peuho, O You Dav district, Ratanakiri	156
8. Girls carving water gourds, Plói Mek	162
9. Sing wearing some of her creations, posing with her husband and son	167

Text Boxes

1. Historical aide-mémoire	39
2. An account by Pol Pot's adolescent Jorai bodyguard	47
3. The Ho Chi Minh Trail	53
4. Memories of a survivor of the US bombing	60
5. Jorai war song in the fashion of a funerary song	62
6. The bombing data: Secrecy, conspiracy, and persistent uncertainties	64
7. Testimony of a former Khmer Rouge soldier	67

Preface

Locating Plói Leu

The first time I went to Andong Meas district, Ratanakiri province, a tropical typhoon was hitting Vietnam, and the rain had flooded most of the roads winding through the forests and the mountains of this remote area of northeastern Cambodia. As I looked for traces of the conflicts of four decades earlier, which had dragged this hitherto-neglected region of Southeast Asia into the eye of a global political storm, the feeling I experienced upon reaching my final destination was one of utter remoteness.

The village to which I had traveled—named Leu (or Plói Leu in the Jorai language)—was formerly part of what Americans called the Ho Chi Minh Trail, a complex transportation corridor of immense military and political significance. Today Leu can be reached only by tracing a single-track dirt road that threads its way from the small market town of O'Kop through the forest to the southern bank of the Sesan River. The village is home to some three hundred people, comprising twenty-seven families of the Jorai ethnic minority and three families of Khmers, the dominant ethnic group in Cambodia.

Jean Delvert wrote that the penetration of the Jorai into Cambodia started from the east, along either side of the Srepok River, a tributary of the Mekong, but neither he nor any other scholar has offered a precise time frame during which this migration took place (Delvert 1961).[1] Jacques Dournes once described this area, which straddles the highlands of Vietnam and Cambodia, as an "axe naturel" (natural axis) or as a major "artery of the Jorai country" (Dournes 1972: 18). My Leu informants told me that the Jorai had been settled in this part of Cambodia for several generations, and Ratanakiri province is now officially home to around 20,000 of them; the main population concentrations are found in the districts of Bokeo, Andong Meas, and O You Dav (Ironside 2013; Bourdier 2014).[2] Vietnamese official records, meanwhile, estimate that the Jorai population in Vietnam is 330,000 people, who are mostly spread across the Central Highlands of the southern Annam Cordillera (Goy and Coué 2006; Michaud 2006; Lap 2009).[3] Every Jorai I worked with in Leu has relatives living near Pleiku (Plói Ku) and Kontum. Regardless of their age, all my informants, from village elders to teenagers, claimed that the Vietnamese highlands were the place where their forefathers had been born, where they had waged wars, and from where they had traveled extensively.

Ratanakiri province, which is bordered by Laos to the north and Vietnam to the east, forms an integral part of what James Scott described as "one of the largest remaining nonstate spaces in the world, if not *the* largest, . . . the vast expanse of uplands, variously termed the Southeast Asian *massif* and, more recently, Zomia" (Scott 2009: 13). According to Scott, the multiple and diverse communities who lived "relatively free" in Zomia (Scott

---

1. The Sesan and Srepok are both tributaries of the Mekong River.

2. "The Jarai number around 320,000 in Central Vietnam and 20,000 in Ratanakiri" (Ironside 2013: 391). According to Frédéric Bourdier, there are 20,781 of them living in Ratanakiri (Bourdier 2014: 7).

3. Siu Lap provided the following figures: 350,766 Jorai living in Vietnam (sourced from the Vietnam News Agency 2006), 20,149 in Ratanakiri province and 93 in Mondulkiri province (according to the Ratanakiri Provincial Department of Planning 2006 and the Mondulkiri Department of Planning 2004 respectively) (Lap 2009: 8).

2009: 19) used different approaches to elude the control of the state. Such approaches to escape "subordination, assimilation or annihilation" (see Michaud 2006: 23–25) included exploiting geographic remoteness and difficult terrain, avoiding use of scripture, and having a diverse and adaptable livelihood. Scott suggested that it may well have served the purpose of these societies to become "barbarian by design" (Scott 2009: 8). Although Scott acknowledged that his main arguments cannot be supported beyond the Second World War, the livelihoods of the villagers I worked with may demonstrate how particular skills necessary to the art of not being governed were and today still are much practiced by resourceful, ingenious, and creative individuals who may want to evade—and sometimes appropriate—various manifestations of external power.

Inspiration for My Research

The original source of inspiration for my research came from my experience working with Norwegian People's Aid in the field of land mine and unexploded ordnance (UXO) clearance in northwestern Cambodia and southern Laos between 2002 and 2005. In Cambodia, most of the national mine and UXO clearance work focuses on the northwestern part of the country along the international border with Thailand, where successive ground battles and guerrilla incursions left vast swathes of overlapping minefields.

The northeastern and eastern sides of the country, where the defining physical legacy of the conflicts is UXO left by US bombing, have been perceived very differently. Mine-action experts generally assume that because of the nature of the explosives used in the area (larger explosive items that are more visible on the ground), local populations have been better able to cope with this human-made source of risk. This assumption is further supported by the relatively low number of yearly casualties. Data collected between 1979 and 2015 by the Cambodian Mine Action and Victim Assistance Authority reveal 64,579 recorded accidents that were caused by antipersonnel landmines and explosive remnants of war (ERW). The northwest provinces of Battambang (with 15,523 accidents), Banteay Meanchey (8,854), and Siem Reap (8,029) are the most affected nationwide. In comparison, casualty data for the province of Ratanakiri show that 270 recorded accidents (of which 103 due to antipersonnel mines and 167 to ERW) have occurred in the space of 36 years.

The low population density that characterizes the northeastern part of the country and the difficult road conditions are other factors that make the region a low priority in national plans for combined clearance and development projects. One of my motivations for conducting research in this part of the country was to get better insight into the ways people were living amid the remnants of war.

The Jorai

This book focuses on the Jorai in Ratanakiri province for three reasons. The first reason is that they are one of the ethnic minorities in Ratanakiri whose cemeteries were strikingly beautiful, integrating modern weapons and scenes of armed conflict through sculptures and painting. The second is that the inhabitants of Leu were the most welcoming when I proposed to settle in their village and study the ways in which they adapted to past conflicts. The third is that in both Cambodia and Vietnam, the Jorai have been traditionally perceived by others as the most belligerent and skilled at the art of war. For this specific reason, their role in major conflicts is historically significant. Accounts of the great Jorai warriors, whose formidable reputation was well described by Christian missionaries, French colonial officials, and foreign travelers, date back to the nineteenth century. In the 1970s, the US Army trained Jorai people to join its special forces, while Pol Pot employed them as his bodyguards because he felt that their knowledge of the jungle, combined with their interest in revolutionary ideas and their fighting skills, made them the most dependable fighters.

I examine the encounter between technological warfare and a group of people who until the second half of the twentieth century were still widely considered the most remarkable warriors in the region, and I explore the ways in which the inhabitants of a Jorai village in northeastern Cambodia have adjusted to thirty years of conflicts that have destroyed their human-made and natural environments. This is an ethnography of how a subsistence farming village has rebuilt life after successive wars, which featured the Americans' intense bombardment of the region from the mid-1960s to 1973 and the brutal Khmer Rouge regime in Cambodia from 1975 to 1979.[4] To this end, my central focus is to investigate the wide range of local coping mechanisms that people have used since the beginning of these protracted conflicts, which continue to shape the social, political, and spiritual life of the people of Leu. In postconflict areas where bomb remnants and ritually unburied dead may lie dormant under the surface, coping mechanisms include individual and collective bodily and symbolic practices that enable people to manage the violence brought on them by the succession of wars.

Ethnic-minority villagers living in these northeastern fringes of Cambodia—older and younger generations alike—continue to find new meanings in these traumatic events and new ways of adjusting to their multifaceted and lasting consequences. There is now an emerging body of literature devoted to postconflict life in countries affected by land mines and unexploded ordnance. However, few of these studies provide a comprehensive analysis of the resilience of rural life in environments contaminated by ERW. Investigating the day-to-day livelihoods of Leu subsistence farmers in this historical and physical context is an attempt to increase our understanding of postconflict communities.

A Note on the Concept "Ethnic Minority"

Various terms, such as "montagnards," "highlanders," "ethnic groups," "indigenous peoples," and "indigenous hill tribes," have been used in the literature on the region to describe its inhabitants (Meyer 1965; Salemink 2002, 2004; Bourdier 2006, 2014; Michaud 2006; Baird 2011). For Ian Baird,

> The meaning of "indigenous peoples" is, however, far from obvious or simple. Its application is complex and frequently in flux, and like so many other identities associated with nationality, religion, class, ethnicity and gender, its use has political implications and is thus often contested. Its meaning varies greatly depending on the places where it is applied, the time and context it is used, and the different peoples who employ it. Some fully endorse the concept, others acknowledge that indigenous peoples exist but deny efforts by

---

4. The bombing campaign affected Vietnam, the Lao PDR, and Cambodia; official data show that the bombardment of Cambodia started in 1969, but unofficial records indicate that it started much earlier (Kiernan 1996; Shawcross 1993; Taylor and Kiernan 2006).

certain groups to be classified as such, and there are many who refuse to accept the idea at all. (Baird 2011: 155)

I use the term "ethnic minority" to mean "an ethnolinguistic group, which differs from the majority of the population owing to their distinct culture, language, economic or political practices and their relationship with their environment and the land of their ancestors." Although this definition often does not reflect the ways people view themselves but rather takes the perspective of the outsider looking in, it nonetheless serves two related purposes. First, it highlights the cultural distinctiveness of the various groups of peoples who live in this particular region. Second, it differentiates them from the more numerous and politically dominant Khmers, who mostly live in Cambodia's lowlands.[5]

The population of Cambodia is officially composed of 90% Khmers (*chonchiet Kmay*) and 10% Chinese, Vietnamese, Lao, Cham, and highland peoples (NGO Forum 2006; Bourdier 2014).[6] Joanna White, an anthropologist who conducted research among ethnic-minority villages in northeastern Cambodia, commented that the Khmer word *chonchiet* (nationality) was in widespread use locally as a label for minorities (White 1995: 48). On its own, *chonchiet* has limited value as a means of describing or identifying people. However, this does not stop many Khmers from using it as a generic term to designate all the peoples living in the highlands, regardless of the kaleidoscope of cultural differences that exist between and among them.[7]

---

5. According to Jean-Michel Filippi: "Some minorities can be immediately located on the map. They are essentially the 'Proto-Indochinese' minorities from the Austroasiatic and Austronesian families who have occupied the same territory without substantial changes for centuries if not millenniums. The territories concerned are located on the periphery of the actual Kingdom of Cambodia, in the northeast and the northwest, as well as in the Cardamom Mountains" (Filippi 2008: 58).

6. For Bourdier, however, "Some villages are starting to include non indigenous individuals, mostly in the central part of Preah Vihear and to a smaller extent in some locations in Ratanakiri where they cohabit with Lao, Cham and Khmer peoples" (Bourdier 2014: 8).

7. For Jean Michaud, the word "group" was equally problematic because it mistakenly conveys the idea that people may form a homogeneous entity, which, as he pointed out, is often not the case (Michaud 2006). According to Jacques Dournes, the Jorai consider themselves part of a large family, but they differentiate themselves on the basis of local distinctions, which have generated group names as follows: Arap, Hödrung, Pö'uh, Cöbuan or Töbuan, Cor, Hroai, and Mthur (Dournes 1972).

The people I worked with in Leu, as well as in other neighboring Jorai villages, used the term *chonchiet* together with the word "Jorai." My informants, regardless of age or gender, called themselves *chonchiet Jorai*. Conversely, the ethnonym Khmer Leu (literally "Khmer above," used by Sihanouk during the period of the "community of the common people," more commonly known as the Sangkum Reastr Niyum, in power from 1955 to 1970), which differentiates people according to mere geographic elevations, as the colonial French had done previously (Diguet 1908), bears resemblance to what Christian Postert described in Laos as the predominance of geomorphological variations over cultural differences that construct ethnic-minority identities. For Postert, "Affiliation to a different ethnic identity is conceived to be less important than affiliation to a preferred area of settlement, for instance the valleys, the mountain slopes or the mountain tops of Laos. The result is a trinomial model that only knows three meta-ethnic groups" (Postert 2004: 103). Lao Loum or "Lao of the Valleys," Lao Theung or "Lao of the Mountain Slopes," and Lao Soung or "Lao of the Mountaintops" became the three major categories that were imposed on them. Likewise, Sihanouk's coined expression Khmer Leu absorbs the diversity of the ethnic minorities living in the north into one discrete group. Khmer Leu is not an expression that my Jorai informants use as a mode of self-representation. As White noted in the case of the Brao: "None of the villagers we met during this research referred to themselves as Khmer-Leu, though some were aware of this term as a label applied to them from the outside. This does not mean they have no notion of themselves belonging to the country of Cambodia, but this is defined in their own right, through their membership of particular ethnic groups."

According to Ian Baird,

> After Cambodia achieved independence from colonial France in 1953–4, Norodom Sihanouk embarked on a nation-building programme. As part of this effort, a new classification system was developed that resulted in the application of the terms *Khmer Loeu, Khmer Kraom* and *Khmer Islam*. The majority Khmer population became known as the *Khmer Kandal*, or middle or central Khmer. . . . Sihanouk also introduced *bong pa-on chun chiet* (ethnic brothers and sisters), a term with a neutral literal meaning (equality and relationship between peoples), yet very paternalistic overtones, with the Khmer seen as being the elder sibling in the relationship. (Baird 2011: 162)

Leu villagers use ethnonyms like Jorai Kampuchea or Jorai Vietnam to draw attention to perceived discrepancies between Jorai living in Cambodia and those living across the border. Many Jorai people in Cambodia perceive their cousins in Vietnam as enjoying a greater level of prosperity, for example (see chapter 3). Memories of the great Jorai warriors are primarily associated with areas within present-day Vietnam. Charles Meyer, a former adviser to King Sihanouk, observed: "Among the neighboring tribes the Jorai earned the reputation for being very warlike. Their relatively recent raids against the Rhade, Bahnar, and the Brao are still fresh in people's minds and are mentioned with some dread. Moreover, the Jorai are the only true horsemen in the region, and people say that in the past, during their expeditions, the warriors gave strength and courage to their mounts by feeding them the livers of their enemies killed in combat. Truth or myth, nobody knows" (Meyer 1965: 14). My informants in Leu linked their recollections of the Jorai who waged war on their neighbors and raided entire villages to capture slaves to a particular time and place. As some of them put it, "They were living at the time of the great-great-grandfathers in Vietnam."

Leu villagers often travel back to those places where their ancestry is deeply rooted, spending a few days in the villages that their grandparents came from and sometimes returning in the company of some relatives. Jacques Dournes described the Jorai with whom he lived as always trading, hunting, and conducting explorations across the border, for there was "no frontier for them, of course" (Dournes 1972). At the time of my research between 2007 and 2009, cross-border movements between Cambodia and Vietnam remained frequent despite severe restrictions imposed by both governments. These restrictions were introduced in the context of waves of ethnic-minority families fleeing political repression in Vietnam over the course of a decade (Hickey 2002; Lap 2009).[8] This issue remains a source of anxiety for people living in Leu and other Jorai villages in the same commune whose kin live only a short distance across the border. Indeed, those hosting family members from Vietnam for long stays without official ap-

---

8. "In 2001 and the following years, thousands of Montagnards in the Central Highlands protested against the Vietnamese government's exploitation of their lands, the closure of their local churches, and the imprisonment of Montagnard church leaders. As a result of harsh government reaction to these protests, many Montagnards fled to Cambodia" (Lap 2009: 10); *Human Rights Watch Report* 2011, 2015.

proval risk heavy fines and even incarceration in jail. As Jean Michaud argued:

> At present, perhaps only Cambodia does not have issues with its very small number of highland minorities, except ... when these are actually ethnic Vietnamese who settled in the eastern provinces during various waves of pioneering migration, the latest being during the decade-long occupation of the country by Vietnamese troops from 1979 to 1989. A mild concern is currently expressed about some other highland minorities presently filtering through from Vietnam's Central Highlands, looking for economic opportunities or taking refuge from their government's political exactions. (Michaud 2006: 25)

Although the imposed international border has today acquired physical, legal, and economic manifestations (local inhabitants are officially required to submit a request and pay a fee at the district level to cross the border), this has not proved a sufficient deterrent to some of my informants, who continue to travel back and forth and try to bring in relatives in order, as they told me, "to all live together!"

Literature on the Jorai

Most of the literature portraying the Jorai dates from the late nineteenth century. Since that time French colonial administrators' reports, Christian missionaries' memoirs, and explorers' notes have contributed to the construction and representation, often critical, of the Jorai person (e.g., Pavie 1898; Cupet 1900; Maître 1912; Simonnet 1977).

Jacques Dournes, who was ordained a priest in 1945 and was subsequently sent to Vietnam by the Missions Etrangères de Paris, took a rather different spiritual and professional route in his interactions with Jorai people, however. After living for twenty-five years in the Vietnamese Central Highlands, "L'homme des Jarai," as he is known in the anthropological milieu in France, found in the "anarchic" belief system of his informants an illustration of genuine faith (Goy and Coué 2006; Hardy 2015). Using the most meticulous ethnographic approach to record the daily livelihood, language, surrounding flora, myths, and cosmology of the persons he lived with, Dournes built a remarkably rich and comprehensive literature on the Jorai of this particular area. One of my objectives in this book is to further the existing limited literature on the Jorai of northeastern Cambodia, who comprise a less studied ethnic minority. Where references to the Jorai of Vietnam are possible, relevant, and illuminating, I have used Dournes's ethnographic materials, which include tales and legends, in order to provide greater perspective on the Jorai of Leu with whom I was living.

The Jorai of Leu village

An Austronesian ethnic minority linguistically akin to the Malays and the Chams, the Jorai of Leu speak a Chamic language that belongs to the Malayo-Polynesian language family (Delvert 1961; White 1995; Lap 2009). The Jorai villagers of Leu organize their social structures along matrilineal lines and attach strong importance to kin- and affine-based relationships (Dournes 1972, 1978; Goy and Coué 2006). In the words of Andrew Hardy, "Central to the question was the division between the inside and the outside, between the male and the female in the matrilineal system. The female holds power, but in public she stays in the background, delegating communication with outside to a male relative. People make the distinction between male thunder and female lightning: thunder makes a lot of noise, but no one has ever been struck down by it" (Hardy 2015: 39).

Leu is situated within one of what conservationist groups in Cambodia identify as the last forested areas in the country, a region that is home to primary forest and a number of ethnic minorities with a profound spiritual and economic attachment to the landscape (Bourdier 2006; see figure 1). This area was regarded by the French explorers—and is still viewed by the lowland-dwelling Khmer—as being particularly wild and inhospitable on account of its rugged mountains, dense forests, malevolent spirits (particularly for the Khmers), and its population of "untamed" and "belligerent" inhabitants (Bourdier 2009: 154) (also see Pavie 1898; Cupet 1900; Maître 1912).

My hosts explained to me that until 1997, Leu was located right on the bank of the Sesan River, but after a devastating flu outbreak, its inhabitants had decided to shift the village's location. As a result, Leu was split into three villages. One group of families went across the river to create the village of Leu Pok, while a second also crossed the river but then traveled up the

Figure 1. Leu villagers. Photo by author.

mountain to create the village of Leu Krong. The remaining families remained on the western side of the river and moved to the present location, which retains the village's original name. I was told that the current site was chosen on the basis of a dream of a village elder. At a time when many villagers had died of illnesses, such occurrences were seen as clear signs sent by the spirits to guide the living.

The livelihood of the Jorai inhabitants of Leu is based throughout the year on a range of subsistence-procurement activities. These include small-scale swidden agriculture to allow the cultivation of vegetable plots and orchards (*hwa*), rice cultivation, hunting, fishing, and the collection of nontimber forest products. A few people find seasonal employment in plantations or large farms and occasionally participate in house building in return for wages. James C. Scott and Jean Michaud argued that this range of livelihood activities is a key characteristic of acephalous or headless societies, whereby their relative autonomy enables them to remain beyond the state's control. As Michaud wrote:

> In economic terms, acephalous societies were one of three possible economic systems: hunting-gathering, horticulture, or a simple form of peasantry, a "prefeudal" one. In all cases, the household (a group of individuals linked by blood or alliance and living under the same roof) was the fundamental building block; it also constituted the smallest economic and ritual unit. Subsistence agriculture was the norm, with various degrees of dependency on the market for the provision of indispensable commodities that could not be grown, gathered, or produced locally. (Michaud 2006: 21)

From a political perspective, the Jorai of Leu do indeed seem to fulfill the characteristics of self-governing peoples. According to my informants, there is no village chief in Leu, although a person from Leu Krong occasionally plays a representative and liaison role (*gŏng čô plói*) on behalf of the three villages. On a day-to-day basis, however, Leu village elders (*prĭn tha*) who have experience, good judgment, and knowledge of the past help guide the life of the village and settle any disputes that arise. This political arrangement is in line with Jorai practices in the Central Highlands of Vietnam, as recorded by a handful of French missionaries (Dournes 1972; Simonnet 1977; Hardy 2015). According to one of the Leu elders, the Jorai people of this region never had any chief, for "they were their own kings!"

Complementing all these activities is the salvaging of explosive remnants of war generated by the US bombing. This is a year-round income-generating activity through which men, children, and women alike can actively contribute to the household's resources. It forms an integral part of their livelihood strategy, which draws on their physical ability to adapt to a landscape that still bears the scars of the past conflicts. As late as my last visit in September 2014, the blacksmith of Leu was confident that the wounds of the land could still yield economic opportunities for people to harvest the metal in return for financial gain.

For Michael DiGregorio,

> Scavenging and junk buying have frequently appeared in development literature as symbols of urban environmental deterioration, human degradation and lost hopes. Beyond these images, however, lies a reality in which these disparaged occupations provide refuge for the unemployed, a secure economic niche for particular ethnic, caste, or territorial communities, material inputs for local industries, commodities for export, and a means of diverting large amounts of recoverable materials from landfills and composting

plants.... The informal sector has thus become, at once, an innovative, adaptive and efficient economic sector, and a refuge of the poor. (DiGregorio 1995)

This livelihood strategy is also deeply psychologically anchored since this salvage is not solely limited to physical recovery and transactions. It lies at the heart of the cultural resilience of the people of Leu, which enables them to transform fragments of weapons and painful shards of memory into refashioned and resymbolized objects used in their rituals and day-to-day life.

Methodology

This book draws on research in northeastern Cambodia from September 2007 to June 2008, followed by an additional period in January and February 2009 to gather further information on local funerary rituals and artistic forms of memory transmission and a further visit in September 2014. Ratanakiri was first selected using US Air Force bombing data, which show that the province was one of the most heavily bombed areas of the country. In addition, social and economic information provided by national institutions, nongovernmental organizations (NGOs), land mine–clearance agencies, and independent researchers confirmed that this part of the country and, more specifically, the districts that are closer to the Vietnamese border (Andong Meas and O You Dav) featured a prevalence of scrap-metal trading and reuse of UXO to sustain the local economy of both Khmer and ethnic-minority villages. However, there is very limited literature on this subject because most research projects exploring such themes focus on areas in the northwestern part of the country. I chose to concentrate on Leu because it was one of the places where the material culture associated with the war was most visibly manifested and also where people showed interest in my research project and agreed to host me.

I conducted my research in Jorai, which I learned on-site to a conversational level, as well as in Khmer, which I speak fluently. My closest informants taught me Jorai in exchange for my teaching them English. Qualitative data were collected through semistructured interviews, informal group discussions, and participant observation. In addition, I spent time working with my various informants while they were busy with their daily activities.

Such activities included wood and bamboo carving with the village carver and participating in various chores like wood cutting, working in orchards, and attending village gatherings and rituals, as well as teaching English to both adults and children. My group of informants included a large number of male and female persons, ranging in age from village elders to younger members of the postconflict generation.

To broaden my analysis, I also spent time traveling and conducting research in neighboring districts (O You Dav, Bokeo, Veunsai, and Banlung) in order to map out the diversity with which other Jorai and other ethnic-minority villages (Kreung, Brao, and Tampuon) remember or reinvent their experience of the wars. To this end, chapter 5 discusses the ways two Jorai and two Tampuon ethnic-minority villages from districts near Andong Meas have conceptualized their past by means of object making and ornamentation that is reminiscent of the past conflicts. Although I am not proficient in the Tampuon language, two of my Jorai informants kindly offered to serve as interpreters and accompanied me to these villages to collect information from craftsmen and craftswomen. My intent was to observe and discuss the different stages of object making, starting with sourcing the raw materials, continuing with production and decoration, and finally use of the finished items. This process enabled me to gain insight into the various meanings assigned to the handmade objects imbued with past and new memories of the wars.

This aspect of my research concerning postconflict material culture entailed the collection of locally manufactured objects. These included carved wooden effigies, sculpted bamboo objects, paper drawings, and hand-woven fabrics, as well as everyday objects refashioned from war debris and materials. Whenever possible, I tried not to pay for the items in cash but to barter alternative items, such as bags of rice, for them or to take away new objects from the local or district markets instead of original ones.

The Anthropologist's Place

Heonik Kwon wrote that the "stranger" is an important concept in the anthropological studies of identity and ethnic relations, "a crucial one in the tradition of existential philosophy and critical thought" (Kwon 2008: 20). In the course of an anthropologist's research, locating oneself vis-à-vis the other who, in this case, is the subject of study can be a daunting challenge. One may eventually end up as a "necessary evil" in the life of the people one lives and works with, as Malinowski described himself (Malinowski 1922: 7–8).

Among people in Leu, my position as a stranger (*toäie*) improved over time as I slowly became part of the social landscape. Children, however, needed more time to get used to my distinctive physical appearance (features and height). For them, my efforts to speak Jorai were even more "frightening," suggesting that they may have perceived their native language as a safe buffer separating us. Indeed, the first time I was able to communicate with some of them in Jorai, they reacted with a mixture of surprise and confusion, as if I had truly penetrated their territory, thus drawing closer to them.

Chapter 1 will discuss the subject in greater detail, so it suffices to say that my hybrid or strange position—having Khmer ancestry but not physically resembling a Cambodian Khmer and living abroad—did not prevent me from moving from one social space to another. In other words, although I was, at first, a strange stranger for the majority of the inhabitants of Leu, I became less a stranger, at least in comparison with Khmer outsiders or foreigners who happened to come to the village.

Returning to Leu in 2009 and 2014 greatly helped me maintain my relationship with friends and villagers. Bringing back pictures that I had taken of them enabled me to finally leave behind the garb of the strange stranger and take on the role of an eyewitness from a not-too-distant time when the forest was still surrounding the village.

Orthography

At present, the way in which Jorai words are written does not follow a particular orthography. In light of this lack of any agreed-on convention, I draw mostly on the spelling used in Vietnam. This system was developed by missionaries, notably via the French-Jarai and Jarai-French lexicon devised by R. Nicolle which dates back to 1940.

In regard to the orthography of the word "Jorai," Siu Lap, a US-based Jorai originally from Vietnam, noted that "various groups of people have used different appellations in labeling the Jarai people. These alternative names include Djarai, Gia Rai, Jorai, Chor, Mthur, Chrai, and Gio Rai. . . . The Viet (or Kinh) people used the term *Người Gia Rai* (Gia Rai people).

The French referred to the Jarai as *Jörai*. We, the Jarai people, call ourselves *Jórai*. The Jórai people are known to the Americans as *Jarai*" (Lap 2009: 6). Similarly, Goy and Coué (2006: 17) noted that several orthographies exist among French anthropologists, who use "Jarai, Joraï, Gia Rai and Jörai." In his *Historical Dictionary of the Peoples of the Southeast Asian Massif* Michaud wrote that "Jarai" has been "their most widely used ethnonym among Anglo-Saxon authors during the second Indochina War (1954–75)" (Michaud 2006: 117). My personal inclination, however, was to use the spelling that is closer to the pronunciation of the Jorai of Leu: "DJorai."

Translations

Where my informants used Khmer vocabulary, for example, to convey their experience of the war, I have indicated these words in brackets followed by "in Khmer" before giving their equivalent in English. This is done to distinguish them from the Jorai words that are mostly used in this book. All translations from the original French (Dournes's textual sources and other French-language literature) are my own.

Persons' Names and Places

To preserve the anonymity of my informants, some names of persons and places have been changed.

Outline of the Book

This book is divided into six chapters as follows. Chapter 1 explores the villager's sense of being and the process by which personhood is constructed in Leu. It examines how the individual perceives himself or herself as distinct from other living organisms. It suggests that the relationship with nature—the forest in particular—plays a major role in shaping the individual. In addition, it looks at ways in which encounters with the "stranger" may further the process of personhood as an individual is confronted with such forms of otherness as an ethnic minority living nearby, a relatively distant Khmer, and a foreigner who comes from even more remote, unknown, and strange horizons.

Chapter 2 discusses the civil and regional conflicts that have had a major impact on the lives of the local populations of northeastern Cambodia. It follows a Euro-American chronological time frame, from Cambodia's colonization as a French protectorate to the establishment of a Vietnam-backed government after the demise of the Pol Pot regime. Drawing on my informants' various narrative accounts of individual and collective pasts, it argues that some episodes, like the US bombing, can be seen as particularly traumatic historical events that have torn the fabric of the villagers' daily lives and shaken their religious beliefs to their foundations.

Chapter 3 investigates how, in times of economic crisis, villagers try to find creative, practical, and effective means to prevent the members of the household from falling below the subsistence margin. Its main line of inquiry concerns how, when faced with various sources of risk, individuals are often compelled to turn to a potentially unsafe or harmful activity as an opportunity to preserve their and their relatives' well-being. Such activities range from bomb hunting to body hunting, whereby material, bodily, and sometimes intangible debris of the multiple violent pasts can be collected for protection and for financial and spiritual gains.

Some of the most heavily UXO-affected villages located on the Ho Chi Minh Trail have bridged the divide between continuity and discontinuity by the subtlest means, maintaining personal attachment to particular places and objects. With reference to the Jorai experience of the US bombing in particular, chapter 4 analyzes how traditional practices have successfully incorporated war-derived objects and how old rituals have been revitalized. I use the words "tradition" and "traditional" within the restrictive time frame of one hundred years, since my informants explained that their accounts cannot stretch back further than a century in time. The chapter argues that encounters with dangerous objects can be reenacted through the reproduction and representation of planes and weaponry, and that this symbolic form of appropriation can become a privileged means for people to reconcile themselves to their violent past. To this end, it demonstrates how the meanings conveyed by a tangible object can be subject to new interpretations and positive inversion by survivors as they help (re)construct a collective memory of war. Indeed, through the acts of making, incorporation, and display, war-inspired practices have become therapeutic, meaningful, and aesthetic features for people living in Leu.

The aftermath of war often calls for processes of healing and memory.[9] The work of remembrance and healing is left to the survivors, who seek to maintain the continuity of life despite the discontinuity brought by the violence of the past (Scheper-Hugues and Bourgois 2004; Kwon 2006). Such traces of the past can be found in local aesthetic practices, which simultaneously crystallize, communicate, and transmit individual and collective memory in tangible forms.

In light of this, chapter 5 looks at the role of the craftsperson as a conscious, dedicated, and skillful individual who does not simply create but creates in a beautiful manner. By means of sculpting, painting, carving, or weaving, the produced object becomes the site whereby memories of the past, perceptions of the present, and predictions of the future are simultaneously made visible in aesthetic form. Each object thus produced reflects ways in which affected communities have dealt with the grievous past. As with the reclamation of war-debris materials, the reuse and recycling of war-associated images through wood or bamboo carving, grave painting, and fabric weaving are the visible manifestations of human coping abilities. The main objective of this chapter is to demonstrate that object making enables the craftsperson not only to express the memory of a painful lived or re-counted experience but also to re-create a better past. This chapter is based on the premise that objects derived from craftsmanship and the act of crafting itself can provide a new framework of analysis for the ways postconflict villages interact with their past and the ways some individuals relate to and interpret their elders' historiographies.

Chapter 6 studies the growing effects of globalization on the small village of Leu. It discusses the ways conflict- and postconflict-generation villagers alike find a new form of identity in embracing the world of consumerism and conversion to Christianity. It explores how Leu villagers adjust to the present changes and how they anticipate future challenges and opportunities. It shows that finding one's path may be fraught with social pressures

---

9. Chapter 2 will examine the ways in which people remember, think, and often speak about the successive wars (US bombing, the Khmer Rouge regime, the Vietnamese invasion) as a whole and undivided period of intense and extremely confusing conflict.

as new practices and beliefs create tensions within the community that separate defenders of the village traditions from ambitious and curious younger people who are trying to carve a social, economic, and historical place that they can claim as their own.

The book concludes with an overview of the Jorai of Leu's cultural resilience and the ways their creativity, persistence and power to adapt to even the most harrowing situations turn them into powerful "homo faber," who refuse to surrender to external and seemingly more powerful forces.

Acknowledgments

Many people provided invaluable assistance before, during, and after I conducted my research. I am truly indebted to all my informants from the village of Leu, who have been very generous with their time, knowledge, and hospitality. Nay, Pou Ksor, Luyin Blen and Siu, in particular, have been a real source of inspiration. Without their welcoming the stranger that I was when I first arrived in the village, this ethnographic work would have not been possible. I also thank Leo Howe for having shown genuine interest in this work and for providing extremely useful comments throughout the different stages of writing. I am also indebted to Susan Bayly who gave excellent suggestions on some earlier chapters of this book. Very special thanks go to Robert Fowler for all his advice on the beautiful translations from French to English as well as to Fenella and John Davis for their reading of the book and subsequent words of encouragement.

I take this opportunity to thank the various providers of funding that made my research and this monograph possible. They include the Evans Fund, the William Wyse Studentship, the Crowther Beynon Fund, and the

Darwin College Finley Bursary, as well as the Center for Khmer Studies, which enabled me to extend my research. I am also grateful to the Cambridge European Trust, which financed my doctorate for three consecutive years.

Portions of chapter 5 were previously published as Krisna Uk, "The Symbolic Appropriation of War-made Objects by the Jorai of Northeast Cambodia," in *Southeast Asian Perspectives on Power*, edited by Chua Liana et al., 81–92, London: Routledge: 2012; and Krisna Uk, "Aesthetic Forms of Post-conflict Memory: Inspired Vessels of Memory in Northeast Cambodia," in *Interactions with a Violent Past: Reading Post-Conflict Landscapes in Cambodia, Laos, and Vietnam*, edited by Pholsena Vatthana and Oliver Tappe, 216–240, Singapore: NUS Press: 2013.

Finally, I will always be most grateful to Eden Davis, Michael Davis, Sean Davis, Boromroat Uk, and Someth Uk, who have been continual and invaluable sources of support throughout the long writing process.

Chapter 1

Ways of Being Jorai

Where do the Jorai living in Leu come from? What makes the Jorai person? How does a Jorai person relate to, or set himself or herself apart from, the multiple forms of otherness? The question of Jorai personhood represents a point of departure from which interrelated themes will weave through the discussions of the following chapters. Using Tim Ingold's working definition of personhood as that "in which the self is seen to inhere in the unfolding of the relation set up in virtue of its positioning in an environment" (Ingold 2000: 11), this introductory chapter seeks to take the reader on an exploration of the Jorai persons I worked with.

The first part of this chapter examines how being a Jorai in Leu is a crafting process that is continually influenced by time, place, and social life. It analyzes how personhood is constructed through humans' relationships with nature and the ways villagers physically and spiritually set themselves apart from it. A potent boundary marker, a person's view of nature is a determining factor of personal and group making, but it is by no means the sole dynamic at work.

The second part discusses how the encounter with the outsider or stranger is a crucial means whereby an individual positions himself or herself vis-à-vis others. Illustrating James Scott's concept of the "self-governing people" of Zomia (Scott 2009: 3) and their effective efforts to keep the state at bay, the local exposure to—and resistance to—successive political schemes and encounters with outsiders has actively contributed to shaping the Jorai person. Simultaneously, this line of inquiry will show the limits of Scott's sharp distinction between upland and lowland people because the history of the Jorai of Leu reveals that their cultural interactions, trade, and political alliances (Meyer 1965) have also served to craft their identity (Michaud 2006; Jonsson 2010). As we will see, otherness translates into the multiple faces the one who is not related by blood or marriage can assume. This other, then, may be embodied by the close neighbor, the distant Khmers, or the foreigner coming from farther away.

Beyond Nature

The Relationships between Humans and Nature

In this chapter, I define "nature" as a complex network that interconnects trees, plants, wildlife, watercourses, mountains, minerals, spirits, and the four elements (see Ingold 2000). I will use the terms "nature" and "forest" interchangeably because people living in Leu perceive them both as pertaining to the same domain—the forest (*glai*) being a metonym of nature—and standing opposite the social human.

Local populations of Indochina have often been described as making a subsistence living in the safe shelter of rugged mountains and dense forests. Some ethnographic writings (French literature of the region in particular) have emphasized how "beliefs, cultures, habitations, resources, and human activities appeared to be deeply connected to the forest, generating the expression 'civilisation de la forêt'" (Guérin et al. 2003: 51). A related idea is Pierre Gourou's concept "civilisation du végétal" (1970), a concept also used by Georges Condominas (1972) and Jean Boulbet (1975) in the titles of their works. In *Paysans de la forêt*, Boulbet used this idea of a symbiosis between man and nature as a leitmotif, describing the local populations with the following phraseologies: "Paysan[s] de la forêt" (Boulbet 1975: 21), "maître[s] de la forêt" (Boulbet 1975: 106), "mangeurs de la forêt" (Boulbet 2002: 8), and so on.

Such terms may call to mind a strong connection between humans and their physical environment, as if nature was conceived of as a nurturing entity. If one draws on Nurit Bird-David's cultural theory, nature can be divided into two discrete categories: the motherly, caring, and giving environment, on the one hand, and the unpredictable, formidable, and possibly harmful one, on the other. The first type is encapsulated in the idea that some societies perceive nature in terms of James Woodburn's "immediate-return system" (Woodburn 1982: 3), which recalls Marshall Sahlins's description of the hunter-gatherers who have "confidence in the yield of tomorrow" (Bird-David quoting Helm 1968: 89). Indeed, Bird-David claimed that this type of relationship entails comparing nature to "a friend, a relative, a parent who shares resources with them. . . . They normally engage with it as if they were in a sharing relationship" (Bird-David 1992: 31). In studying the livelihood strategies of the South Indian Nayaka, she argued that such local perceptions derived from "a confidence born of the view that the environment is morally bound to share food and other material resources with them and that under normal conditions it will" (ibid.).

For the Jorai living in Leu, though, life is conceived in spite of nature. Yet it is by means of their relationships with the forest in particular that the Jorai of Leu lay the foundation of their personhood in the most explicit manner. According to Jacques Dournes, who spent twenty-five years living with the Jorai and the Sre in the Vietnamese Central Highlands, tropical nature is often regarded as a hostile entity. In the eyes of the Jorai he lived with, nature is a reality that needs to be framed conceptually, in which each and every life organism interacts with one another via a vast system of associations or, in French, *correspondances*. Although this process may directly respond to the individual's need for rational boundary markers, in the words of Dournes, it illustrates the "retaliation of Culture over Nature" (Dournes 1969: 155).

In this sense, the Jorai "enslaves nature" only in order to fulfill his or her material needs, feeling neither attachments to the forest nor connections with other forms of life from which he or she carefully tries to stay away (ibid.). It is only through the individual's dreams at night that the forest creeps in, even more powerfully, as a person loses his or her bearings under the thickness of its canopy. For the villagers of Leu, being a person results from the necessary liberation from the state of wilderness, and this emancipation often translates into various forms of behaviors described later.

Setting the Human and the Forest Apart

The village of Leu is located in a relatively isolated area a few kilometers southeast of the small town of O'Kop. My informants commented that until a little over twenty years ago it was inaccessible. Human settlement (both Jorai and Khmer) has since spread in the area and has reclaimed land for subsistence cultivation from the forest. According to a few village elders, clearing the forest is necessary to make human settlement possible. Villagers living in a place surrounded by tall trees were often described disapprovingly by my informants as "living *in* the forest" as if they were completely absorbed by it. As a direct result, Leu's villagers push back nature's encroachment continually by means of seasonal clearance.

Through such physical transformations, nature becomes an environment that gives humans the impression, or illusion, that they are in control via the double imposition of human mind and agency (Ingold 1980, 2000). According to the people living in Leu, there is no direct Jorai translation for the word "environment." A villager claimed that the Khmer word for environment (*parethan*) came into use in 1971–72 under the influence of both the Khmers and the Vietnamese. The word thereafter spread more widely through the work of nongovernmental organizations (NGOs), and some villages like Leu eventually adopted it.

Luyin Blen, a village elder, commented on the local view of the forest as follows: "People don't like the forest. . . . In the past, because the forest was so vast, people were afraid of the tigers and bees, particularly of the tigers' attacks. . . . People did not know so much about the forest." This comment points interestingly to the idea of knowledge, or lack thereof, related to the forested realm. Owing to this lack of knowledge, the villagers associate the forest with uncertainty and, by cutting away the vegetation and domesticating some of its space, feel that they can limit its potentially harmful influences on them. Although attacks from tigers have become extremely rare, a rumor circulated throughout the entire period of my research that a tiger, spotted by hunters, was roaming the most densely forested part of Andong Meas district.

Female villagers in Leu rarely stray from well-trodden paths; their daily itineraries are limited to the *hwa* (fruit and vegetable orchard) for a day's work, to the river to bathe, or to sparse forest areas nearby in order to collect wood and nontimber forest products. Men sometimes penetrate dense forest areas when they are hunting, but, as I will discuss later, the hunter is one of the few "initiated" who can enter the forested realm and emerge from it with relative impunity. For the children living in Leu, the forest (*glai*) is a place where no one will venture because it remains the privileged abode of the spirits (*yang*) and ghosts (*atâo*), especially at night (*mlam*).

Although village paths can be conceived of as safe human-made arteries running through unsafe locations, they are constantly under threat, particularly at dusk, when people, especially children, have a heightened sense of nature invading their realm. This invasion may work in two ways, however. On the one hand, a villager can stray away from the path and get lost in the forest while returning home; on the other, a forest-dwelling spirit harboring malice toward villagers may venture too close to the village. Dournes noted: "People do not go out at night [because] there are tigers (or bombs). The forest is not only the domain of the flora and the frightening fauna. It is also the privileged habitat of the spirits or *yang*, which are as tangible as the trees and the tigers. It is the abode of the fairies who can bewitch you and drive you to insanity" (Dournes 1978: 16).

Darkness at night and the density of the forest during daytime play the same role in restricting visibility. If one conceptualizes the human sense of vision as a form of knowledge, this may explain the villagers' constant desire to transform the village's immediate landscape into something that visibly bears the traces of human presence, thereby changing untamed nature into an accessible or knowable environment.

The village of Leu has very few trees (with the exception of domesticated fruit trees), and most houses (*sang*) are organized around a large cleared area in the middle of which water pumps have been built with foreign aid. Nature can still manifest itself, however, in the form of dense bushes or tree groves, which grow continuously behind houses and gradually invade the orchards. Such manifestations are associated with the persistent return of the forest. Villagers use the term *glai* (forest) in referring even to the smallest of the invading plants that they are constantly trying to cut back (*čong*).

According to Siu, the village wood-carver, Leu men, women, and children alike constantly endeavor to push back the limits of the *glai* in order to construct and maintain a space imbued with social meanings as epitomized by the village. Just as the village space is human made by means of vegetation clearance, the person from Leu is a *homo faber* or "the working man" who also crafts his/her own self and, as we will see in later chapters, is continually in the making. Drawing from his personal experience with the Jorai in the Central Highlands of Vietnam, Jacques Dournes captured this dialectic nicely:

> Toward the forest (and even more toward what is called savage), man's attitude is one of rejection. Traditionally the Jorai loathe the forest. . . . They try to get away from it and destroy the memory of it around them—they do not leave a single tree within the village; they do, on the other hand, bury their dead in the forest, which is the realm of ghosts, spirits, and wild animals. It is also the place from where they originate, but that they want to forget. The Jorai no more believe in the kindness of the forest than they do in its virginity; although it is very useful to them, it remains fraught with pitfalls and foes. By dint of logging they push its limit farther and farther away from their own habitat. They do not believe in Nature's intrinsic kindness either; what is good comes from Culture. . . . Whatever bears the traces of nature is primitive; whatever bears man's imprint is civilized. Through his techniques, man opposes himself to Nature and wants this to be known. (Dournes 1978: 395–96)

The spatial dimension used by each segment of the population shows that each degree of forest density has its equivalent in degree of knowledge and associated perceptions of danger. Children, especially young ones who are looked after by their older siblings, seldom leave the village precincts and therefore operate within the smallest areas. The only time they venture beyond the village is when their mothers take them along for a day's work in the *hwa* because no one within the household or among the neighbors is available to look after them. Older children, from the age of seven onward, may travel to work with their parents but will often need to be accompanied by an adult.

As mentioned earlier, women generally walk and travel within a limited geographic range, and their daily routine creates a well-defined perimeter. Travel beyond these boundaries is infrequent unless it is in groups or to visit relatives living in other villages. For each precise location that is used and regarded as relatively safe, humans have created cleared access routes through the varying densities of the forest canopy. Men, conversely, have the widest and most flexible spatial coverage since their daily activities (hunting) or seasonal work (as well as religious interests in the case of those who have converted to Christianity) can take them farther away from the village and beyond the forests.

This local usage and perception of the environment surface even more forcefully in the ways in which dangerous persons are treated. As I will discuss in greater detail in chapter 4, the land mine victim who has been physically impaired is associated with *glai* (as in bad death) because he or she is a source of risk for the village's inhabitants. To this end, the social reintegration of those disabled by war requires successive steps in order to fully reintroduce the individual inside the village boundaries. This ultimate reunification of the individual's physical body with the larger social body of the village is made possible only through rituals that can open a safe and cleansing channel for the polluted person to become harmless to the rest of the village's members.

The Encroaching Forest: Negotiating Boundaries

Despite humans' attempts to emerge physically and spiritually intact from the potential vicissitudes of the forested realm, they nonetheless remain dependent on it for their day-to-day survival. On the one hand, the forest is a physical barrier that creates an enclosed social space and thus maintains a distance from potential external intrusions. On the other hand, both timber and nontimber forest products are essential in sustaining everyday life in Leu. As Dournes commented: "Inside his house, man remains in a forested setting; he actually never departs from it. He never really leaves this 'evil' forest (one of the meanings of the word *yang*), which thus necessitates exorcising practices" (Dournes 1978: 21).

All construction materials (e.g., wood, bamboo, leaves, ropes) are derived from the forest and are graciously given by the *yang* who dwell in them and to whom an offering is necessary in order to collect the material safely. Once the material is introduced inside the village boundaries, it becomes (imaginatively) domesticated. The same applies to the plants that have been collected in the forest and are used for medicinal purposes. Once they are taken away from the forested realm and replanted inside the village, the plants may lose all their power because they need to grow in the woods, from which they draw their magical properties. On this subject Dournes noted: "All these plants can be found growing in the wild in semidense forest . . . for those who know where to find them. . . . I brought some back . . . into the village and cultivated them in my medicinal plants garden; I was then told that they had lost all their power, for they need to be collected in the forest to be effective" (Dournes 1978: 86–87). The power of sylvan organisms works mostly within a natural environment; it disappears when they travel into the tamed milieu. However, sculpted effigies or house-building materials made out of wood or bamboo taken from the forest can retain their powerful characteristics. Proper ritual or village elders' consent is therefore needed before they are introduced inside the village.

Gaining knowledge of nature as a means of reducing villagers' anxiety can thus take various forms and enables organization of human life within an established system of territoriality founded on daily habits and approved practices. Whether by creating physical separation (clearance) or by setting boundaries through other forms of identification (e.g., naming), each location thus becomes deliberately partitioned, coded, or classified. The following example shows how land that has not been cleared may remain the domain of some powerful spirits or possibly may be reappropriated if local perceptions and knowledge do not oppose this.

Southeast of the village of Leu is Bok, another Jorai village, which is located on the banks of the Sesan River only a twenty-minute walk away. Between the two villages stands a dense patch of tall trees that no one dares to cut. When a Japanese charity came in 2008 to offer to build a primary school for the two villages, this forested site was initially perceived as being the ideal location. Because it was equidistant from the two villages, the children would all be able to reach it on foot in only ten minutes. But after a village meeting, Leu village elders categorically refused to have this area cleared because they claimed that it was the home of "powerful spirits who had always lived there." Building the school on this plot would be an act of negligence that would directly harm the children. Subsequently the school project's site was relocated to what was identified as "neutral ground" beyond Leu and closer to the river. The fact that this obliged the children of Bok to walk for half an hour to school was seen as a small price to pay for avoiding the likely curse of displaced spirits. In the course of her research on the livelihoods of ethnic-minority villages in northeastern Cambodia, Joanna White recorded similar practices founded on animistic beliefs:

> First, there are rules that govern the relationship with the local environment which are founded on religious beliefs concerning the power of the spirits of the forest. . . . Customary law governs the cutting of primary areas of forest

and villages are usually surrounded by areas of dense forest which remain untouched. Villagers described how, when exploring unknown areas of forest to be cut or cultivated, it is often customary procedure to consult with elders to confirm that this is acceptable and these areas are not home to powerful forest spirits. (White 1995: 38)

In Leu, people designate areas that pertain either to the human or the natural domain by identifying a landmark, which in most cases takes the physical form of a particular tree, a change in the vegetation, or a specific crossroads. In the case of the proposed school, a cluster of tall trees was regarded as having been the home of long-established spirits stretching as far back as the elders could remember. Building in its location was therefore interpreted as an offense that no offerings to the spirits could atone for. According to Stéphane Dovert: "The link to the land is indeed not absent. Each location is 'inhabited' by some ancestors and spirits who qualify it in a symbolic and durable manner, but not necessarily in the logic of an influence or an exclusive use. Therefore, for the Jorai, the link to ancestral land is dictated by the memory of the land and the memory of the various places inhabited successively. It does not involve a permanent seizure of the space, however" (Dovert 2005: 58).

In reference to the Jorai with whom he was living, Dournes commented that each place was given a name, whether it concerned an entire forest or a cluster of trees, or a large river or a small stream. He interpreted this naming process as a manifestation of humans' control over nature or the expression of a certain type of knowledge, which was a form of "counter-fear" (Dournes 1969: 104). This ties in with the idea that naming enables knowledge and hence locating oneself in both the physical and the cosmological world (Vom Bruck and Bodenhorn 2006).

Dressing away from Nature

Like clearing the forest to create a *hwa* or expand the village's dedicated space, wearing clothes enables the Jorai of Leu to distinguish themselves from other living organisms. Being dressed (*buh*) plays a potent role in the confirmation of one's liberation from nature. Naked (*blun*), the Jorai from Leu cannot be differentiated from animals, as if nakedness, a potential state of vulnerability, only "serves to bring out, or render visible, its inner constitution" (Ingold 2000: 129). It is thus through the process of wearing items of clothing that the individual can become a person.

Nakedness in the village of Leu is extremely rare for adults even when they are bathing in the river. For young girls, who sometimes bathe with no clothes on, shielding their private parts with the left hand (the side of impurity) when coming out of the water manifests a sense of modesty. Wearing clothes is thus a way to conceal and shield one's body even if this involves only a small piece of cloth. The *tuai blah* or *peung* (in Khmer), which is the traditional loincloth worn by the Jorai, used to be an integral part of men's daily dressing code. For women, wearing locally woven skirts and leaving their breasts bare was the analogous traditional dressing habit. As opposed to more intimate parts of the body, the display of a woman's breast used to be regarded as a "natural clothing item" in the sense that its beauty was an aesthetic and inherent feature of the person (Lewis 1951; Condominas 1957; Dournes 1978).[1]

It is possible to infer that because of external influences (especially the work of foreign missionaries) and access to European styles of clothing, men and women alike have since changed their dressing habits dramatically, concealing more body parts. For children, however, nakedness can be more common and is generally widespread in Cambodian villages of subsistence level. Although Leu infants are sometimes left naked, especially at bathing or feeding times, this remains only temporary because mothers hurriedly put clothes on them (even if they are only rags), especially when they are leaving the house.

Although the very few Khmer children living in the village often played outside naked all day, I never, during my time in Leu, saw a Jorai child left undressed for any time apart from the ones who were said to be insane. In Leu and other neighboring villages, adults and children alike need to wear an item of clothing as soon as they leave the privacy and shelter of the house. Clothes may thus function as a boundary marker that enables the individual to liberate himself or herself from nature and thus make the transition

---

1. Except for Captain Cupet, who, during his exploratory mission in Indochina, noted that the "Phnong" women were "ugly, dirty, and bulky," so when he was confronted by the bare breasts of some females he encountered, he felt the imperious desire to give them his scarf so that they could conceal their nakedness (Cupet 1900: 285).

from bestiality to personhood. Alternatively, being dressed can be seen as part of an established semiotic, providing a concrete sign whereby meaning is constructed, shared, and understood by fellow villagers. The converse perspective also holds true inasmuch as it is considered taboo, if not totally incongruous, to dress an animal. Applying to animals the proper mark of the human would serve only to directly transgress the physical and conceptual boundary that has been carefully established. Jacques Dournes wrote on this subject as follows:

> The Jorai wear clothes; it is taboo to have an animal wear anything that remotely resembles an item of clothing; anyone who infringed this law would be struck down by lightning. Clothing is a specific vector, a sign of an opposition that man wants to express. Men refer to the state of "enslavement" and the state of "total nudity" by using the same word, *hlun*. What can we infer except that man acknowledges the sharing of the same nature (of which he seems to be ashamed) and affirms a transcendence by means of cultural phenomena? (Dournes 1969: 395)

More than a mere signifier of everyday practical use, an item of clothing also serves the essential purpose of constructing and representing a person, the signified. This view gains credibility because if during mortal life it enables an individual to set himself or herself apart from other living organisms (e.g., animals, plants), as we shall see later, it will also play an essential role in the afterlife. As Jane Schneider and Annette Weiner have argued, "Cloth as metaphor for society, thread for social relations, express more than correctedness, however. The softness and ultimate fragility of these materials capture the vulnerability of humans, whose every relationship is transient, subject to the degenerative process of illness, death and decay" (1989: 2).

People living in Leu regard death as a tragic event that partitions the person and hence—to borrow Marilyn Strathern's notion—renders him or her completely "partible" (Strathern 1988: 324). The person is thus reduced to parts as soul, body, social relations, objects, and clothes are left scattered from the moment when the last breath of life has been exhaled. In dying, the villager has to some extent created disconnected and hence meaningless parts of his or her personhood that need to be reassembled. This crucial jigsaw process is the one that close relatives and friends will undertake to make the body complete again at the time of the burial. In such contexts, the clothes of the departed play a central role because they symbolically compose the body of the dead. This further sheds light on the conceptual incongruity of dressing an animal, which would be comparable to giving the animal a human limb. This would in fact create—or remind the Jorai of Leu—of a hybrid entity, showing that their careful separation between humans and animals has been severely transgressed.

Body parts, personal belongings, and items of clothing can therefore signify an individual, and it is in this very meaningful context that the curing ritual of the shaman (*pöjau*) and the search for missing-in-action soldiers takes place. Indeed, if the *pöjau* can extract an illness from someone's body by using an item of clothing (*hnim*) in the absence of the owner, by the same token, the missing soldier can be brought back home via his body parts or personal objects. With respect to these inalienable objects, Simon Harrison described the act of "restitutive giving" as military personnel returned war trophies to their "rightful owners":

"Soldiers who collected enemy possessions as combat trophies, and the surviving kin of the original owners, to whom these artefacts return as mourning or funerary objects, seem to have shared very similar assumptions about the relation between persons and things: namely that the remains of the dead, and memorial objects associated with the dead, are not entirely separable or, more broadly, that the body does not have precise boundaries" (Harrison 2008: 775).

For my informants, naked persons are people who are spontaneously associated with nature, for whom the call from the forest may be insuperable, and who are inevitably drawn back into its depths. In Leu and other neighboring Jorai villages, insane people are often left naked, chained, or put in a cage out of fear, as some of my informants told me, that they will wander and get lost in or be reunited with the *glai*. The association between insanity and nakedness is not fortuitous. Leu villagers call the insane *ving* or *möhlŭn* in Vietnamese Jorai; the latter term is also present in the Vietnamese Jorai expression *möhlŭn mötah*, meaning the hunter who returns empty-handed or "naked" and "raw" (Dournes 1969: 395). In this context, the issue of hybridism (by conceiving it as "a mixture of two pure forms," according to Bruno Latour) is often a source of anxiety (1991: 78).[2] Falling

---

2. Also see Mary Douglas (2002) on the subject of purity, boundary transgressions, and taboos.

into this ambiguous category of the hybrid are the *ving* (the insane), the *mötah* (the hunter), the *pötao* (the master of the element), and the *pöjau* (the shaman). What they all have in common is this ability to incur relatively little harm while traveling through dense forests.

Siu, the village wood-carver, explained that there are different Jorai terms for the insane that correspond to various degrees of madness and associated violence. At the bottom of the perceived scale of insanity is *ving*, which designates an insane person who is harmless; at the top of the scale is *jung* ("someone who is aggressive and hits people," according to him), which identifies the violent mad person who can be a threat to the entire community. An example of *ving* is provided here that involves the attraction of the individuals concerned to the dense forest, reinforcing the local belief that the sylvan space remains a potent and unfathomable realm that the sane individual is not naturally well equipped to live in. Dealing with the insane is regarded as both a personal and a collective problem because the person's relatives must handle it, but its solution has to assure the rest of the community that it will not affect them. With respect to the following case, I was told that the solution sought by the family and the village elders, which was to physically isolate the individual, was common in other Jorai villages in the commune.

Than, a thirteen-year-old boy who had been born mentally challenged, spent most of the day shackled to the main pillar of his parents' house in Leu. His mother was usually the one who attached his foot in the morning before leaving for a day's farming work, and she was also the one who untied him late in the afternoon when she returned from the fields. I was told that the boy was constantly left shackled out of fear that he would run into the forest. It was only late in the day that the boy was left to walk naked in the village, when he was often taunted by other children. Villagers regard this particular state of mental illness as being made visible by the nudity of the person. My informants generally described an insane person as close to the state of bestiality, which is reflected by nakedness, dishevelled hair and a long beard, and peculiar language and perceptions of the world. Because an insane person belongs to the ambiguous world of the forest, he or she is often physically isolated (and hence socially marginalized) as a way to protect him or her and the villagers.

Than eventually reunited with the forest, however. One afternoon in December 2012, the boy walked away from his mother and disappeared into the forest, never to return. The villagers of Leu set off to look for the boy but could find no trace of him. I was told that a few months later someone had found his bones in the depths of the forest. The villagers brought back his remains and organized his funeral. Than is now buried in the village cemetery, a sacred space where tall trees are left to grow free near the forest. "A forest somewhere, with its faeries and wild beasts, a haven for those who dream all the way to madness" (Dournes 1978: 16).

My informants described to me physical particularities that may associate an individual with animals and that are socially rejected if not culturally banned. For example, the persons I worked with considered hair on the chest (but not on the legs) (*arăt*) a revolting physical attribute among men, and one that was often viewed with repugnance. In contrast, a smooth-shaven and muscular chest was regarded as a sign of beauty and virility. The connection between hair and the human chest in particular is the link that places the individual in the local category of the animal (e.g., the tiger) or the hideous (e.g., the bearded foreigner).

Tooth filing plays the same role in some ethnic-minority communities of Southeast Asia where long teeth are associated with animal fangs. Such customs, which are often the subject of specific rituals, as in Bali, demonstrate the transition from nature to culture by means of a rite of passage. Although tooth filing is no longer practiced in Leu, some of my informants claimed that it was a means to differentiate one ethnic group from another, as illustrated in the following Jorai myth: "In the absence of their parents, two brothers were living together. The youngest bit the penis of the elder, who screamed. The parents returned home and punished the younger brother by filing his incisors and chasing him out into the mountain. From then on, Vietnamese and Jorai have lived separately, the Vietnamese with a slit penis and the Jorai with filed teeth" (Dournes 1972: 17).

The local categorization of various forms of otherness often finds its basis in aesthetic characteristics, which are illustrated in mythical stories.[3] Siu, the wood-carver, commented that "foreigners have a long nose because they descend from the beautiful mythological black dog." The Jorai, he said, came from another dog species, which was "much smaller and less handsome." Most of my informants knew a few myths describing the origin of the world, and according to them, "There are very very ancient stories; these

---

3. As I will discuss later, the colonial categorization of various ethnic groups was also based on aesthetic characteristics, as well as perceived levels of belligerence.

are the ones our great-great-grandfathers used to tell." One of these stories describes the human race as descended from the union of a black dog and a woman. The following is a version of the story I was told:

> Men knew that the sea would soon overflow. They took a woman and a black dog and placed them inside a drum. The woman's name was H'Bia. When the water receded and the earth started to dry, H'Bia cut through the skin of the drum and came out; there was not a single man left. From her union with the dog, she had a single child: a boy. The boy grew up. The mother and son set off in different directions in search of food but eventually met up again, and from their union the human race was created. God [*Öi Adei*] then came to earth to separate the families; there were eight of them, and he gave them the following names: the Siu, the Kösor, the Nei, the Röcom, the Römah, the Köpa', the Rahlan, and the Rö'ô. These families wanted to know the pure from the impure, and God told them, "Acknowledge your families; do not marry within a single family, otherwise your impurity will spoil both the earth and heaven." God also gave them *yang*, . . . and, as they became more and more numerous, he also gave them a Master [*potao*], who was to look after them. (Dournes 1972: 47)

In the village of Leu, people still adhere to the long-established rules of matrilineal descent and matrilocality, meaning that at marriage a husband will move into his wife's house. When asked whether marriage was still forbidden between people bearing the same family name, as illustrated in the preceding legend, my informants Siu and Luyin Blen both said that this was still generally the case. However, they indicated that sometimes people believed that as long as the two spouses did not come from the same village, they would still be able to marry each other even if they were both descendants of the same family (whether both descendant of the Römah or Röcom).

The Realm of the Yang

My informants said that most people living in Leu (with the exception of the Christian converts) believe that each and every feature of nature is inhabited by a spirit called *yang* (or *areak* in Khmer). This belief system plays a pivotal role during main agricultural cycles, when the propitiation of the spirits is instrumental in the planting, growing, and harvesting of crops. It also dominates the everyday life of the villagers since the spirits dwelling both inside and outside the village ensure the well-being of the entire community. In a similar vein, Frédéric Bourdier wrote:

> The sacred is omnipresent in the life of the peoples of the forest. Most human actions—ranging from the building of a house, leaving on a hunting trip, weddings . . . to the establishment of a new field—as well as any occurrence of misfortune or illness stem from a complex cosmology that puts man in touch with powers that are beyond him. This does not necessarily mean man's submission to or apprehension towards a world whose mechanisms he cannot grasp, but rather a desire to establish a profound relationship with a natural environment with which he feels interconnected. (Bourdier 2006: 49)

Luyin Blen, one of my older informants, explained that the people of Leu village believe in the presence of both *yang* and gods in their environment. The two types of supernatural entities are considered different. Some ancestors, I was told, can become *yang* and remain inside or close to the village in order to guide their descendants, while other *yang* are spirits that may become benevolent through ritual actions, and still others remain unknown and may be inauspicious.

Gods, however, are perceived as very powerful deities who manifest themselves only on particular occasions, which necessitate a large number of sacrifices. I discuss such manifestations further in chapter 2, which describes how the villagers of Leu associated the American planes with an appearance by the powerful gods. As Guérin noted: "The villagers also think that the souls of their ancestors remain near the village, observe them, bless their good deeds, and punish those who violate traditions. They are particularly terrified by the souls who resulted from bad deaths. Some rituals involve the entire community and are the responsibility of the committee of elders; others concern the household or the family only. However, everyone participates in the religious celebrations" (Guérin et al. 2003: 47).

In a large number of ethnic-minority villages that I visited in the course of my research, the presence of the *yang* is specifically marked in the form of a cluster of fruit trees (often banana trees) planted beside the communal house. A singular type of collective property, this dwelling of the spirits is frequently watered by different people in the village. In exchange, it connects the entire village together and helps its inhabitants take decisions during village meetings. According to Gordon Paterson, "A grove of sacred banana trees is planted in the centre of the village next to the communal meeting hall. It is believed that the spirits of the ancestral elders reside in these sacred areas and sacrifices are made here if the village faces problems or troubles. One such sacrifice is to sprinkle the blood of a pig over the banana trees to ask for rain in times of drought. The ancestral spirits are known as 'areak' in Khmer and they protect and govern the village area" (Paterson, n.d.).

Other familiar *yang* or *areak* may well reside in particular trees growing outside the village that one is not permitted to cut. As in the example mentioned previously, such parts of nature are the elected abode of powerful spirits, which are crucial in maintaining the balance of power between benevolent influences and evil ones. This balance can be maintained only via ritual practices, whether individual or collective, for propitiatory or reparation purposes, with the spirits participating in the flow of exchanges that govern the life of the individual who needs to be at peace with his or her environment (see Guérin et al. 2003). This flow of exchanges is manifested at times of sacrifices through the circulation of blood (*drah*), which is regarded as the sacred vehicle par excellence with which to connect oneself with the spiritual world. Indeed, as Guérin claimed, "Making a sacrifice, hence offering blood to the divinities, appears as the principal means to preserve the harmony between human, nature, and the cosmos. Conversely, menstrual blood or blood generated during labor is regarded as particularly impure. Women need to give birth outside their house to avoid polluting their home and disturbing the protecting spirits" (Guérin et al. 2003: 48).

Despite humans' desire to free themselves from the uncertainties of the forest realm, the Jorai from Leu know that they originate from nature and are still capable of communicating with the spiritual world through either ritual actions or dreams. In the latter case, Kluen, the village healer, explained that the soul of the villager (*böngat*) is the part of the person that travels outside the body and is capable of interacting directly with the world of the spirit. It is thus possible to infer that the soul and the spirits dwelling in parts of nature have the same origin since "plants suffer from ill treatment, they cry, and they complain. In days gone by they were able to speak like any other living beings; without our knowing where appearance ends and reality starts, mythological characters appear as plants and humans, animals and humans. This converging entity illustrates an acknowledged co-nature that is mediated through *böngat*" (Dournes 1969: 402).

If the world of the forest permeates the social existence constructed by the villager in multiple ways, the world of the spirits similarly slips into the recesses of the individual's daily life. The villager is never really safe from losing his or her soul, which may set off on a journey triggered by fatal accidents, sudden illnesses, or even night dreams. In this case, the protection of the spirits is essential to help guarantee the return of the soul to the individual's body, a request that, according to Luyin Blen, is also formulated by the bomb hunter before leaving the village.

The soul is thus a medium that is free to travel in the spiritual world at times of death and night dreams; dreaming is regarded as a temporary death. Luyin Blen told me that it was through dreams that his grandfather Sol Luagn was directly contacted by the gods: *preah tchang ban koat* (the gods wanted him) (in Khmer). The villager explained that his grandfather had the same dream over and over again for seven nights, in which the gods told him what he needed to do. Later his grandfather became a very successful trader who traveled a great deal. He eventually became the richest man in the district, owning between ten and twenty hectares of land, a large number of cattle, and some elephants and having nearly a hundred people working for him. Luyin Blen said that at the time of the Pol Pot regime, the Khmer Rouge confiscated all his assets and eventually killed him "because he did not follow them."

Most of my informants commented that the best way to communicate directly with the spirits and gods was through dreams. As I will explore later in further detail, dreams open up a window to the other world whereby ghosts, ancestors, spirits, and gods can freely connect with the human sphere. Inasmuch as dreaming is a liminal state that enables ordinary persons to travel in a relatively safe way, some individuals have the ability to travel back and forth between the two realms in order to serve the interests of the wider community. The first of these is the *pöjau* or village shaman, who occupies a special space within the local Jorai community.

The *pöjau* is the local healer who by means of these ritual actions can find the cause of an illness or intercede with the spirits on behalf of his fellow villagers.[4] My Leu informants told me that there had been no *pöjau* for a

---

4. As Dournes noted, "[*Pöjau*] forms a great and discrete category, as if in the eyes of a Jorai inflicting death and giving life (killers and healers) were located on the same single chain" (Dournes 1978: 170).

long time in the village. Some elders dated this absence to the time at which the village split during the period of the Vietnamese-established government. Siu said that although there was no longer a *pöjau*, there was still a healer within the village who was "very knowledgeable about the Jorai rituals." Kluen, one of the village elders, thought that his role consisted only in "helping decipher signs sent by the spirits so as to help cure an illness" or contributing to the appropriate performance of a ritual. The old man felt that he was only the repository of such traditional practices rather than one who—by means of spirit possession, for example—could converse freely with the spirits.

Siu explained that when a sick villager from Leu could not be cured by Kluen, he used the services of a *pöjau* from a nearby Jorai village. The power of the *pöjau* is regarded as the result of a long apprenticeship or a "gift sent by the spirits." In this regard, Dournes noted, "The art of *hian* was taught in Jal-Mal, near Laos. The Lao knew best; they would make a snake out of a belt; if they hit the snake, it would turn into a belt again. People would come from everywhere to learn: the Jorai, the Bahnar, the Hodang, the Mnong; and over there all of them spoke only one language, which was neither Jorai nor Lao, but the language of the *yang*" (Dournes 1978: 168).

Another hybrid person with the ability to straddle the boundaries between the humans' social sphere and the untamed is the "master of the element," the *pötao* (also called *sadeth* in Lao), who, more dramatically than the *pöjau*, has vanished from the villagers' social and regional landscape. According to Siu, although the *pötao* have now disappeared in northeastern Cambodia, they still exist in today's Vietnam.[5] As masters of the elements, three chosen individuals would be associated with a particular element (and magical object) from which they derived their cosmic and social power: the *pötao apui* (associated with fire), the *pötao ia* (associated with water), and the *pötao angin* (associated with air) were, according to Dovert, "the guarantors of social cohesion" inside a Jorai community. This cohesion is largely explained by the fact that by mastering the elements, the *pötao* were able to offer the villagers who relied on them a safety buffer against the uncertainties of nature, of which lack of rain and flooding were some of

---

5. According to Siu, there was still one *pötao* living in the northern province of Siem Reap.

many harmful manifestations (Meyer 1965; Dournes 1977; Salemink 2004; Hardy 2015).

I was told that one fine example of the power a *pötao* demonstrated would occur during the dry season, when the *pötao ia* would summon water by "planting his sword into the earth after smearing its long thin blade with pig and chicken blood." Considered hybrid individuals, with their long hair and beards and their isolated houses, the *pötao* were endowed with the power to command parts of nature. As my informant Siu said,

> They do not live in houses like us. The *pötao* will have his house [*sang*] placed in the middle of a field or inside the forest, in which case it would have to be made of stone. The *pötao* never travels by car or motorcycle; he always walks accompanied, and local inhabitants would walk him from one village to another as some sort of god. . . . The *pötao* was also the guardian of the Jorai people, so if they wanted rain, [the *pötao*] would bring the rain, if they wanted heat, the heat would come. The *pötao* never wore any clothes, only a *peugn* [loincloth].

Even if one cannot find any more *pötao* in northern Cambodia, the mere mention of their name still reminds most Leu villagers of a time when the supernatural was made visible in their life.[6]

A former US military soldier who trained a group of male and female Jorai enrolled in the special forces in the 1960s near Cheo Reo in Vietnam described the *pötao apui* (master of fire) who was then living there as follows: "The king of fire was so powerful that he could not live in a village or near other people's houses. Villagers had to build his home outside human settlement because when walking he could well destroy all the houses around by the mere swinging of his arms."[7] In fact, the power of the *pötao* extended well beyond local communities and was well known to the rulers of Cambodia and Vietnam, who would treat them as their royal counterparts; hence the word *pötao* is sometimes translated as "king" (Meyer 1965; Guérin et al.

---

6. "Only the *pötao* Jorai have a religious power, which spreads well beyond the village circle, for they occupy a special place in the imagination of the Jorai group. Besides, they are acknowledged and respected in some neighboring ethnic groups like the Edde" (Guérin et al. 2003: 47).

7. M. Lund, personal communication, June 2008. Another former US soldier commented that the burial site of the king of fire was easy to find because "it is the only one where the grass does not grow." K. Worster, personal communication, June 2008.

2003). According to my informants and the legends they know, the *pötao apui* was the owner of a sword with supernatural powers that he appropriated from the Chams.

In his traveling notes, Norman Lewis described the power of the sword as follows: "The mere act of half-drawing this weapon . . . would be sufficient to plunge the whole of living creation into a profound slumber; while to draw it completely would cause the world to be devoured by fire" (Lewis 1951: 118). However, the *pötao apui* saw their influence decline when their first encounters with foreigners bearing firearms revealed that the sword was not in fact able to cast thunderbolts, as had previously been believed (Goy and Coué 2006: 23).

Encountering the Multiple Faces of the "Other"

The Melancholy of the Jorai Warriors

The reputation of the nonstate peoples of Zomia as "crude, unrefined and barbaric" (Scott 2009: 28) has, as Scott argued, "been socially constructed" (Scott 2009: xii). The description of the Jorai by the French during the colonial period in Vietnam is similarly unsympathetic (Scott 2009). This construction of the Jorai person appears throughout the early literature on Indochina (Pavie 1898; Cupet 1900; Diguet 1908; Maître 1912) and in the colonial efforts to classify ethnic minorities from the most docile to the most pugnacious groups. Owing to their perceived belligerent characteristics, the Jorai were often placed at the latter end of this spectrum. According to Meyer, "The Jorai have always had a bad reputation with Westerners. The murder of Odend'hal and a few French administrators, and the 'pacification,' which was achieved only in 1932, help give some explanation for this. Credited with every sin under the sun, they were consequently somewhat neglected in favor of the Rhade and the Bahnar, who were deemed infinitely more docile" (Meyer 1965: 14).

The following description by Father Pierre Dourisboure, one of the first French missionaries sent by the Mission Catholique to the Central Highlands of Vietnam, is also illuminating: "In the South of the Bla started the immense territory of the Jorai, a population still largely unknown to the missionaries. Sufficient unto the day is the evil thereof, for the Jorai were in fact the most formidable of all the savages" (Simonnet 1977: 64). In order to set up their first Catholic mission among the ethnic minorities of central Vietnam, the French missionaries headed by Father Etienne Cuenot undertook numerous explorations, sometimes, compelling them to traverse long, difficult, and dangerous routes that necessarily passed through the Jorai territory. It was not without apprehension that Deacon Dzo reflected on this test of his faith, concluding, "The tigers and the elephants will show us more mercy than will our human kin" (Simonnet 1977: 19). Most of the villagers I worked with maintained the memory of the great Jorai warriors and talked about this aspect of the Jorai's history with unconcealed pride. Village elders and younger people alike often described the strength of their warrior ancestors, their resourcefulness in making weapons, and their reputation among other ethnic-minority groups. Pou Ksor, one of the village elders, associated the great warriors "who [once] raided entire villages and traded slaves" with the time when the ancestors of the people of Leu were still living in the Central Highlands of Vietnam. As he put it:

> Before going to war, those "who had the knowledge" would sacrifice a pig or a buffalo to the spirits. The war always opposed one village against another. The greatest warriors commanded two to three persons who owned a shield and a sword. Those who were the most skillful ones were the ones who had studied the art of war. The study of war stopped during the French period as people were enrolled to fight against the Japanese. It has fallen into oblivion ever since.... The Jorai were strong and they were feared among others, especially the Kravet, the Kreung, and the Kachok. Ultimately these ones formed an alliance with the Jorai because they didn't want to fight them.

Phel, who was born in the 1980s, had heard many stories about his ancestors and explained how strong they were: "When the Jorai were about to attack a village (Jorai or other), they would warn their enemies a month before launching the attack. The main purpose of such village raids was to capture two to three families and use them as slaves." Furthermore, he told me that they were capable of fabricating a type of firearm (*phao*) similar to the ones that his grandfathers used to improvise: "They didn't need very much to make it.... It was made out of bamboo and other materials from the forest. It was so powerful it could kill people a few hundred meters away! Even the French could not survive it!"[8]

For Siu, who also belongs to the postconflict generation, the Jorai warriors belong to the past because their strength derived from the fact that in old times people were not afraid of death. As Siu explained: "Before, the Jorai were powerful people, they were not afraid to die. But not anymore. People have become afraid because of the wars and the disabilities." As we will see in greater detail in chapter 2, the conflicts of the twentieth century generated new warfare strategies, involved new types of enemies, and used new sorts of weapons, all of which brought with them new forms of bad death.

The First Features of Otherness: The Neighboring Stranger

With respect to where the "community of our own people" ends and where the "other" starts, Jean Boulbet once wrote, "We are always the barbarian for someone and especially for our neighbors" (Boulbet 1975: 1). Likewise, Dovert, who researched the various ethnic groups of the Southeast Asian highlands, regarded the local concept of "stranger" as spatially bound:

> The "stranger," a notion which makes sense within a logic of separation and assertion of one's identity, was not an inhabitant of the plains, but the neighbour, the local "other," the person who speaks another language and lives differently or, simply, the person who shares your culture but with whom you have built no alliances.... For the Jorai for example, the word *toaï* designates the stranger in the village, the person who is neither a relative nor an ally, whether Jorai or not. *Gop jjuei* (the community of our own people) is opposed to *phung toaï* (the host of others), a vague and collective term which indicates less affinity. However you define yourself, it is with the local "other" that you trade or fight much more than with the distant strangers. It is he at any rate whom you meet on a regular basis. (Dovert 2005: 55)

---

8. Phel did not indicate where the powder may have come from, but it is reasonable to assume that at the time of the French colonization, when the Jorai of northeastern Cambodia were first introduced to firearms, they may have been able to access gunpowder.

Studies of highlanders living on either side of the Cambodian and Vietnamese border reveal that there are differences in lifestyles and beliefs within the same ethnic group (Dournes 1972; Matras-Troubetzkoy 1983; Guérin et al. 2003; Bourdier 2006; Paterson, n.d.). At times, substantial disparities can be found between one Jorai village and another, as well as between individuals, with respect to time, places, and social contexts. For example, funerary rites may differ in the making of the grave, as well as in the beliefs regarding what may happen after death (Goy and Coué 2006).

The diversity of the ethnic groups living in the highlands of the region opens up a multitude of lines of inquiry because the notion of ethnicity is intimately connected to the sense of belonging and identity. However, in a context where borders are being constantly renegotiated, geographic proximity and habits play a significant role in repositioning oneself vis-à-vis the other. I have been told that interethnic influences are most frequent when Jorai villages are located near Tampuon ones and thus have access to sources of inspiration that may affect customary laws, death rituals, and aesthetic forms of memories. Such rapprochement is especially visible in the domain of the arts, where geographic proximity, interrelations, and reciprocal influences have to some extent united them. As Siu, the local wood-carver, put it, "[The Jorai and the Tampuon] are the same, we live next to each other, we copy them, and they copy us."

When the ordinary Jorai confronts a farther-removed and more different other, this horizontal and mutually beneficial relationship is often replaced by a vertical rapport, whereby various manifestations of power exacerbate prejudices based on classificatory and hierarchical differentiations. For Guérin and especially for Jacques Dournes, the Jorai person remained "inachevé," or, in other words, still in the making as he or she changed over time and with respect to spatial distribution and encounters. Again, as Dovert insightfully pointed out:

> Alongside the local "Other," someone who belongs to an unrelated clan or a different ethno-linguistic group whom long proximity has taught you to know well if not like, an "Other" of a different nature has now become established, an "Other" who is the embodiment of material power and coercion (still relative but nonetheless real) on earth. The intrusive Other, who is synonymous with pressure and oppression, carries with him cultural references that are so radically divergent that the local Other, despite his differ-

ences, becomes more and more alike. Without fading away, the difference with this *alter ego* is forgotten by virtue of what unites you when confronted by one or more of the strangers. (Dovert 2005: 68–69)

Beyond the Neighboring Others: The Khmers

The village of Leu is composed of thirty families, three of which are partially Khmer (for example, a Khmer marrying a Jorai) or fully Khmer. At the time I was living in the village, I did not witness any disputes or strong disagreements between the Jorai and the Khmer members of the village. Members of one of the Khmer families who own a very small shop claimed that they "had been there first" and had arrived at the time when Leu was only covered with thick forest. It was a few years later that the original village of Leu split, and that the remaining inhabitants came to the present location, near the first Khmer family, to rebuild their village.

Although differences in language mean that some Khmer individuals feel socially separated from their Jorai peers, some members of the very few Khmer families have developed close and mutually beneficial relationships (either by being from both ancestries or by having spent their childhood with them). Siu, for example, called the Khmer lady who owns the shop *ming*, meaning "aunt" (in Khmer), and talked about her with affection. He told me that she had once loaned him some money without her husband's knowledge and that she was kind. This fits with a comment made by the *ming*, who said that she tried to help people who could not pay but found it more difficult when many villagers were in this situation simultaneously, even if only on a temporary basis.

Beyond the village domain, where this cohabitation of a handful of Khmer families and a Jorai majority seems to show that with time and habits people have adjusted to each other well, my informants often expressed their general distrust (*đing đaŏ*) of the Khmers, most of whom they often described as "mean" and "malicious" (*mónă*). My informants from Leu and other neighboring villages regularly shared stories of experiences in which visits to the local clinics or travels on big roads proved to be opportunities for the Khmers to financially exploit them. The latent tension between ethnic minorities and Khmers thus prevails in part as a result of the frequent acts of extortion—euphemistically styled as "taxes" or "fines"—by the district police and the corrupt practices of health workers and shopkeepers. The negative perceptions engendered by these incidents are reinforced by the knowledge that the fines imposed on Jorai persons and members of other ethnic minorities (e.g., for not having renewed their motorcycle license plate) are typically higher than those imposed on Khmers who have committed the same infringements. The anxiety caused by encounters with the stranger (in this case, the non–ethnic-minority individual) stems mostly from the belief that the latter cannot be trusted.

In discussing this particular issue, my informants indicated that they felt that they could do very little to avoid the kind of precarious situations just described. Compounding the sense of division and exploitation is the fact that legal and administrative positions are rarely open to Jorai candidates, who have limited access to school, educational training, and social networks in towns. Most find it difficult to access socially and politically meaningful positions to advance their career, a situation that mirrors the obstacles faced by ordinary Khmers in Cambodia who aspire to obtain the positions (and salaries) enjoyed by expatriates.

To some extent, the hierarchical scale of values in which the colonial French felt superior to the Khmers is being replicated here as the Khmers in turn feel superior to ethnic-minority persons. In the course of my research, I frequently observed Khmers making condescending remarks regarding my Jorai informants. In some cases, the Khmers I dealt with openly disapproved of the close relationships I had with Jorai people. Whether they were business owners, police officers, NGO workers, or even missionaries, their comments and body language continually stressed a divide that they felt set them culturally, socially, politically, and economically apart. In the same way in which the Jorai of Leu regard the forest as an inauspicious space, the Khmers consider the sylvan domain within the binary system of the "wild and tamed, of dark haunted bushland versus inhabited open spaces—*brai* and *sruk*—runs like a leitmotiv through Khmer cultural consciousness" (Mabbett and Chandler 1995: 26) of which the Jorai and other ethnic-minority groups form an inseparable feature.

This hierarchical classification is illustrated and justified by numerous mythical stories that often convey the sense that Jorai illiteracy or the absence of script is a result of their inherent negligence and inferiority.[9] Reminiscent of the

---

9. The Jorai script based on roman script was created only in the early twentieth century with the help of French missionaries in Indochina.

legend of the loss of scripture mentioned by Scott, which in effect might be an effective means to evade the state (Scott 2009), Luyin Blen told me the following Jorai myth, which resonates with the biblical story of the tower of Babel:

> Humankind used to live in a very high tower, where all races were cohabiting with one another. So tall was the tower that a lady known as Hipuik pounded on the vault of heaven whenever she was using her mortar and pestle. The Jorai people also used to live in this tower, yet they were so busy eating tamarind all day that they did not realize that a dog was busy eating the book in which all their language was recorded. After the destruction of the tower and the spread of all the races on earth, the Jorai found themselves with no book and knowledge of the language script, whereas others had managed to preserve theirs.

After Cambodia's independence in 1954 and the waning of French political influence, one of the main objectives of Cambodia's ruler, Prince Norodom Sihanouk, was to assimilate the ethnic minorities of the northern part of the country, whom he labeled the Khmer Leu (the Khmer from above, near the Lao and northern Vietnamese border) as opposed to the Khmer Krom (the Khmer from below, near the southern Vietnamese border). The creation of these two geographic categories was the first move to integrate the ethnic minorities semantically into the majority ethnic Khmer population in Cambodia. It implied, moreover, that the officially classified thirty-five diverse ethnic minorities[10] blurred all the distinctive characteristics inherent in their identity in order to fit them into a single grouping. We can infer that this new attempted categorization was a major step in the process of integration. "In Cambodia, during the *Sangkum Reastr Niyum* period in the 1950s and 1960s, Prince Norodom Sihanouk implemented a policy of 'Khmerization' of the population. The word *Phnong*, which had hitherto been used to describe them, was banned and replaced by *Khmer Leu*, "the Khmer from above," as part of a logic of negation of particularisms. In the Cambodian rhetoric, which has not moreover developed much since, the Khmers form the Cambodian nation. In order to integrate the

---

10. According to a study conducted by the Center for Advanced Study in Cambodia (Centre for Advanced Studies 1996), the results of which were used by the Cambodian government, as well as NGOs.

marginal populations into the nation, they must first be considered Khmer" (Guérin et al. 2003: 55).

Aware of being trapped in this new set of classifications, ethnic-minority persons nonetheless remain firm about their sense of belonging and identity. As a Brao villager explained to Joanna White, "Khmer-Leu was the name given to us in the past. It is not our real name. We are all people of Cambodia . . . but I am Brao" (White 1995: 48). By being called "Khmer," the minorities lose their particularities and gain in exchange the privilege of being integrated into a wider, seemingly homogeneous group. Only the term Leu (above) still marks this geographic distinction, although, metaphorically speaking, the people from above are being virtually displaced and joined to the Khmer lowland majority in order to create this single entity. This displacement took on violent physical form under the Pol Pot regime, when highland populations were transferred to the south and were forced to intermarry in order to suppress disparities between highland and lowland people, as well as between highland groups (Becker 1986; Chandler 1994).

Adopting one of Scott's state's strategies to control the periphery and eliminate nonstate spaces in Zomia, Prince Sihanouk's policy of integration was officially driven by the conviction that ethnic minorities were living in a state of utter underdevelopment and therefore were in need of Khmer culture (reading, writing, and dressing skills), Khmer education (hygienic and environmental), and Khmer progress (e.g., a market-based society). One practical manifestation of this policy was the relocation of Khmer families (mostly former soldiers) to the northeastern provinces with the aim of developing the region. Interestingly, the same phenomenon of acculturation occurred simultaneously in neighboring Vietnam under the government of Ngô Dinh Diêm. While Prince Sihanouk pursued his desire to integrate ethnic minorities through a process of Khmerization, people in South Vietnam were likewise forced by a provincial subdecree to join the nation by renouncing the *tuai blah* or *suu troany* (piece of loincloth attached around the waist, which constitutes men's traditional dress) or else face fines by government agents (Guérin et al. 2003; Scott 2009). As Guérin wrote, "The prohibition of traditional clothing and body tattoos is meant to make the inhabitants of the highlands resemble the Viet and the Khmer. They must learn how to live like their fellow countrymen. The national right supplants customary laws; slash and burn need to be replaced by rice cultivation, names of places change as well, and the teaching of local languages is banned (Guérin et al. 2003: 54)." In the same way in which the French colonizers constructed and represented the identity of their Khmer counterparts as being inferior to their own, the Khmers thought that they needed to teach European values to their counterparts living in the highlands in the name of their "mission civilisatrice" (ibid.). Dovert stated:

> Within these dynamics of segregation, the "montagnard" is probably not [yet] himself conscious of being [a montagnard], although he is indeed one in the eye of the other, whether as a whole or through particular identities. By fixing ethnolinguistic groups through its "scientific" and administrative grids colonization redistributes, here as elsewhere, the maps of otherness.... People carefully record the customs of each and every ethnic minority group [the customs particular/specific to each ethnic group], which are associated with a number of stereotypes designed to establish a hierarchy. Ethnic minority groups are classified in the light of different scales. (Dovert 2005: 64)

When Cambodia gained independence, Prince Sihanouk's Sangkum Reastr Niyum replicated the French colonization practices and used the same discourses imposed on the Khmers in the late nineteenth century against the ethnic minorities. Although this cultural process of Khmerization of the Cambodian highlanders appeared as a condition for them to actively participate in this nation building, for Guérin, "Their integration into the nation implied their disintegration from their own culture" (Guérin 2003: 57). As I will discuss in greater detail later, the violence and ambition of this policy of integration would play a significant role in rallying ethnic-minority forces to the Communist cause led by Saloth Sar (aka Pol Pot) from the late 1960s onward.

Ian Baird observed,

> During the Khmer Rouge period, during the 1970s, all "Khmers" were considered to be equal, with class identification being, instead, the key way of differentiating various people in the country. However, many highlanders were frequently given a higher designation than Khmers, being referred to as "base people." At least some of the Khmer Rouge leadership, including Pol Pot, believed that the highlanders represented a primitive form of Khmer (and Communism), relatively untouched by monarchism or capitalism. Their egalitarian natures were believed to give them the potential to become more easily adaptable to the radical socialism that the Democratic Kampuchea state desired. (Baird 2011: 162)

Elizabeth Becker further explained:

> For Sar and the party, the people and the hills reflected their own problems and were at one with them in fighting a common enemy. Moreover, the poverty of these people appealed to Sar's vision of himself as a liberation leader. These people, he later wrote, were "like beasts under an extremely cruel regime of exploitation.... [They] had known only humiliations and contempts [*sic*]." There was no ambiguity here as in the plains, where Sihanouk was still revered. Sar went to the hills for safety and ended up adopting for his cause the hill people who needed revolution. When his troops won the war eight years later, witnesses remarked on the high proportion of dark-skinned tribals fighting in his ranks. Sihanouk, even later, blamed these "savages" for the cruelty of the Cambodian Communist Party, a classic case of the long-standing royal prejudice against the simple tribespeople who themselves became the victims, not the perpetrators, of Khmer Rouge violence, when the Khmer Rouge later lashed out against the minorities. (Becker 1986: 123)

Chapter 2 will explore this particular issue in further detail, discussing how some villagers in Leu have been involved in a series of violent conflicts, which, owing to their intensity, complexity, and overlaps, have caused them great confusion about who was the other and who, then, was the enemy (*ayat*).

The Stranger from Far Away

The presence of a stranger (*ga gnao*) or foreigner (*ga gagn*) in Leu is often a source of suspicion and sometimes fear, especially on the part of children. Usually regarded as an intruder from the outside, the stranger is conceived of as someone unknown and hence often untrustworthy. This lack of trust stems not only from physical differences but also from the capacity of the stranger to inhabit two different places simultaneously, the village site and the space beyond. This idea resonates with Georg Simmel's sociological research on the stranger, in which the latter is characterized by his mobility because he has "a distinct structure composed of remoteness and nearess, indifference and involvement" (Simmel 1971: 145). Of the Jorai people he worked with, Dournes noted, "Outside the (extended) family a human can only be *toäie* (stranger) or *ayat* (enemy)—these two terms do not contradict each other. The stranger, if he is indeed strange (the French, for instance), will be first regarded as a *yang* (superhuman power)" (Dournes 1972: 10–11).

When I was living as an anthropologist in Leu, my greater physical size and different features were the main reasons the village children mentioned in explaining their fear or lack of trust. Indeed, for most children, their encounter with the anthropologist increased their personal vulnerability because, as they used to tell their parents, "she is too tall and looks different from us." However, when they were faced with multiple sources of hazard at the same time, they could find ways of grading and managing them. For example, when they were faced with walking in the dark at night, children might have to weigh the risks of returning home on their own (and facing potential ghosts alone) versus walking with the anthropologist (and facing the ghosts accompanied). It seemed that in such cases some children thought that the anthropologist was less a source of hazard than the ghost, and as a result they often walked very closely behind her. When children were asked why they followed me so closely at night (the opposite of what usually happened during the daytime), they responded that they were afraid of the "white shadows" that often appear in the dark. Another possible scenario is that others may have found the two sources of hazard (facing the anthropologist and the ghostly appearance simultaneously at night) too daunting and may have decided to wait until another adult walked them home, but of this I was not made aware.

The adult population first viewed my presence with genuine curiosity and sometimes suspicion, which dissipated only over time as I extended my visits throughout the months. It was only through my participation in daily chores (cutting trees, working in the *hwa*, and so on) that seeing me daily became a habit. This habit became a means to integrate slowly as my status shifted from being the stranger to the guest and eventually the "niece" of my landlords. In the same way, Meyer Fortes's mentor and friend Naabdiya described how his status among the Tallensi changed progressively as he slowly made his way from the village boundaries to the close ties of kinship: "When you first came here you were a stranger [*saan*], now you have become our kinsman [*maabi*]" (Fortes 1975: 230).

Throughout the months I was in Leu, I had many opportunities to observe the villagers respond to their encounters with foreigners with a mixture of anxiety and fascination. Reactions differed according to age and gender. Female villagers would be (or pretend to be) less curious than their male counterparts. Younger generations would tend to gather closer and observe the features of the individual in detail, especially if he or she was not Caucasian. One of the village elders commented as follows: "There was a time when we were all afraid of strangers. Both village elders and children ran and hid in the forest or in the *hwa* (orchard) whenever a stranger came into the village, whether he was Khmer or else. Not anymore, as we have grown accustomed to them. However, people see some differences between strangers. For example, we call a foreigner with a dark face (e.g., an Afro-Caribbean) *Plagn Tchu*, which means 'coal.'"

In such situations, however, identity boundaries would sometimes shift spontaneously between the villagers and the anthropologist and the foreigner. My original and hybrid status as a *ga gagn* (Khmer and foreigner from Europe) would sometimes be renegotiated because for the villagers I was suddenly closer to them than the foreigner coming from more distant horizons. This was due not only to the fact that with time I slowly integrated into the local landscape but also because of what were perceived as more closely shared physical, linguistic, and cultural characteristics between myself and the villagers.

At the same time, one's acquaintance with and proximity to a stranger/foreigner is often considered a source of multiple opportunities, especially in regard to access to commodities (e.g., basic medicines) and outside knowledge, which may carry the potential to improve one's social status or advance one's career within the community and beyond. However, the presence of a foreigner can also be a source of risk to the well-being of the individual and the entire community. As I will show in chapter 2, the various historical encounters that the villagers of Leu have had with the multiple variations of the other have often resulted in dramatic and irreversible life changes.

In this chapter, I have sought to describe and analyze the practical relationships that the Jorai of Leu maintain with their natural environment in order to emerge as persons. For Maurice Godelier, "Man has a history because he transforms nature" (Godelier 1984: 10). In the case of the Jorai of Leu, it is through emancipation from nature that the individual founds and maintains his or her identity as a social human being. Despite awareness that humans rely on nature to build their livelihood, this imaginary domestication often gives Leu villagers the impression—or the illusion—of being autonomous. As Clifford Geertz once wrote, "Man is an animal suspended in webs of significance he himself has spun" (1973: 5). To this end, being dressed is a form of praxis that has both personal and cultural meaning, in which an item of clothing becomes an index whereby such conscious human action deliberately creates partitions and fixes the individual in a safe place.

This place can in turn be challenged through broad-ranging types of external encounters, which may cast uncertainty over an individual's social status vis-à-vis the multiple faces of the external others. Indeed, the more remote the origin of the stranger, the less predictable and more dramatic the consequences may be. As Norman Lewis commented when traveling in Southeast Asia, "If someone offends the tutelary spirit of the village things can be resolved without too much trouble, but if a commercial company comes with a concession and cuts the banyan tree which houses the spirit and carries it away, what can be done? It is the end of the world" (Lewis 1951: 100).

As I will explore in greater detail later, the encounter with the other coming from farther and new horizons and with the technological weapons the other brought along has played a major role in threatening the villagers' attempt to clearly separate themselves from nature. Traditionally regarded as a place to avoid since it is the locus of the spirits and the untamed, the forest became in various times of uncertainty and conflict a place where the people of Leu could hide and protect themselves from more formidable threats. Owing to this fact, the relationship between humans and nature has always remained ambiguous, while increased exposures to various others have given birth to new forms of spiritual beings. As Guérin argued, "With the colonial period, new *yang* appeared, associated with novelties that seemed endowed with a supernatural power; the *yang xe dien* (car), the *yang nhac nuoc* (state)" (Guérin et al. 2003: 49).

In a similar way, the apparition of the bombing plane in the cosmological landscape would appear to the villagers of Leu as a formidable harbinger announcing tumultuous times. For Luyin Blen, for example, the succession of violent wars in the last century showed the descendants of the great Jorai warriors from the Central Highlands of Vietnam how they could be afraid of death.

Chapter 2

Local Lives Caught in the Storm of Global History

Although the Jorai had established a formidable reputation as warriors in the highlands of Cambodia and Vietnam (Meyer 1965; Simonnet 1977), the twentieth century brought with it new types of weapons and new military strategies that engendered unprecedented levels of violence and impacts on the human, physical, and historical landscapes. By teasing out how people conceive of their involvement in this tumultuous recent past, this chapter aims to investigate the identity of villagers who belong to this generation of conflicts and how this has consequently shaped individual testimonies. It argues that the episode of the US bombing can be conceptually framed as a historical event distinct from the sequence of local and regional conflicts because it had wider implications for the villagers' sense of historical consciousness. The objective is not to offer an in-depth clinical examination of war survivors' posttraumatic disorders. Rather, the premise is that the traumatic event of the US bombardment resulted in violent disruptions and lasting physical and spiritual injuries that affected all forms of life.

The following is divided into three main sections. For practical purposes it follows a Euro-American or linear chronological order commencing with the relationships between the Jorai and the Khmer from the seventeenth century onward. The first section gives an overview of the main historical events from an outsider's historical perspective to give the reader a better idea of the issues at stake, as illustrated in text box 1. The second section focuses on the ways in which Leu villagers themselves perceive, remember, and reflect on the same episodes while placing greater emphasis on the ones that, according to them, have shaped the history of their village most dramatically. The last section examines the ways in which the past has actually carved out a discursive and physical space among war survivors and how this is now part of the reality of Leu everyday life.

Historical Overview

The Jorai Nephews of the Khmer King

The first historical record that describes the relationships between the Khmers and the Jorai dates back to 1601. The text is the founding charter of the monastery of Sambok, situated on the left bank of the Mekong River. This document illustrates the privileged rapports between the Khmer king and his two Jorai counterparts, the *pötao apui* (king of fire) and the *pötao ia* (king of water), by which they had secured peace in their respective kingdoms and pledged assistance in times of war. The charter details the sumptuous gifts the Khmer king sent to the *Srok Ayonapar* every three years to ensure the longevity of this mutually beneficial relationship.[1] It offers a description of the regalia proffered on the occasion of what Charles Meyer interpreted as the enthronement of the two *pötao*, who became henceforth the "nephews" of the Khmer sovereign (see also Mourat 1883: Mikaelian 2009).

---

1. *Ayonapar* is derived from the Sanskrit *aya-na-pura*, "fortified location used as a shelter" (Meyer 1965: 21). The bibliographical notes of the Bulletin de l'École Française d'Extrême-Orient mentions "We can find in Mr. Odend'hal's notes an explanation for this name. The country of the sadets is located in the Ayoun and Song Ba valleys; the latter river is called Apah by the Moï. Ayonapar = Ayoun Apah" (BEFEO 1904: 488).

The enthronement ritual of the *potao* entailed a lustral bath, anointment with oil and powder, invocations recited by the *Chau Ponha Thuk Chrya*, and the proclamation of the dignity conferred upon the *potao* stipulating that he was thus elevated to the rank of "nephew" of the Khmer sovereign and endowed with the honor of representing the king, his "uncle," as guardian of the sacred sword, governing the Jorai and the Phnong in accordance with their traditions, maintaining the forest paths, and uncovering enemies.... Finally, this text adds that "The King lays down that news of the King of Fire and the King of Water be sought once every three years." (Meyer 1965: 18)

Posted in Cambodia from 1886, French colonial administrator Adhémard Leclère mentioned that all the gifts were given in pairs (one for each *pötao*) and included, among others, elephants, palanquins, parasols, rice, salt, spices, betel leaves, tobacco, clothes, silk, musical instruments, knives, and metal bars, some of which were made by the Kuy, who had been renowned fire and iron masters since Angkorean times (Dupaigne 1997; Diffloth 2013; Bourdier 2014). In return, the *pötao* sent ivory, rhinoceros horns, and items of clothing that the Khmer sovereign used in rituals to expel drought and invoke rain (Meyer 1965: 19–21).

According to Baird, "The Khmer appear to have given the Jarai goods of considerably greater value than what they received. One explanation for this is that the Khmer were indebted to the Jarai for defending the northeasternmost part of the Khmer domain, either from Vietnamese or possibly Cham or Lao invasion.... Another possible explanation is that the Jarai goods were considered to be as valuable, or even more valuable, as the goods that the Khmer provided because of their alleged magical powers, making them important for certain palace rituals" (Baird 2011: 161).

Both Meyer and Leclère surmised that this relationship must have predated the 1601 Sambok Charter by some considerable time: "If the renown of this dual kingship spread, as we have argued, into southern Indochina; if it has nevertheless come down, albeit diminished, to the current generation; and if it still today enjoys some prestige, this means that it must in the past have shone with a certain resplendence and exerted some degree of influence on the political affairs of the region" (Meyer 1965: 15).

Although written records of the origins of this alliance and the regular exchanges of gifts are probably lost, we know with greater certainty that they ended under the reign of King Norodom, who ascended the throne in 1859.

Leclère claimed that this dissolution was mostly due to the political conflicts (internal rebellions) that affected the Khmer kingdom, as well as the arrival of the French in 1863 and the institution of the French protectorate.

During the first half of the twentieth century, French administrators, missionaries, and anthropologists avoided contact with the *pötao* because of their religious powers, which in Vietnam extended over the Jorai, Rhade, Bahnar, and Sedang populations. After the murder of French explorer and administrator Prosper Odend'hal on April 7, 1904 by the Jorai, the French limited their contact with them, whom they deemed too bellicose and unpredictable, although their greater physical size and their arts of waging war were perceived to make them highly suitable to join the French military. Leclère stressed that in Indochina, people believed that the king of fire could break the path of the sun, while the king of water could trigger floods, but "what remains of the mystic royalty and the powers of the Potao in the midst of the upheavals brought by the French administration and the American military occupation?" (Meyer 1965: 26).

The French Colonial Period

When the French first settled in Cambodia in 1863, they were already well established in Vietnam. The priority of the French government was to maintain a solid base in Indochina, of which Vietnam would be the geopolitical center. This helps explain why the French presence in Cambodia took the form of a protectorate rather than a colony. The establishment of the protectorate followed an appeal from King Norodom,[2] who, caught up in Siam and Vietnam's fight for control over the region, wanted to offset the threat posed by his neighbors by requesting that the French intervene (Shawcross 1993; Chandler 1994).

The French presence in Cambodia was first concentrated in the capital city, Phnom Penh. Subsequently, however, administrative units were introduced in the provinces to better promote commerce, notably in the form of plantations, and, most important, tax collection. According to Scott, tax

---

2. Grandfather of Prince Norodom Sihanouk, Cambodia's first postindependence head of state.

collection played a key role in the efforts of the state mechanism to expand its control and thereby bring people living at the periphery closer to the center (Scott 2009). The vast majority of the Cambodian population at that time was concentrated in small hamlets, and people seldom traveled to the capital city or even to towns. In the localities, the main power brokers were landlords, who endeavored to maintain their positions and social and political stability through a long-established system of patron-client relationships (Vickery 1986; Chandler 1994).

At the same time, the northeastern part of Cambodia, which was an integral part of Laos until 1905 (Baird 2010), started to attract increased interest from French entrepreneurs who thought of the region's microclimate as an ideal place for the development of a cash-crop economy. As in Vietnam, the fertile upland areas of the provinces of Ratanakiri and what would later be called Mondulkiri subsequently became the focus of efforts by outsiders to develop plantations for rubber, coffee, and other crops, and large-scale cultivation intensified in the 1960s (De Koninck et al. 2005).[3] According to a Jorai elder from Leu, "The Kreung and the Tampuon have worked in the plantations with the Khmer since the beginning. Other ethnic-minority groups like the Jorai would only work there occasionally, for example, twice a year for five days, because at that time, they were living too far from the Khmers." Ethnic minorities continue to provide seasonal labor in the rubber plantations to this day.[4] Henri Locard, a historian specialist on the Khmer Rouge who was in Cambodia in 1966 researching rubber plantations in Ratanakiri province, claimed that most of the ethnic-minority labor working in the plantations near Banlung was Kreung. At that time, he commented that while exploring the district of Bokeo, he could hear the bombs hitting the ground in the distance.[5]

In the early twentieth century, commerce in the country progressively expanded and was facilitated in the northeastern region by the construction of roads linking Cambodia directly to Vietnam. The construction of these roads provided employment for some members of ethnic minorities; others enrolled

---

3. Between 1951 and 1953, the French started gold mining in the district of Andong Meas (meaning "the golden well"), which today constitutes a source of daily livelihood for ethnic-minority villages located in the area.

4. For more information on the history of rubber plantations in Cambodia, see Meyer 1971; Aso 2013; and Boucheret 2013.

5. Henri Locard, personal communication, September 2014.

Text box 1. Historical aide-mémoire

Dates	Major Events in Cambodia and the Region	Leu Villagers' Involvement[1]
1863	• French protectorate in Cambodia.	• A few join the French Indochina army.
1945	• Japanese invasion. • Cambodia takes the Northeast from Laos.	• Villagers fight the Japanese with the French. • Transborder movements and exchanges continue.
1954	• Cambodia achieves independence; Sihanouk becomes its first president.	• Villagers become the target of "Khmerization."
1959	• Ratanakiri province is officially created.	• All ethnic minorities living in the northeast become Khmer Leu.
1961	• First surveillance planes spotted over Ratanakiri province.	• Planes are identified as "flying gods."
1964–65 —	• Vietnamese Communist guerrillas infiltrate Cambodia. • US planes start bombing the area.	• Villagers provide support to the Vietnamese, who explain the planes. • Villagers seek refuge in the forest
1967	• Cambodian Communist Party leaders establish base in Ratanakiri.	• Villagers provide support to, and in some cases join, the Communists. They are seen as of "pure Cambodian race."
1970	• General Lon Nol overthrows Sihanouk.	• Villagers take up arms against Lon Nol's government with the Cambodian Communists.
1968–75	• KR extreme ideology firms up.	• Villagers are no longer exempt from the KR's escalating political repression.
1975	• KR takes over whole country. Forced displacement and labor, executions.	• Villagers are sent to work in agricultural cooperatives.
1978–79	• Vietnamese invasion, KR demise and retreat to northwestern Cambodia. Creation of People's Republic of Kampuchea (PRK).	• Villagers return to village location to rebuild it; some enroll as soldiers serving under the Vietnamese occupation.

(continued)

(Text box 1 continued)

Dates	Major Events in Cambodia and the Region	Leu Villagers' Involvement[1]
1979–98	• KR wages guerrilla war against PRK government from sanctuaries in northern and northwestern Cambodia and Thailand	• A small number of villagers continue to fight for the Khmer Rouge during this period.
1992–93	• United Nations Transitional Authority in Cambodia (UNTAC).	• UN peacekeeping operation planes are seen in the provincial town of Banlung
1997	• Coup d'état by Hun Sen's Cambodian People's Party.	• Leu villagers are not involved because northeastern Cambodia is not directly affected by the conflict
1998	• Remaining Khmer Rouge leaders surrender; conflict in Cambodia ends.	

[1] This time line summarizes major events that have directly or indirectly affected the villagers living in Leu and is for readers to use as an aide-mémoire only. For the sake of clarity, villagers' responses and experiences based on informants' accounts are summarized in the right-hand column.

in the military forces levied by the French colonial authorities. After an interview with a Jorai villager, Joanna White reported that "many people died during heavy, dangerous road construction work carried out with the use of explosives, and some villagers described how those who had contact with the French and who had been 'named' by them were expected to pay annual taxes to the colonising power" (White 1995: 20). Indeed, the French felt that they could better exercise their authority over people by attributing new names to ethnic-minority workers, as well as to their Khmer counterparts. In the same way, Leu villagers used specific naming practices as a way to gain knowledge of or better control over places, persons, and objects, as I will illustrate later.

Despite the progress of French influence in Cambodian economic life, the northeastern region was still largely considered unsafe by both the French and the Khmers. As White pointed out, "Some parts of the region were infamous for not being 'subdued' until the late 1930s." Indicative of this was the fact that local protests against the encroaching presence of foreigners took the form of violent attacks on outposts, which led to the death of French settlers in the province of Mondulkiri. "Again, this perpetuated the warrior-like reputation of the highlanders, in this case the Phnong" (ibid.).

During the Second World War, the Japanese invasion of Cambodia triggered conflicts with the French, who enlisted both ethnic-minority and Khmer soldiers to fight for them. In the village of Leu, a few older individuals had vivid memories of their role in this fighting, during which the French provided them with clothing and weapons. In one case, a village elder recalled with unconcealed nostalgia how he used to converse in French and how he had felt a part of a social and military elite. For this villager, like others I met in neighboring communities, getting to know the foreigner can be a source of pride and social influence inside and outside the village's boundaries.

The Sangkum and Beyond

"RENDERING KHMER": THE POLITICS OF ASSIMILATION

After the signing of the Geneva accords in 1954, Cambodia became an independent country. Prince Sihanouk, who became the president at the head of a political party called the Sangkum Reastr Niyum (People's Socialist Community), envisioned the Cambodian nation as a homogeneous entity (Chandler 1994). In line with this vision, his government redrew the map of the northern part of the country with the official creation of Ratanakiri province in 1959 and neighboring Mondulkiri province a year later (Chandler 1994; White 1995). The redesign of the national map and the attempted integration of ethnic-minority groups heralded an unprecedented period of intrusion into the lives of those groups. From then on, the influence of the Khmers and their trade and agricultural activities progressively expanded through the forest, reaching out to more and more remote villages.

THE LATE 1960S AND EARLY 1970S

In the late 1960s, this policy of acculturation, combined with the government's fight against Communist movements (threatening both the country and the region), persuaded members of ethnic-minority groups to join forces with the Communist Khmer Rouge (KR) and Vietminh guerrillas. According to Guérin, the revolutionary movement seemed to enjoy much popularity among ethnic-minority inhabitants (2003: 73–74). A Jorai who in 1964 was employed as a KR guide explained to the historian Sara Colm, "People were very interested in Pol Pot's ideology in the beginning. During the Sihanouk regime the civil servants and military worked separately from the people and only came if there was a problem. But the Khmer Rouge worked closely with the people—even if people had less food under the Khmer Rouge, the people were interested in them. We knew the Khmer Rouge wanted to build a strong society and would change leaders if they did wrong" (Colm 1998).

Similarly, Phi Phuon, Pol Pot's Jorai bodyguard, told me, "[Before the Khmer Rouge] people lived in darkness. They didn't know anything. They only knew how to do their orchard and look after themselves." As will be shown in his forthcoming biography written by Henri Locard and Frédéric Bourdier, Phi Phuon was a very interesting Jorai figure who espoused the revolutionary ideals as a form of emancipation. During the time of Democratic Kampuchea, he became the head of the bodyguard unit and then the head of logistics at the Foreign Ministry, a battalion commander during the 1980s civil war against the Phnom Penh government, and deputy governor of Malai district in Banteay Meanchey after the Khmer Rouge's defection in the 1990s (see Sikoeun 2013).[6] The following is an excerpt of an interview he gave in 2001 while describing Pol Pot and the Jorai espousing the revolutionary cause:

> I observed his relationship with the people of Ratanakiri who respected and loved him very much. As for the messengers, they were filled with the spirit of responsibility; they loved him and regarded him as a *Yuthmit* (brother in arms). We took over the duties we thought we were able to fulfill, [duties] we thought we understood, which were not difficult for us. Before we were given a task, he would first ask if we were able to do it or not. The geography was our geography. So there was no difficulty. We could do it and we could achieve it. We were determined to accomplish it. . . . His relationships with the people [here] were the same as with other people and with the army. He showed great politeness and sweetness; he was very gentle, neither crude, nor

---

6. Henri Locard, personal communication, September 2014.

rude; he was good hearted, he had smooth words. He inspired a lot of confidence. We could lay our lives in his hands. We could entrust our lives to him. He had nice words for us. We tried hard to fulfill the tasks as best as possible. We responded to his demands. We lived with him periodically. There was no blame for him. There was no mistake.[7]

In 1968, with the support of their new allies, the inhabitants of Ratanakiri launched a rebellion against the national army. Thousands of government soldiers were sent to counteract the guerrilla offensive, but they did not succeed in regaining control of the province. In 1970, Sihanouk's regime was overthrown by a coup d'état led by General Lon Nol, who established a US-backed government focused on curtailing the spread of communism in the region. As it was increasingly drawn into the Vietnam War, Cambodia became the battleground of various guerrilla movements, or what Shawcross reported as "a land of blood and tears" and Hanoi radio described as "hell on earth" (Chomski and Herman 1979: 359). The simultaneous civil and regional conflicts affected the lives of the highlanders to an unprecedented extent. As the Communist insurgents reinforced themselves with alliances on each side of the Cambodian-Vietnamese border (Kiernan 1996; Guérin et al. 2003), Ratanakiri found itself at the center of what came to be known as the Ho Chi Minh Trail, a complex set of logistics and infrastructure designed to supply the Vietnamese Communist forces in South Vietnam. This made the province a prime target of the increasingly intensive US aerial bombardment.

LIVING AT THE TIME OF THE KHMER ROUGE

The province of Ratanakiri was the first area where the leaders of the Cambodian Communist Party (and the future Khmer Rouge regime) attempted to implement their concept of an ideal agrarian-based society (Becker 1986; Kiernan 1996; Guérin et al. 2003). The Communists' decision to locate in the remote northeastern part of Cambodia in 1967 was driven by the need to escape the police sent after them by Prince Sihanouk and to build up an insurgency then in its infancy. It was reinforced, however, by KR leaders'

---

7. Interview of Phi Phuon by unknown researcher, 2001, originally translated from the Khmer by Kouy Theavy. This transcript was given to Henri Locard.

interpretation of the ethnic minorities' social and economic structures, which they considered close to the Marxist-based ideals that they themselves espoused. Indeed, KR leaders associated the life of the ethnic-minority population with a pure form of "primitive communism," and Pol Pot often described them as his "faithful allies in the revolutionary cause" (Guérin et al. 2003: 73). As a village elder in Leu explained, "For Pol Pot, the Jorai were pure because they were a race without rulers, which means they were not following anyone. They were their own kings!"

Although purity was an essential Khmer Rouge value in regard to race, social structure, and economic self-sufficiency, fear of betrayal was the other key tenet that would become the cause of pervasive paranoia and summary executions throughout the KR regime. Yet at the time the Communists first took refuge in the northeast, ethnic-minority groups were considered the most loyal because they were still uncorrupted by any forms of imperialism. Becker argued: "In 1967, the Cambodian communists depended on the goodwill of the hill people, and for once, these allies responded generously, never betraying them, guiding them through the forests and protecting them from Sihanouk's attacks on their headquarters" (1986: 123). Indeed, the physical landscape provided the Communist insurgents with the dense forest canopy they needed to remain physically concealed, while the lack of communication with the outside enabled them to live relatively undisturbed by external influences and hence made it possible for Saloth Sar (later known as Pol Pot) to lay the foundations of their utopian society. For Elizabeth Becker,

> The hidden jungles of Ratanakiri province were ideal for those ideas. The terrain was nearly impassable. The thick malaria-infested jungles were feared by the people of the plains and considered unspeakably hostile by Khmer of the cities. Life in the hills has changed little since the famous French naturalist Henri Mouhot first explored the region one hundred years earlier. Even though a number of the Cambodian communists had spent their childhood in rural villages, they were as unprepared for life in the hills as the French had been. But like the French naturalists, the communists felt the horrible conditions were more than made up for by the kindness of the tribal people who lived there. These were the Khmer Leou, Khmer of the Highlands. Mouhot said of them: "The most perfect equality and fraternity reign in these little [tribal] communities. . . . Quite alone and independent amidst their forests, they scarcely recognize any authority but that of the chief of the vil-

lage.... [The Cambodian king's] emissaries scarcely dare pass the limits of the kingdom, so fearful are they of the arrows of the savages and the fevers which reign in their forests." (Becker 1986: 122)

As late as 1968, the escalation of the rebellion in the northeast to some extent reinforced the popular opinion that highland people were particularly violent (ibid.). The Jorai were traditionally regarded as proficient warriors and were well known for their strength and fighting skills (Simonnet 1977). For Hiom Ro, a village elder, Pol Pot chose to stay with the Jorai because "the Jorai knew the forest, the trees, the stones" and therefore knew best how to enlist nature itself as a key component of guerrilla warfare. As Philip Short described in his biography of Pol Pot, Phi Phuon, a Jorai aide-de-camp to Pol Pot, "in early 1972 escorted him through the 'liberated zones' for three months to see how the new political and military structures were taking shape" (Short 2004: 227–28).

In an interview, Phi Phuon[8] told me that the Jorai, the Kachok, the Kraveth, the Kreung, and the Tampuon, as well as the Lao, were selected to join the Khmer Rouge because of their skills in hiding in the forest and running fast.[9] But in addition to that, the Jorai were best known to be "ferocious warriors." Suong Sikoeun, who worked at the Ministry of Foreign Affairs of Democratic Kampuchea, added, "[The Khmer Rouge] used the Jorai as bodyguards because they were loyal, faithful and disciplined.... The Jorai were essentially hired as bodyguards and drivers, not decision makers... no, very few were.... Pol Pot chose Phi Phuon because he was the first to volunteer and because he was strong!" The KR leaders employed many Jorai as their personal bodyguards, although this did not stop them from later subjecting the people whom they had once trusted to political repression (Becker 1986; Chandler 1994; Guérin et al. 2003; Bourdier 2006).

As the Khmer Rouge ideology of race and purity further developed, a sentiment of pervasive paranoia ensued whereby Pol Pot's Kampuchean Revolution[10] could survive only if all elements of pollution were purged.

---

8. Phi Phuon was born Rocham Tuon in 1947 in Talao village, Andong Meas commune, Ratanakiri province.
9. Phi Phuon, interview with the author, September 2014.
10. The name Kampuchea was used in titles such as the Democratic Kampuchea (DK) or Khmer Rouge–established regime, as well as in People's Republic of Kampuchea (PRK), which succeeded it. "The name 'Kampuchea', or *kambuja* in conformity with traditional orthography,

Consequently, all of Cambodia's ethnic minorities were targeted because they constituted a threat to the edification of a real Khmer nation. In a sense, Sihanouk's past vision of national unity was implemented to its logical conclusion, this time, however, by the use of the most extreme violence. To this end, a KR decree was issued that clearly conveyed the excessiveness of this vision: "There is one Kampuchean revolution. In Kampuchea there is one nation, and one language, the Khmer language. From now on the various nationalities . . . do not exist any longer in Kampuchea" (Becker 1986: 253).[11]

For Elizabeth Becker, who covered the war as a journalist, the decree was implemented with various degrees of violence, ranging from "outright massacre and pogroms" to sparing the lives of ethnic-minority groups who would forsake their identity by leaving their language, religion, and practices behind. In Ratanakiri, which was part of what the Khmer Rouge regime termed the Northeastern Zone, it seems that the purges were less systematic thanks to the fact that the Communist insurgency had originally settled there in 1967 and "because of other factors including this previous attachment to the central committee and the strength of minorities in the zone committees, who successfully ignored most of the Center's orders to absorb or eliminate the 'imperialists' and minority elements" (ibid.). In Leu, as well as in neighboring Jorai villages, people confirmed that in order to survive, they had to follow orders closely, negate their ethnic distinctiveness, abandon swidden cultivation, and sometimes intermarry with other ethnic minority groups. The testimony in text box 2 comes from a Jorai, who described how life at the time was hard even for those young people who were chosen to be part of the Khmer Rouge elite.

In contrast with other provinces, cooperatives and working camps in Ratanakiri were set up relatively close to the villages. To some extent, the northeast seemed to have suffered less from major displacement than other parts of the country, where people were sent to work in distant regions. When the collectivization plan was implemented to its full extent, elephants,

---

first appears in Cambodia in tenth-century inscriptions to refer to the people, the *kambu-ja*, 'born of Kambu'—a figure of Indian mythology. . . . The name 'Cambodia' then . . . is a well established English equivalent of the native name" (Vickery 1986: xiii).

11. Minorities that were persecuted included the Chinese, Thais, Chams (Muslims), the Vietnamese, and the hill tribes, among others.

Text box 2. An account by Pol Pot's adolescent Jorai bodyguard

In 1967 I went to stay at Plói Tang Chiet, a Jorai village that is half an hour away across the river from Plói Leu. Pol Pot, Ieng Sary, Ta Ya (aka Ney Saran),[1] and Thok, who formed the core Communist clique, were settled there, while other Communist rebels chose to live among Tampuon communities. We still have vivid memories of this period, and the banana tree where Pol Pot used to tie his hammock still grows there. I believe this period of conflict was the most difficult time [in the recent history of warfare] because of all the executions and because there was no food and no more sense of family.

At the age of fifteen, I was chosen as an *angkarech* [bodyguard, in Khmer] as part of eight personal bodyguards who were very close to Pol Pot. From 1968 to 1975, *angkarech* were recruited among what Pol Pot considered the *koma klahang* [strong children, in Khmer]; we were the ones who knew how to follow and obey orders. Yet the assignment was temporary because seven of us would be regularly replaced since KR cadres were afraid that if people stayed too long, they would get to know one another and *bayk ka* [fail their duties, in Khmer]. After 1975, Pol Pot decided to remove all the Jorai from their bodyguard duties and had them replaced by the Khmers; the Jorai were instead sent to work in agricultural plantations near the provincial capital of Banlung.

As one of Pol Pot's *angkarech*, my daily chores included working in the *chamkar* [orchard, in Khmer] to look after the crops, feeding the cattle, boiling water, carrying stuff, and cleaning Pol Pot's house. Pol Pot used to convene regular meetings, and as a bodyguard I was regularly subjected to indoctrination sessions, which were meant to stimulate one's pride and loyalty. At that time, he had already started to separate out the "good" [*neak leuho* in Khmer] from the "bad" people [*neak akroch* in Khmer; see Hinton 2005]. Executions were rampant because we needed to fit in his bodyguard scheme; otherwise, we were put to death. We could not escape; if we tried to; the KR would have thought that we were people "with knowledge" [*neak tcheh* in Khmer]. They were watching us closely. ○

---

[1] Ney Saran, alias Ta Ya or Number IX, was the secretary for the Northeastern Zone. According to David Chandler, "[He] joined Pol Pot and a handful of others in Office 100, the Vietnamese base on the Cambodian-Vietnamese border, where [he] remained until 1965" (Chandler 1999). He was later imprisoned and tortured in the infamous S-21 prison in Phnom Penh, where he died.

buffaloes, rice-wine jars, traditional gongs, and all objects that constituted local wealth were confiscated. A survey conducted in 1992 concluded that the KR had seized more than twelve thousand rice-wine jars and an equivalent number of gongs from the local villages (Hawk 1995). Village elders in Leu claimed that the Khmer Rouge destroyed the jars violently, although some of "the ugliest" were kept in order to store vegetables. As Luyin Blen described, "You had to forget!" The same applied to the village gongs, which were either destroyed or buried and sometimes later repossessed. Illustrating this systematic seizure, a Mnong villager from Mondulkiri province reported to Guérin, "When the KR came, they took all the elephants with them. We have never seen them again. Some people said that the KR had killed them" (Guérin 2003: 75).

As a few villagers of Plói Leu were sent to collective agricultural settlements in other districts of Ratanakiri, groups of ethnic-minority inhabitants from neighboring Mondulkiri province were displaced from the plateaus to the lowland plains, where they were compelled to carry out irrigated rice cultivation (an activity with which many of them were not familiar) in order to fulfill the larger collectivization plans (Guérin et al. 2003). A feature of the Khmer Rouge regime that affected the daily life of all ethnic minorities was the ban on all religious practices. Although many animists abandoned the traditional cult of the local spirits (but in most cases resumed it after the war), others nonetheless maintained their religious life in secrecy.

In the course of her study, White recorded, "Traditional rituals such as animal sacrifices and spiritual ceremonies were outlawed and villagers who had played a vital role in religious activities, such as spiritual healers and elders, did not dare speak of this for fear of being killed. One Kreung spiritual healer described her experience of this time: 'I still saw the spirits in my dreams and they asked for animals to be given to them, they still made people sick, but I did not dare make offerings to them. I only sometimes gave a chicken in secret'" (White 1995: 27).

Phi Phuon, Pol Pot's bodyguard, explained that from 1970 onward he was not allowed to speak Jorai. He had to forget the language entirely, excluding it from his speech and banning it from his thoughts, along with leaving all traditional Jorai ritual practices behind. He explained that when his mother died in 2003, he did not have enough money or time to carry out a proper funeral. But when his father passed away in 2012, he resumed past traditional rituals for the first time. He subsequently sacrificed fifteen cows and buffaloes and brought in rice-wine jars to ensure that the soul of his father would be granted a better life.[12]

Facing eradication of their culture and punishment of its practices, large numbers of people started to escape across the border, seeking refuge in Laos and Vietnam, especially when ethnic-minority villages were razed to the ground and when purges against potential enemies (both internal and external) were at their highest (Guérin et al. 2003). In 1978, before the Vietnamese invasion that deposed the Khmer Rouge, new waves of executions were being ordered, and entire populations of border villages were displaced to lowland areas (ibid.).

In examining the Central Highlands of Vietnam, Gerald Hickey described the highlanders as "buffer people" because they were caught among Communist soldiers arriving from the north, both Cambodian military forces and colonizers coming from the southern plains, and Americans flying in from overseas (1982: 290). With similar geopolitical forces at play, the volatile situation that spread onto the Cambodian highlands has been perceived in a similar way by the Jorai of Plói Leu. Pou Ksor remembered that when he was a teenager, the district of Andong Meas was already littered with bombs, but at that time he did not know why the Americans were attacking the region. Later he could reflect on the complexity of the situation and described it as follows: "There were a lot of Vietnamese soldiers hiding in the forest who later on—as we would be told—were backed up by the Chinese. Pol Pot was fighting Lon Nol, while the Vietnamese were fighting against the Americans. It was *sangkriem total* [total war, in Khmer]!"

In this unstable environment, a large number of ethnic-minority families decided to escape because they faced life-threatening forces coming from all directions.[13] "All these antagonistic forces end up violently colliding with each other in the highlands; and although some ethnic minority people may choose one camp or another most are 'accidental victims of the struggle'" (Hickey 1982: xvi). As Guérin explained, "The question for them is how to survive the storm that is blowing across Indochina. Their migrations may be voluntary, their departure being freely decided by the villagers who are

---

12. Phi Phuon suddenly passed away in April 2015 in the former Khmer Rouge stronghold of Malai district in Banteay Meanchey province. His brother promised that he would have a Jorai funeral organized back in his village in Ratanakiri.

13. For Guérin, this process started as early as 1971 (Guérin et al. 2003: 76).

well aware of the risks they would take if they stayed. Entire villages prefer to run away in order to escape the American bombardments and the Communist incursions" (2003: 80).

Ben Kiernan estimated that nine thousand people, or 15% of the ethnic-minority populations of northeastern Cambodia, may have died under the KR regime (Guérin et al. 2003: 81). This figure appears very low, and Guérin thought it likely that the actual number of victims was higher because the total population was originally underestimated. Figures concerning death tolls vary widely from one source to another. In the northeastern region, the killings perpetrated by the Lon Nol government's soldiers, added to human losses from ground fighting, illnesses, malnutrition, executions, and the heavy bombardment, may have contributed significantly to increasing the overall number of victims in this particular part of the country. Taking all these factors into account, Guérin offered one of the highest estimates of deaths, suggesting that one-third of the total highland population living in the south of the Indochinese peninsula died during the years of protracted conflicts.

Most war survivors from Leu, as well as from other communities, agreed that the major cause of civilian death was malnutrition rather than systematic executions or aerial bombings. Luyin Blen, a village elder, commented that the hardship of living with the KR taught people how to become less wasteful. The fact that animal sacrifices were forbidden made some individuals realise that they could save their livestock, especially in times of privation, without being systematically punished by the *areak* (the spirits). For Thol Khloy, another village elder, "At the time of the KR, people were doing agricultural work. We only had one rice saucepan for everyone. We were very hungry. But before 1970 things were *thwameda* [as usual, in Khmer]. We did not suffer any particular maltreatment from them."

Highlanders in general have since been associated with the KR and to some extent improperly labeled "pro–Khmer Rouge" by the Khmers because they had been in contact with the Communist insurgents since the end of the 1960s (White 1995: 26). Despite some genuine endorsement of the KR ideology, as illustrated by the case of Pol Pot's bodyguard, this claim lacks nuance and gives a flawed picture of the real life of ethnic-minority communities at the time. Luyen Blen recalled that then people were afraid to die: "We were like chickens in a cage." On the basis of her study of a variety of ethnic-minority villages, White concluded that "the majority of villagers, however, remember this time as one of fear, physical hardship and living on a near-starvation diet; one Kreung villager compared the current rice shortage to these times: 'This year there was not enough rice. People say the soul of the rice is lost, it has gone away, just like in the Pol Pot times'" (White 1995: 27). The northeastern zone was under the control of the KR from 1970 to the end of 1978. In the first years, the intensity of the bombing was so severe that it delayed the implementation of Pol Pot's revolutionary social and economic program. In such a context, it is possible to infer that the general anger and frustration generated by the bombardment of the country played in the KR's favor because it rallied active supporters to be volunteers and soldiers (Chandler 1994; White 1995; Kiernan 1996).

RESUMING LIFE AFTER THE KHMER ROUGE

After the Vietnamese invasion of the country in December 1978, which later forced most of the KR armed forces to retreat to encampments in northwestern Cambodia along the Thai border, displaced ethnic minorities returned to their villages in order to reunite with their relatives and rebuild their homes. Some Jorai called this resettlement in their original villages "retreading the rice husk" (White 1995: 29). For some inhabitants of villages close to Leu, however, resuming life at the site of their original settlement was a daunting challenge they were not able to face. As one elder of Plói Pok said to me, "Oh, we could not rebuild anything there; there were too many deaths and too many ghosts around." Although people established the new settlement away from the old site, the cemetery remained in its original location where the village ancestors are buried.

Under the Vietnamese-backed government of the People's Republic of Kampuchea (PRK), the ethnic-minority communities of the northeast region demonstrated that they could mix the old with the new. For example, people resumed their swidden agricultural practices while maintaining ricefield cultivation as it had been imposed on them under the KR. According to White, "This post–Khmer Rouge period appears to have been one of relative calm and stability" (White 1995: 29); villages benefited from this autonomy and were able to govern themselves as they had in the past, albeit with distant control from the government. This relative stability continued despite the 1997 coup d'état.[14] According to my informants, the worst of the physical and psychological violence generated by the war ended at the time of the Vietnamese occupation, when most resumed the seasonal pace of subsistence farming. For a few others who carried on their army duty as PRK soldiers or continued fighting for the KR, the conflict was to leave a final and enduring mark as they fell victim to explosive remnants of war (ERW).

The US Bombing: A Historical Event

Although profound disruptions have occurred since the establishment of the French protectorate and particularly during the Khmer Rouge regime, Leu villagers seem to frame the period of the bombing as a particular event that can be singled out from a relatively long and unbroken sequence of conflicts. In light of this, I use Marshall Sahlins's working definition of the word "event": "An event is not simply a phenomenal happening, even though as a phenomenon it has reasons and forces of its own, apart from any given symbolic scheme. An event becomes such as it is interpreted. Only as it is appropriated in and through the cultural schemes does it acquire an historical *significance*" (Sahlins 1985: xiv). For most of my informants, the bombing experience appeared to be a particularly chaotic time not only because of the nature of the event itself but also, and most important, because of the meaning it held for the war's survivors.

In the mid-1960s, the Americans began their bombing campaign aimed at eliminating the Ho Chi Minh Trail (text box 3), targeting Vietnam, Cambodia, and Laos. The Cambodia Mine Action and Victim Assistance Authority estimated that more than a million tons of bombs were dropped on Cambodia alone, with the highest concentration in the northeastern provinces. Surveillance planes were first spotted by the local population as early as 1961, however, at which time they were flying over the region in order to locate the North Vietnamese Communist troops.

---

14. Factional fights between the FUNCINPEC (Front Uni National pour un Cambodge Indépendant, Neutre, Pacifique, Et Coopératif) supporting Prince Ranariddh and the Cambodian People's Party (CPP) in support of Hun Sen (the present head of state) started in July 1997 and lasted until August. The fights and political tensions ultimately resulted in a coalition government with the CPP as the leading party of the country that has remained in power to the present.

Text box 3. The Ho Chi Minh Trail

> The Ho Chi Minh Trail was a complex logistical system using jungle paths, trails, and rivers running through Laos, Vietnam, and Cambodia that enabled North Vietnamese Communist troops to supply members of the South Vietnamese Communist National Liberation Front (NLF) with manpower and matériel during the Vietnam War (1959–75). It has been estimated that the NLF received sixty tons of aid per day from this route, and that up to twenty thousand soldiers a month were traveling through it (Shawcross 1993; Kiernan 1996).
>
> "Since the early 1960s, too, US Special Forces teams had been making secret reconnaissance and mine-laying incursions into Kampuchean territory. In 1967 and 1968 about eight hundred such missions were mounted, usually by several American personnel and up to ten local mercenaries, in most cases dressed as 'Viet Cong.' One Green Beret team 'inadvertently blew up a Cambodian civilian bus, causing heavy casualties.' Then, in 1969, the number of these secret missions was more than doubled; over a thousand more were mounted before the March 1970 coup. And in the same fourteen-month period, over 3,600 B-52 raids were conducted against targets in Kampuchea under the Menu operation. As William Shawcross described, "Night after night through the summer, fall and winter of 1969 and into the early months of 1970 the eight-engined planes passed west over South Vietnam and into Cambodia. Peasants were killed—no one knows how many—and Communist logistics were disrupted. To avoid the attacks, the North Vietnamese and Viet Cong pushed their sanctuaries and supply bases deeper into the country, and the area that the B-52s bombarded expanded as the year passed. The war spread" (Shawcross 1993: 35). ○

The Formidable Encounter

When the Jorai inhabitants of Plói Leu saw the first plane in the sky, they immediately said to themselves, "Now the gods know how to fly." The association of the plane and the object coming from the sky meant that the villagers believed that the plane was the manifestation of a god in its most symbolic and formidable form. After a decision of the elders, the entire community was closed off to organize a propitiating ceremony that lasted for seven days and seven nights. This ceremony involved the sacrifice of seven chickens, seven pigs, and seven rice-wine jars.[15] Luyin Blen, a village elder, recalled, "People could hear a voice coming out of the planes, and they thought that the planes were talking. We didn't know that there were men inside. We were so scared that all the villagers went hiding in the forest.... The planes would also drop lots of leaflets to warn us about the impending war. They were written in Khmer on one side and in English on the other, but we could not read, and because of that we could not know."

Luyin Blen was my only informant who remembered this episode to the extent of recalling the blue and red colors of the papers and the multitude of them that fell from the air and littered the ground. His comment raises the issue of knowledge in times of war and in this particular case the type of knowledge that is denied because of lack of ability to read and write. Because most villagers were illiterate at the time and had limited Khmer proficiency, Luyin Blen felt that the villagers' inability to decipher the leaflets was a sign of their vulnerability. With reference to James Scott's "art of not being governed," although the lack of scripts may have contributed to freeing some groups from the yoke of the state, in this particular context, the lack of reading and writing skills enabled some people to remain invisible to the state and thereby out of its control. "If swiddening and dispersal are subsistence strategies that impede appropriation; if social fragmentation and acephaly hinder state incorporation; then, by the same token, the absence of writing and texts provides a freedom of maneuver in history, genealogy, and legibility that frustrates state routines" (Scott 2009: 220). Past conflicts have shown that literacy can conversely instigate a real sense of hopelessness, however. Looking at the First World War and British journalist Henry Hamilton Fyfe's article "British Propaganda and How It Helped the Final Victory," Nicholas Saunders referred to Paul von Hindenburg, who, while observing the Allied counteroffensive, reflected on the British, "[who] bombard our front not only with a drum-fire of shells, but also with a drum-fire of printed paper. Besides bombs which kill the body, they drop from the air leaflets which are intended to kill the soul" (Henry Hamilton Fyfe, quoted in Saunders 2003: 2).

---

15. Seven is considered a sacred number and is frequently used for ritual purposes (Lafont 1963; Dournes 1978); however, other neighboring Jorai villages have performed the same rituals, but with slight variations in the time frame, e.g., five days instead of seven.

Villagers also emphasized the fact that at the time that the first planes appeared, they had limited contact with the outside world since they were keeping their distance from the Khmers, whom they did not trust (*đing daŏ*). As long as they believed that the flying objects were powerful gods, villagers from various Jorai communities in the area sought refuge in the forest and performed rituals to propitiate them. Luyin Blen remembered, "At the beginning, planes often flew over the village, but they would carry on beyond the border to fight in Vietnam. A few years later, the Vietnamese came here and the planes followed them. As soon as we knew what they really were, we stopped sacrificing animals to them." The village elder noted further, "The first planes flew above the village in 1961. Nobody told us that they were planes; we just thought that they were *preah* [gods, in Khmer]. We did not have any written language and did not have any books, so we could not know.[16] This lasted for three years until the Vietnamese soldiers came in 1964–65. They were the ones who told us that they were not gods but planes piloted by men, and they also gave them a name: *Tchai Pol*; *Pol* means 'to fly' in Vietnamese. This is where our Jorai word for plane [*sepol*] comes from."

Local conceptual frameworks may struggle at first to comprehend an unexpected encounter with a formidable unknown, be it an object or an individual. As Luyin Blen indicated, the villagers' immediate reaction was to understand the unfamiliar by using their existing body of knowledge and hence associating the planes flying in the sky with their gods, who were regarded as the only ones capable of such power. In reexamining the case of Captain Cook, Marshall Sahlins highlighted the fact that the Hawaiians rapidly found a logical explanation for the phenomenon (in Kant's definition as what can be directly accessible through observation) that was based on their religious beliefs and cosmology. Drawing on the elders' knowledge, mythical stories, and collective experience, they comprehended Captain Cook's appearance as a manifestation of their god Lono. "History has been known to reenact this cosmic drama. Consider what happened to Captain Cook. For the people of Hawaii, Cook had been a myth before he was an event, since the myth was the frame by which his appearance was interpreted" (Sahlins 1985: 73). By naming the unknown (as both a creative and

---

16. Literacy was introduced forty years later in the village by means of Christian missionaries based in Vietnam.

an acquisitive action) and subsequently attributing a rational explanation to an unusual manifestation, they made the unexpected the expected and hence incorporated it into the normality of daily life.

In a similar way, during the Vietnam War, when the Americans flew helicopters to northern Laos to train the Hmong ethnic minority and equip their leader, Vang Pao, with new weapons, Hmong insurgents thought that the Americans were their long-awaited god. In the eyes of the local insurgents, this extraordinary occurrence was the fulfillment of an old myth, which foretold that a god or messiah would reunite their diaspora and give them their country back, a country that had been lost to them in the past. This belief had a profound impact on the Hmong insurgents working with the CIA to fight the "secret war" against the Communists. It is possible to infer that the landing of the Americans to some extent inspired a Hmong revivalist movement called the Chao Fa (Lord or God of the Sky) that in 1976 promoted the creation of a "true Hmong society" while awaiting the return of the legendary king who would save them from oppression. Although the messianic freedom fighters were equipped with old rifles, they felt that they were invulnerable because they believed that they were placed under the protection of their god (Lee 2000).

In Leu, however, village elders claimed that there were no legends or stories to prepare them for this formidable encounter. Although the identification of the planes with the gods was immediate, people had no alternative interpretations of their manifestation, and therefore they continued their propitiating ceremonies. Later, when Vietnamese Communist troops infiltrated, the villagers were given an explanation for the planes, which most of them then understood as the real cause of the occurrence (a flying object piloted by a human).

Although today a few village elders like to think of the planes as a hybrid entity combining human pilots and superhuman power, the Vietnamese had communicated to them the unambiguous idea that foreign powers were responsible and were about to profoundly disrupt their day-to-day lives. Villagers (especially those who would join the various fighting factions) felt that they owed to their Vietnamese neighbors an increased knowledge of the war. In addition, the Vietnamese gave the plane a name, which for the villagers helped them understand better its power. As one of my informants put it: "Before that we did not know what it [the plane] was; we just called it *preah* [god, in Khmer]! So we carried on making sacrifices for three years until we knew what it was." Naming the cause of fear can be an effective way to fence off the danger that seems to emanate from it, enabling people to better comprehend it and place it within the expanding boundaries of their conceptual framework (Vom Bruck and Bodenhorn 2006).

Surviving the Bombs

Villagers told their stories with heaving sighs or shaking heads as if to physically emphasize how difficult surviving at that time was. Many of the villagers' narratives highlighted the scale of the attacks and the damage they created in obliterating entire villages or destroying swathes of land. Today large bomb craters still act as visual testimonies of such damage, forming a part of the landscape of local communities and agricultural fields.

In narrating their survival experiences of the bombing, people systematically used the words *rot* and *pouwn* (run and hide, in Khmer). In describing life during the bombardment, villagers emphasized the discrepancy between the power of the attacks and the means people had either to respond to them or to properly protect their families. My informants remembered how this period constituted a regression to the past when they could barely cook food. Thol Khloy recalled that in 1967, when the bombs were already falling from the sky, he hid in the forest with his wife and daughter. The war then escalated against the Communist insurgents, and the bombing intensified in 1972 and 1973. He recalled, "We forgot how to light a fire, we had no plates or saucepans, and we had to hide in caves all day, which we could leave only during the night."

In reflecting on thirty years of long-drawn-out conflicts, most people identified the time of the heavy bombing as the most difficult warfare experience of their life. Others regarded the period of the Khmer Rouge as the most difficult because they felt that they had to struggle harder to stay alive. For Ban Lagn, surviving the bombing was an extraordinary ordeal. Ban Lagn was never a soldier, and at the time of the aerial attacks, he sought refuge in the forest with his family for nine years. He commented that the hardest time was when people felt useless because they had to hide and live in caves without being able to grow their own food.

People's accounts of this return to nature illustrate how degrading the period of the bombing was, but none of them compared themselves to animals explicitly despite the fact that their descriptions highlighted their personal shame of having to live in the wild inside forest caves, human-made wells, or animal dens. As discussed in chapter 1, the villagers of Leu have a profound aversion to untamed nature and all forms of bestiality. Although their views are often socially constructed, they feel the need to guard themselves against their various manifestations.

In drawing a comparison with Nurit Bird-David's study of the Nayaka hunter-gatherers, one can argue that the inhabitants of Leu conceive of enclosed village life as being a haven that protects them from the unpredictable effects of nature. Yet at the time of the aerial bombardment, people were so afraid of the American planes that the forest became a place of temporary safety where they could *top dam glai* (hide in it, in Jorai). As a survivor put it, "In times of war, people always run into *glai* [the forest] to hide even though they are not used to living in it because of the *yang* [spirits]. When the planes came, we looked to the forest as a place to hide. In fact, we are more scared of human beings than we are of the spirits, because humans can be crueler."

As mentioned previously, the various manifestations of nature are believed to be endowed with life. Trees, rocks, rivers, seasonal crops, and portions of land are seen as being inhabited by natural *yang* and ancestral *areak*.[17] For the villagers of Leu and nearby Jorai villages, nature, like humans, has been affected by and continues to suffer from visible and less visible forms of distress generated by the conflicts. According to one villager, "[At the time of the bombing,] men and spirits were altogether confused." As a result, in spite of having spent years taking refuge in the forest, Leu villagers insisted that life in the forest remained inhospitable for humans. Moreover, some village elders claimed that since the end of the war, the forest had also become a haven for new malevolent dwellers, such as ghosts of foreign soldiers and unexploded ordnance (UXO). Therefore, the traditional thought that humans should protect themselves from the untamed forest continued to prevail. Research on postconflict communities living in high-risk areas (with a high density of UXO) shows that villagers have divergent opinions about whether the greatest source of risk comes from what can be seen or from what remains unseen

---

17. The villagers distinguish between two kinds of spirits: the ones that originate from nature *yang* and the ones that are the reincarnations of ancestors *areak*, who tend to settle near villages to protect and guide their descendants.

(Uk 2007). In the case of Leu, life during and after the conflicts illustrates the common opinion that what is visible (a live bomb or an enemy soldier) may be a greater source of danger than what is invisible (an ill-intentioned spirit).

One villager commented that although the time of the bombing was particularly onerous, they were still able to forage for food, and communication between villages was possible, albeit risky. A number of people shared this view, mentioning that they managed to get used to the bombing by adjusting to life in the forest, gauging when and where the raids were likely to occur, or simply making use of all their senses. Testimonies of soldiers involved in armed conflicts elsewhere in the world likewise emphasize the sensory side of the survival experience. With reference to the First World War, Saunders described the individual as "folded into the landscape" as he struggled and survived in the trenches. Indeed, in such a physical environment, Saunders argued that "soldiers experienced 'being in' the landscape and contributing to its transformation through their own woundings, sufferings and deaths" (Saunders 2003: 128). Text box 4 relates one of many similar stories of a bombing survivor, describing how people struggled to build their everyday resistance to the devastations caused by the increased intensity of the war.

Physical and Cultural Disruptions

Most testimonies have in common an emphasis on how the bombing was a lasting cause of multiple disruptions: the excessive violence of the bombardment, the constant hiding and running, the loss of relatives, and the absence of the gods and protective spirits. The account of a bombing survivor in text box 4 offers an interesting perspective since it describes how some local beliefs were shaken to their foundations. For some villagers, the relentlessness of the aerial attack meant that even the supernatural world must have plunged into chaos, thus affecting the course of life of the spirits and the gods themselves (as one informant once told me, "Especially with all the ghosts roaming around"). Others thought that the intensity of the war (often compounded by ground fighting) was such that it was beyond the gods' power to withstand this human-induced destruction. Because the villagers found no evident signs of the gods' and spirits' retaliation, some people started to lose faith. With the advent of the KR regime, which banished all rituals,

Text box 4. Memories of a survivor of the US bombing

> Most *boh pó čah* [bombs, in Jorai] were originally dropped in Vietnam, but when the Vietnamese entered Cambodia, the planes came after them. The hardest time was when they came to bomb us: the planes were flying low, and they were targeting watercourses. They knew that people would always hide along the river because we needed the water. The planes came every day and dropped their bombs on each side of the river because they knew we would be nearby. However, we became familiar with the raids, and knowing when they would start, we were able to organize ourselves to collect water from the river. Sometimes they would drop chemicals in the river, which meant that we became sick, suffering from headaches, diarrhea, nausea.... It is possible that these chemicals have caused permanent disabilities, but probably less so here than in Vietnam. In any case, people would be afraid to spread this kind of information because it might generate a new war.... But we had our own doctors, and people would then look for another water supply. We were continually changing water sources to avoid being dependent. Changing habits all the time was key to our everyday life.
>
> Because the planes were mostly targeting rivers and forests, people started to dig wells in the middle of the fields because they knew that the pilots would overlook them. Villagers would hide and live in them, but it happened that a bomb hit the well, in which case everyone in it would die. When people die from the bombs, there is seldom any corpse [*čô*] to bury. Yet some families would try to make an offering and call the spirits of their dead relatives. If someone lost a child, for instance, he would tell the spirits, "My child died and disappeared" (no body found), and ask them to protect the dead one. But most of the time people would not dare to set out and look for their missing relatives because they were afraid of being killed. There was so much war at that time that in the course of these six years of intense conflicts we even started to doubt the existence of the gods! ○

people felt that they had been abandoned by the gods and spirits and concluded that they could carry on their life without resuming past rituals and see whether they would ultimately be punished by them (Keane 1996).

A few villagers admitted that after the bombardment and the cruelty of the KR period, they had lost their faith in their local spirits; some of them, like Luyin Blen, later converted to Christianity, as I will show later. One of the village elders, though, voiced his own interpretation, wondering whether it was possible that both gods and humans were actually involved in the conflicts, with the gods guiding the pilots of the planes. But the few villagers present dismissed this hypothesis as completely foolish. After the others' mocking reaction, the village elder remained quiet but smiling while intently gazing at me as if silently asking whether he was indeed being foolish to believe in such a possibility.

Another major source of disruption resides in people's unsuccessful efforts to situate themselves at the time when the event unfolds. Most informants described how confused they were (and sometimes still are) as they tried their best to find their role amid historical developments. In fact, former soldiers often said that they had joined various fighting factions, switching from one side to another because of the confusion generated by the intensity and overlaps of the conflicts. Former alliances turned into new feuds, which changed into renewed alliances again. According to Pou Ksor, a village elder, "We could not tell apart the good from the bad, differentiate our ally from our enemy, as the conflicts started to overlap with each other." The past lives of some war survivors show that as they were caught in the middle of different battles and conflicts of interests, people had to make important choices while trying to keep their head above the dangerous waters of the time.

In the village of Leu, people remembered changing sides continually. For instance, some supported the Vietnamese Communists in 1964–65, then fought against them in 1977 as they sided with the Khmer Rouge, and then later still collaborated with the Vietnamese-installed puppet regime of the PRK in the 1980s. These various testimonies reveal that despite the dramatic changes that occurred in the second half of the twentieth century, some people endeavored to become agents of change rather than mere victims of overpowering historical events. In the Central Highlands of Vietnam, Jorai war songs sometimes describe the attempted return of the Jorai warrior who, despite trying to honor his ancestors' reputation, tragically falls victim to the various foes of the twentieth century, as illustrated in text box 5.

When Pou Ksor earlier described the chaos of the war as *sangkriem total* (total war), his description of all the parties involved revealed that the individual had suddenly become more aware of a world beyond the Jorai everyday world (see Biersack 1991). In a sense, the violent exposure to foreign horizons meant that Leu villagers could not live, view, and represent their own history independent of the intrusion of external forces.

Text box 5. Jorai war song in the fashion of a funerary song

Brother, the dead did not take you back
You did not die a victim of the spirits
You died for having joined the army
For your wish to collaborate with the Americans

Brother, you smashed you head at the Mang-Yang pass
Your jaw torn near Ankhe
Your legs broken at Dak-Sut
Your breath silenced near Kontum

O! Youth of our villages
At the time of the French you became soldiers with them
At the time of the Americans again soldiers for them
It is suicide, can't you see?

Brother, you got shot at Dak-to
You got trapped at Plei-mrong
You were struck dumb at Plei-me
You destroy yourself for believing in liars

Attack, let's fight back
Let's turn these weapons against the Americans
But let's not kill ourselves
As they would wish us to

Brother, your disappearance is a waste
You are game, shot like a squirrel or a civet
I would like to save you from your fate
to pick you up, to carry you away
brother, O! brother. ○

(Dournes 1987: 151–52)

To some extent, one can argue that the influence of the French colonizers, as well as the Khmerization policy of Prince Sihanouk at the time of the Sangkum Reastr Niyum, may have also proved to be critical times for the ethnic-minority population in general. But an event like the US bombardment was often described as more violent, unexpected, and disproportionate in scale. In addition, the brutal intrusion of far-flung foreigners whom no one had seen or even heard of before may indeed have constituted a greater threat to the village.

A village elder asked me, "Why did they bomb us?" Many other people similarly felt that the reason for such violence still evaded them. Despite that, the people I worked with were conscious that, with the arrival of the first bombing planes, a larger world had actually collapsed into their own. Text box 6 briefly discusses the absence of quantitative data as an additional perspective on historical disruption, in which missing records, falsehoods, and political scheming constitute yet another dramatic legacy of the intense aerial bombing.

Local Narratives and the Persistence of the Past

Narrating the War: Language, Time, and Embarrassment

In discussing the war in general, my informants regularly used the words *blah ngă* or *sangkriem* (war, in Jorai and in Khmer, respectively). On several occasions, I witnessed that when villagers were talking among themselves, they would spontaneously switch to the Khmer language, as if the Jorai locutions lacked sufficient accuracy to convey the speaker's message faithfully. Indeed, old and young villagers alike sometimes found it more convenient to express themselves in Khmer when they were debating development or political issues since for these subjects of conversation, new words were often introduced in their Khmer form. Debates concerning war and the description of its violence in particular also often resulted in the use of the Khmer language.

In gathering people's testimonies of their involvement in the various conflicts, I discovered that for most people living in Leu, the general concept of war was conceived of as a discrete and self-contained notion, as if it encompassed a long series of battles generally starting from the fight against the

Text box 6. The bombing data: Secrecy, conspiracy, and persistent uncertainties

According to William Shawcross, "Cambodia was a test, a trial through which Nixon was putting the American people, let alone the Cambodians, so that if a real crisis did come one day, the world would beware. 'This is not an invasion of Cambodia,' Nixon insisted. (Officials were ordered to call it an 'incursion' instead). At one level this was just another lie, but at another it was true. Cambodia was a testing ground for United States resolve" (Shawcross 1993: 148). The US bombardment of Cambodia has generated many conspiracy theories, fueled not least by declassified documents revealing covert operations across Cambodia's borders, regarding decisions taken (or ultimately endorsed) by Nixon and Kissinger in the face of congressional opposition to maintain an intensive assault on Communist forces present in the country. The bombardments were labeled Operations Menu, Breakfast, Lunch, and Dinner, which all fell under the "Menu strikes" program and involved carpet bombing in the vicinity of the capital city of Phnom Penh, in addition to eastern and northeastern Cambodia. Today, as previously, although top secret documents have been fully declassified under the thirty-year rule (during the Clinton administration), full data concerning the total numbers of plane sorties and tons of bombs remain incomplete. These persistent uncertainties derive to a large extent from the destruction of bombing records and the falsification of documents at the time when Congress was undertaking an official enquiry into the president's involvement in the military operations in Cambodia. For William Shawcross, "The bombing of Cambodia had evidently become an important symbol of [Nixon's] embattled presidency" (Shawcross 1993: 293).

According to a Southeast Asia mine and unexploded ordnance database specialist, "[Today] the US Department of Defense only has 15% of the data available." "By 15th of August 1973, when the last American planes dropped their cargoes, the total tonnage dropped since Operation Breakfast was 539,129. Almost half of these bombs, 257,465 tons, had fallen in the last six months. (During the Second World War 160,000 tons were dropped on Japan.) On Air Force maps of Cambodia thousands of square miles of densely populated, fertile areas are marked black from the inundation. The immediate and the lasting effects of that massive, concentrated bombardment will probably never accurately be known" (ibid.). The consequence of this lack of clarity in the amounts that were dropped and when the bombardment effectively started not only underlines the violation of Cambodia's neutrality

> at the time but also prevents researchers from properly assessing the impact of the aerial campaign in a quantitative manner. Official data show that the US bombing effectively started in 1970 (at least five years after the date given in testimonies by local people), while tonnage estimates vary widely between 500,000 and 2 million tons of bombs over the entire estimated period of the US bombardment (1964–73). ○

Japanese and continuing to the Vietnamese invasion and the subsequent creation of the PRK in 1979. In this regard, the Jorai term *blah ngă* (war) most often encapsulated personal ordeals, collective experience of foreign attacks (US bombardment), forced labor, military enrollment at the time of the KR, and the fighting against multiple and ever-shifting enemies. When my informants wanted to talk about a specific conflict, they instead used the word *peublah* (fighting, in Jorai), for example, in phrases such as "fighting with the French" or "fighting against the Americans." Such qualifications thus enabled them to identify and extract a single event from the large and seemingly coherent war category that appears to have defined the individual and collective past. To this end, the concept of war, with its intrinsic notions of violence, survival, loss, and painful memories, may provide us with an analytical framework to better understand Leu villagers' perception of their place in time.

Furthermore, people's use of the Euro-American dating system was quite widespread when they were inscribing a particular incident in time, especially among former KR soldiers, who were usually more accurate in locating specific historical occurrences. The villagers' more traditional sense of time has been increasingly replaced by the Gregorian calendar as years, months, and days have been used to record, and to some extent remember, particular tragic events. Conversely, births and ordinary deaths were not framed in the same manner; people were vaguer about locating these particular social events in time or simply seemed to find it irrelevant.

Luyin Blen, for instance, was one of the people I worked with who seemed to use years in a rigorous manner in giving accounts of the violent past. Cross-checking of information with other informants, literature reviews, and other discussions I had with him at different times enabled me to verify a date, a development, or a narrative detail he told me, thus confirming his remarkable ability to place each episode he remembered in a wider chronological context. Occurrences that were beyond or not directly connected with the war seemed to have slipped into the dusty haziness of history, however. Events that had taken place a long time ago, before the fight against the Japanese (1945), for instance, were dated "at the time of my grandfather(s)," a spontaneous time marker that was very often used by both the older and younger generations in the village. On the other hand, relatives' births or deaths were located in time in connection with a particular bad harvest or epidemic or with reference to someone else's birth or death. Pou Ksor, for instance, told me that his nephew, Siu, had been born when a close relative died in combat.

Another important feature of my informants' accounts relates to narrating the time of the Khmer Rouge period, especially when these informants were directly involved in building the revolution. Because of the sensitivity of the subject, many former KR supporters were reluctant at first to talk about the KR in a way that would expose their past involvement. Indeed, because of the shame associated with the KR regime, a few villagers often remained silent about this period of their history or resorted to the personal pronoun "we" instead of the first-person singular "I," thus engaging in a general and anonymous narrative on how this was a very painful period of their life. At the time when I conducted my research, the indictment of main KR players in the Khmer Rouge tribunal was drawing worldwide attention, and its historic initiative to bring perpetrators to justice had been broadcast in the country through various channels; hence one's past contribution to the KR revolution might have been a source of particular embarrassment, guilt, or shame. It was only later in my research that I was able to develop relationships with former KR soldiers and thus learn about some of the darker details of personal and collective histories (see text box 7).

It was only after I had known one informant for more than nine months that he felt comfortable talking about his personal experience living with the KR in greater depth. Thirty minutes after the start of one of our conversations, he admitted that he had deliberately enlisted as a KR soldier, saying, "Oh, all right, let's say it, I was a member of the KR revolutionary army and I am not ashamed. . . . These were hard times and I had to survive." There-

Text box 7. Testimony of a former Khmer Rouge soldier

Before settling here, Pol Pot was in Vietnam, and one person from my village went away with him and I never saw him again. The Vietnamese were fighting the Americans and the Khmers were fighting the Khmers. The Khmer Rouge (KR) pushed Lon Nol back all the way to Phnom Penh, and all the *chonchiet* [ethnic-minority groups] fought Lon Nol. I joined the KR in 1977 to fight against the Vietnamese. *Samdech* [his highness] Pol Pot asked the Jorai to work with him to ensure surveillance, protection, and the organization of the network. Meanwhile the KR took away all the adolescents to [the northern province of] Stung Treng for labor and study. A lot of people died under the Khmer Rouge but fewer from the ethnic-minority side. Deaths amounted to 2 to 3 million in total, with the highest death rates between 1977 and 1979, although the KR started its purges as early as 1974.

Under the KR, people could not talk. There was only a cup of rice to share among five people. If someone protested, he would get killed. Food was served twice only during the day. The *kampong peitseup* [the eighty cup, in Khmer], as they called it, was divided, and people were given a few vegetables that were boiled in a huge saucepan. There was no nutrient in it, and the water was pitch black. But I have never eaten that.... I had to follow; otherwise they would have killed me.... For us who became KR soldiers, we shared a cup of rice between two people, which was all right. To avoid being hungry, people always listened and obeyed the orders....

School [indoctrination] was from 6:00 p.m. to 2:00 a.m. People would sometimes be taken away during the night to be executed. Others left and managed to escape into Thailand, Laos, and Vietnam.... They were afraid. If I had stayed one more month, I would have been killed like the others, but the Vietnamese came in time. As a soldier, I knew how to get to the Vietnamese border. I was one of the first to defect, and I gathered a group of three hundred people to march toward Vietnam. But we met the KR on the way, and we were asked what we were doing. I told them the truth and said that there was nothing to eat, no potatoes, no crops, nothing! So I was going back to my village where I knew there would be something to eat, but they made us turn around. The other leader of our group got punished and died under torture; as for me, it was only a matter of time. I was keeping a grenade in my hand all day and all night; if they had wanted to torture me, I would have killed all of us. They did not dare. I escaped again and this time managed to cross the border. I surrendered myself to the Vietnamese, placing my hands above my head. The Vietnamese helped me and gave me some food. ○

after the discussion lasted for more than an hour. For most people living in Leu and neighboring villages, personal connection with the KR remains a taboo subject, especially in talking to outsiders. The concealment of one's past KR activities is known to be widespread in Cambodia (Dunlop 2005; Hinton 2005). In remote places like Leu, people know what others have done in the past but do not talk about it anymore because they may well have been involved themselves or find that it is now part of the past that needs forgetting. It was by gathering information from various individuals (those who experienced the KR time and younger persons from the postconflict generation) that I discovered that some of my informants had been more active in the revolution than they had previously told me. Whether they joined deliberately (inspired by the Marxist-Leninist ideas) or were forced to join (under threat), some of the personal underlying motivations remain a complex issue that is now very difficult to elucidate clearly.

In his account of his time spent among the KR, Luyin Blen used the term *samdech* (king or highness) once or twice to refer to Pol Pot. A highly deferential Khmer term that is commonly used to refer to the royal family or the current head of state, *samdech* conveys a particular sense of authority, respect, and allegiance. At the start of my research, I was interested in knowing who among the people I worked with had actually joined the KR in their revolutionary movement. At the completion of it, I realized that most of them had in one way or another. In the late 1960s, Pol Pot had chosen Ratanakiri province as a first Communist base, and thirty years later a wave of former KR soldiers (some of Khmer origin) had moved into the area after the peace agreement in 1991 to leave their past behind and rebuild their life. As a result, people may have felt that they were bound by a common past, and it was thus not unusual to hear similarly vague or even entirely made-up accounts of personal experiences at the high point of KR influence in the region.

Entrapped by the Past

Leu is one of many villages located on the infamous Ho Chi Minh Trail, and therefore, large bomb craters have become ordinary and characteristic features of this postconflict environment, scarring villages, forests, and orchards. According to Leu villagers and a few Jorai villagers living near the

Vietnamese border, this area is also largely known to be affected by *luk tek* (bombs) that were dropped by American planes to obliterate the Ho Chi Minh Trail and to a lesser extent antipersonnel land mines and improvised explosive devices used during ground battles along the border at the end of the 1970s.

For Luyin Blen, the threats from land mine and bomb explosions in general could be seen as the persistence of armed conflicts into the present. In other words, each time an accident occurs, the violence of the past swells to overflow the present, leading to a superimposition of past and present times. Therefore, one may want to venture that the modification of the physical landscape—through vegetation cutting, for example—is a way for the Jorai villagers to once again push back the limits of a hazardous, albeit this time human-made, environment. From time to time, accidents happen as people till their land to seed their new crops, dig in bomb craters to salvage metal, or use recycled explosives for river fishing. In such cases, the memory of the war reactivates itself since its dormant presence (in the form of buried explosives) suddenly erupts. According to the survivors of the conflicts, especially those who have been maimed by explosive remnants of war (ERW), the memory of the war is deeply embedded in one's mind and body. As Luyin Blen explained, "[For them,] the war is not over; it is still going on!"

For Pou Ksor, key historical developments were associated with specific years inspired by the Gregorian calendar. In talking about his accident, which cost him an eye, a forearm, and three fingers, he associated the tragedy of losing his body parts with the accuracy of geographic space and date: "In 1982, I was in Preah Vihear [a northern province], where the mine accident happened on the 18th of August." Most of my informants who had fallen victim to land mines connected their injuries to an inauspicious date as if this particular moment in time was deeply etched in one's body and memory. In the same way, Pou Yeng was regarded by other villagers in Leu and Bok as having been closely involved with the Khmer Rouge when he lost his right leg to a land mine. Like Pou Ksor, Pou Yeng recorded the accident using space and time references: "I became disabled in Stung Treng [province] in 1979 when fighting against the Vietnamese." Yeng described his time living under the US bombardment as an extended period of hiding in the forest with his wife and disabled child, while, during the KR regime, he claimed that he was a bodyguard whose main chores consisted in boiling water, carrying things, and helping gather people for meetings.

In the eyes of some of the young villagers who were born in times of peace, people who have fallen victim to a land mine are forever marked with the seal of the past war. After I had met Yeng, nineteen-year-old Nay, one of my young informants, commented that Yeng's involvement in the KR revolution movement was well known by the rest of the villagers to be more substantial than the menial chores, claiming, "He lost his leg.... He was Pol Pot's personal driver! That day he left his car to check a booby trap that was placed across the road." As if sharing an important piece of information that was well known to others, Nay talked about Pou Yeng's disabled condition as if it was a logical consequence of (or possibly retribution for?) his closeness to Pol Pot.

In this case, the individual accident was reframed by the larger historical event because it had left visible traces on the human body. The use of antipersonnel land mines by the KR soldiers allowed them to act at different places and times simultaneously, thus enabling the various warring factions to act across time, stretching the temporal boundaries of their troop advancements into the future (Gell 1998). As I will discuss in chapter 3, in such a war-torn landscape, unexploded ordnance constitutes a tragic legacy of past violent conflicts that has the ominous potential to directly affect future generations.

In his study of agency, Gell noted that the use of antipersonnel land mines (APM) enabled the KR soldier to act out a "distributed personhood" (Gell 1998: ix). This disposition allows for a crystallization of identity whereby the APM (as the vehicle of his intention to hurt) is employed as a tool by the user so that it becomes an extension of his own body. Once the land mine is activated, it earns the ability to distribute itself because its detonation will send land mine parts (shrapnel) into various parts of a single or multiple bodies. The concept of distributed personhood can be understood through its ripple effect once the mine has been set off. As a function of dynamic distribution, a single agent can (by means of APM) create multiplicity. In fact, a single soldier can replicate his presence in as many land mines as he chooses to bury and activate. In the same manner, albeit on a smaller scale, a single antipersonnel land mine can in turn disseminate its presence (by means of shrapnel) to as many body parts as it affects.

Ironically, one can use Gell's notion of distributed personhood and the inherent process of multiplying the single to frame the way the KR administration was established and managed. Pol Pot, at the head of the establishment, had through layers of management and delegated duties gained the ability to be simultaneously invisible and present within each and every one of the cadres who dutifully carried out orders from above. This capacity to replicate and distribute his authority (or the idea thereof) down the chain of command and control constituted one of the most striking mechanisms of the KR administration (*angkar*), one that ultimately would suffer from its own (mal)function through the spread of paranoia, suspicions of betrayals, and summary executions.

In the preceding case, both the acts of land mine laying and explosion produce a distinct distributive effect by occupying various spaces at various points in time. For most land mine and ERW victims, the distributive impact of a land mine explosion often means that physical pains may persist, especially when fragments have remained locked inside the body and are impossible to remove because of their continuous movement. However, as Maurice Merleau-Ponty interestingly pointed out, pain may also remain inside a phantom limb as if it is locked in the missing limb, which somehow remains connected to the rest of the body (1962).

In this instance, war shapes not only people's minds in the form of tragic memory or trauma but also the physical body as if the body is a transformable material in itself, henceforth making the violent historical moment the unique possession of the individual's body part. This transformation can often lead to the creation of what can be called the "man-machine" or the "man-object" within the process of "remaking men" as Jeffrey Reznick puts it in referring to former soldiers who lost limbs during the Great War and benefited from prosthetic or orthotic support to compensate for the loss of body parts (2004: 53). Pou Yeng used a wooden stick in lieu of his right leg, while Pou Ksor had decided that he did not need any replacement for his lost left forearm. As he said to me once, "Some organizations came a while ago and offered to replace my [left] arm, but I don't need one; I grew accustomed to not having it anymore.... I can go on about my life this way.... What preoccupies me, though, is my eye; do you think they can fill in the blank and not leave it empty?"

More than worrying about their incomplete bodies, Pou Ksor and other disabled persons have mentioned their common anxiety caused by the unaesthetic aspect (the ugly appearance) of their injuries. The trace left by the war is not only marked by the absence of body parts but also characterized by the body's perceived unattractiveness for both the disabled and the rest of the community. In this particular instance, people may feel that a wider divide between the generations has been effected through physical disabilities.

But when an accident occurs in times of peace, the victim falls into a trap that enables the two generations to collapse violently into one another, thus removing the time difference that originally separated the generation that lived through the war from the following one that tries to make a livelihood out of its remnants. As Alfred Gell noted,

> The trap is therefore both a model of its creator, the hunter, and a model of its victim, the prey animal. But more than this, the trap embodies a scenario, which is the dramatic nexus that binds these two protagonists together, and which aligns them in time and space. Our illustrations cannot show this because they either show traps awaiting their victims, or victims who have been already entrapped; they cannot show the "time structure" of the trap. This time structure opposes suspended time, the empty time of "waiting," to the sudden catastrophe that ensues as the trap closes. (Gell 1996: 27)

This idea, which illustrates Gell's "network of intentionalities," is explored in greater detail in chapter 3.

In studying Ilongot head-hunters, Renato Rosaldo argued that

> it makes a great deal of difference, to take a number of examples, whether one speaks about history as a river running slowly to the sea or as the fierce gales of change, an irretrievably lost moment, a seed grown into a blossoming flower, the good old days, an ugly duckling become a swan, a green betel quid chewed into red saliva, a walk along the path of life, or an oscillation between the focus of inward movement and the diffusion of outward dispersal. . . . Often imaged as spatial movement, the Ilongot sense of history can be represented, on the one hand, as a group of people walking in single file along a trail and, on the other, as an alternation between the focus of inward concentration and the diffusion of outward dispersal. (Rosaldo 1980: 289)

For more than a century, the villagers of Leu have gone through periods of violent conflicts and political transformations as they have tried to set the course of their communal life through changes brought by the collision with military and political forces, walking, like the Ilongots, in new directions, engaging in new paths and retreating, or merely trying to seize new opportunities as the stability of the entire community (or the safety of the household during the KR regime) was endangered. People's exposure to external powers that were beyond their control seems to have culminated at the time of the US bombardment, which has played a significant role in locating the individual in a wider geopolitical context. Such a historical event can be interpreted as a "sign" or a "text" that creates "a conscious relationship between past and present" (Dening 1988: 3). In light of such collateral effects, the Jorai of Leu may view their history of the past 150 years as inseparable from the history of foreign others.

This sense of historicity that surfaces through individual testimonies is often passed on from one generation to the next as older inhabitants make use of individual memories to inform the youngest villagers of the collective past. Gayle Morrison called this particular form of historical consciousness "*perceptual history*, a history that gives voice to the human variety of experience as much as to the chronological sequence" (2007: 2). But this kaleidoscope of voices only tells the same story of self-preservation at a time when the last fence against the external world was irreversibly destroyed. Today, as the village's life seems to progress at the pace of subsistence cultivation despite the growing influence of materialism, the remains of the past still intrude into the villagers' lives as buried matters surface to help shape the present.

Chapter 3

Postconflict Strategies of the Jorai *Homo Faber*

How do people cope with the physical legacy of war? How does one build a livelihood from the rubble of the natal landscape and the material debris of technological warfare? To what extent do leftover armaments partake in the everyday life of postconflict societies? In a natural environment that is perceived as inauspicious to human life, maintaining a subsistence livelihood in times of peace was often described by Leu villagers as being "arduous." For people who live in the presence of foreign and sometimes treacherous objects, the salvage of physical remnants of war can provide new economic prospects, however.

Although there is a growing body of literature related to postconflict reconstruction in countries affected by land mines and unexploded ordnance (UXO), few researchers have conducted comprehensive ethnography to examine the resilience of Southeast Asian rural communities and the variety of their modes of survival (Boholm 1996). Investigating the Jorai subsistence farmers' coping strategies in the most affected areas thus is an attempt to increase our understanding of these postconflict societies. This chapter aims to discuss the different survival strategies used by the villagers from two distinct but interrelated perspectives: first, how they contribute to the economy of the household, and second, the way they affect an individual's place within the wider group. Throughout this chapter, the term "household" refers to a discrete social and economic unit that is composed of kin- and affine-related individuals who share food and material goods and often sleep under the same roof. It examines the different mechanisms that enable the members of the household to maintain the pool of common resources they need to live on during difficult times.

The chapter is divided into four sections, beginning with an overview of household day-to-day survival mechanisms, which will shed light on what is conceived of as a crisis that may threaten the well-being of the household members. This overview provides a thorough examination of how the ordinary Jorai living in Leu identifies, translates, and responds effectively to risk, meaning such potential threats as illness, food scarcity, insanity, UXO, ghosts of war, and unburied bodies.

The second section investigates local attitudes and responses to risk factors whereby pragmatic, albeit sometimes unsafe, initiatives enable risky activities to be seen as, and transformed into, opportunities. Among these activities, the collection of already exploded or unexploded ordnance illustrates the economic incentives a war-torn landscape can offer subsistence farmers.

The third section turns to the local recycling and consumption of salvaged materials and in this regard is an analysis of the biography of war-related objects in parts or as a whole. In transforming the object, personal creativity and psychological resilience are at work in modifying and extending its life cycle, thus breathing new life into objects originally programmed to cause death.

The last section explores the other face of the hunter in pursuit of the dead body of the foreigner. As with bomb hunting, the perceived economic gains generated by the activity of body hunting have created a market that is difficult to enter but potentially profitable, since confronting, retrieving, and returning the remains of a former enemy can bring both financial reward and spirit appeasement.

Leu Villagers' Day-to-Day Survival Mechanisms

Risk and Theories Regarding Southeast Asian Peasants' Survival

The notion of survival encompasses the fields of politics, economics, and social and medical sciences, thereby lending itself to varying interpretations. Related anthropological debates have been stimulated by work such as that of James C. Scott (1976, 1985) and Samuel Popkin (1979), who offered contrasting analyses of the survival strategies developed by Southeast Asian peasant communities. The following discussion uses the expression "survival strategies" in the subsistence-farming context of Leu, where people's coping mechanisms consist of all the available means that enable them to save the household from falling below its livelihood margins. Coping involves pragmatic attitudes, individual skills, technical knowledge, new ideas, and difficult decisions, the use of which enables a householder to effectively expand his or her security buffer and thus reduce the vulnerability of household members to various sources of livelihood stresses.

The school of the moral economy of the peasant, which includes James Scott, Eric Wolf, and Karl Polanyi, argues that the peasant is ontologically risk averse. Because peasants often live close to a subsistence margin, security is perceived as a crucial element of livelihood preservation, since even a small decline can jeopardize the survival of the entire household. "[The subsistence peasant] works close enough to the margin that he has a great deal to lose by miscalculating; his limited techniques and the whims of weather expose him, more than most producers, to unavoidable risks; the relative absence of alternatives for gainful employment offer him precious little in the way of economic insurance. If he is even more cautious about endangering his livelihood, he has a rational basis for his reluctance" (Scott 1976: 25).

Scott termed peasants' continuous anxiety with respect to subsistence and security the "safety first" principle, meaning that farmers concentrate on avoiding economic shortfalls rather than maximizing potential surplus. This form of response is justified by the confidence that communal fallback mechanisms will act as both a social and an economic safety net to ensure that any individual crop failure is automatically compensated by some redistribution of village resources. Indeed, "All moral economists stress that the individual will go under if, and only if, their communities go under" (Popkin 1979: 10).

As an exponent of the political economy approach to analyzing Southeast Asian peasants' behavior, Samuel Popkin conversely believed that moral economists have substantially exaggerated the peasants' virtuous qualities. By contrast, he portrayed the peasant as a rational problem solver whose thoughts and economic behaviors belong more to an effective corporation than to a community bound by reciprocal trust and moral duties. Popkin hence critiqued what he saw as the moral economists' misleading depiction of a homogeneous community and their claim that peasants do not need markets. He argued instead that moral economists falsely posit that peasants are antimarket individuals with an aversion to buying, selling, and investing for personal gain and social advancement within the community's hierarchical structure. For the political economist, "As long as there are multiple economic levels, an interest in advancing from one level to the next, and an interest in avoiding falls, peasants will be concerned with both insurance and gambling, that is, secure and risky investments" (Popkin 1979: 21–22).

The ordinary Leu villager is neither a risk-averse nor a corporate-driven individual. It is with respect to particular contexts and situations, which I will discuss later, that a villager decides whether to take risks. In Leu, the household survival strategy essentially works within the framework of kin and affine relations. Such networks through blood and marriage enable the household to call on a significant pool of individuals who can help in times of need and crisis. Because people live close to the survival margin, with just enough food for a day or two, events that do not allow the household to stretch its endurance buffer any further cause a crisis. Therefore, children start contributing at a young age (nine or ten, or even younger for some bomb hunters) by working in the garden, collecting fuelwood and water, hunting for birds, snakes, and frogs, and fishing.

Children's active participation thus emphasizes the fact that each person contributes individually while relying on other household members at the same time. Coping entails mutual rights and responsibilities and thus spreads risk across a wide group. For example, a villager relies on other members of the household to bring in food or cash on a daily basis. Food is shared equally among the members of the family, and it is always offered, even if in limited quantity, to a neighbor or a visitor who happens to be present at the time. In spite of an unproductive day (e.g., no fish caught in the river), the people I worked with hoped that someone would bring in food for the evening; hence the larger the household unit, the less anxious (and the more reliant on one another) its members may be. However, my informants could hardly foretell what they would eat beyond the present day, and they sometimes had to skip a meal because their relatives had returned home *blun* (naked) or empty-handed.

Nonetheless, for the same reason, the opposite conclusion could be drawn: village elders commented that they had stopped building and living in Jorai traditional longhouses (only one remains in the village) since the greater the number of persons sharing the same accommodation, the more individuals felt encouraged to sit back and wait for other members of the household to work and bring in food. Some villagers claimed that such uneven contributions were the source of family arguments that were solved by physical separation into smaller houses and family units.

The Repercussions of a Global Crisis on a Local Village

The Jorai of Leu are subsistence farmers who rely heavily on their annual production of rice. The planting season starts in June, when the monsoonal rain nourishes the fields for four months before the harvest at the end of the year. The Jorai living in the region have in the past (except the period of the Khmer Rouge regime) carried out swidden agriculture, which entails rotating the cultivation of the land and allowing long fallow periods. However, since the conflicts, a growing dearth of land has caused people to progressively abandon their traditional lifestyle and convert to wet-rice farming (Guérin et al. 2003). In addition, people cultivate other crops, like corn, sweet potatoes, and cabbages, and sometimes raise cattle. Other major sources of livelihood derive from the collection of nontimber forest products, seasonal labor (burning and cutting trees), game hunting, and fishing, as well as hunting for bomb remnants in order to recover metal and explosive materials.

In the first months of 2008, an unusual global rise in the price of a barrel of petroleum had direct repercussions on Southeast Asian countries and severe effects on the lives of the villagers living in Leu. As a non-self-reliant country in regard to main crop production, Cambodia imports rice and many consumables from Thailand and Vietnam. As a result, the price of rice rose significantly and ultimately doubled in isolated districts like Andong Meas.

For the Jorai subsistence farmers, the daily diet is essentially rice, which constitutes a meal on its own three times a day. Indeed, large servings of rice are crucial in order for people with a limited food supply to fill the stomach and compensate for the lack of meat or other sources of proteins. My informants commented that if they did not consume large portions of rice (at least two full plates for each meal), they would lack the energy to work in their *hwa* (fruit and vegetable gardens). For example, in a household where six adults and a young child live (with fluctuations over the months because family members from other villages often come to stay), the monthly average amount of rice was estimated at 100 kilograms. The price of a kilogram of rice in the local market of O'Kop usually varies between 6,000 and 8,000 riels (1.5 to 2 USD), depending on quality, but at the height of this abnormal inflation, a kilogram of the lowest-quality rice cost 12,500 riels (more than 3 USD), double its usual price. The regional inflation in the price of rice was thus seen as a dramatic blow to households trying to sustain their livelihood, especially since it occurred at the beginning of the lean season, when people were about to exhaust the supply of rice from the last harvest while waiting to plant again. Because the inflation lasted for months, all the households in the village became reliant on the local market, where rice progressively became the most coveted commodity.

Subsequently, Leu villagers tried to respond to this crisis in a variety of ways: first by borrowing rice from relatively better-off families within the village (although this lasted only a relatively short time because these more affluent families were themselves hit by the inflation) and then by traveling in small groups across the Vietnamese border to borrow rice and money from relatives. Villagers from various communities living near the border started smuggling rice from Vietnam, but this practice became more and more difficult as increasing taxes needed to be paid on the Cambodian side and as the Vietnamese government took the drastic decision to ban all rice exportation in order to ensure its own national consumption needs. Last, people resorted to working as seasonal laborers in large plantations or construction sites (e.g., house building). But in this case, the use of motorcycles for daily transportation was severely limited as a result of inflation of the price of gasoline.

In these months, the first risk-causing factor identified by Leu villagers as making the household increasingly vulnerable was the shortage of rice. This in turn created the conditions for indebtedness and chronic illness, which ultimately resulted in a lack of labor because people felt too ill to work. At this time of scarcity, the general inflation triggered multiple adverse effects, which led people, especially those with several young children, to think of this period as a difficult time.

In early 2009, Kluen told me that he had just returned from a two-hour motorbike ride to visit his relatives in Vietnam, from which most of Leu villagers' ancestors had originally come. He explained that he was forced to seek help beyond the village to borrow rice since his family had run out of food and could not borrow from anyone. Furthermore, his wife was repeatedly ill because she went without eating enough in order to feed their three children. In times of scarcity, the possibility of relying on kin living across the border is an important safety net. It is a crucial component of the villagers' "social space," to use the term coined by Georges Condominas (Condominas 1980: 11–96), that is created, used, and constantly negotiated by the villagers. Kin who reside outside the village in a foreign land are often considered—and perceived by the rest of the community—as being of invaluable support in minimizing the household's everyday exposure to risk. As Joanna White commented,

> Extended family groups assist each other at key stages of the agricultural cycle when work is particularly pressing or difficult, such as when trees must be cut to clear new areas of forest, or during the harvest, or in times of labour shortage due to death or illness. When rice stocks run low it is also common for borrowing to take place between members of the extended family. This exchange of labour and goods amongst kinship groups often takes place on an inter-village basis. Groups with a clan kinship system, such as the Jorai and Tampuan, also have these wider allegiances to draw upon. (White 1995: 42)

The Anthropology of Risk

The concept of risk has been applied to an ever-growing range of situations in Europe and America in the past forty years (Douglas and Wildavsky 1983). The *Collins English Dictionary* (1994) defines risk as "a source of danger; a possibility of incurring loss or misfortune" or "a venture undertaken without regard to possible loss or injury." As described in Ulrich Beck's research on the modern society at risk, the term has come to be used and accordingly redefined in a multitude of sectors (e.g., health, law, banking, finance, politics, and the military) as it has gradually pervaded all layers of current social, political, and economic life (Beck 1995; Boholm 1996).

In the past thirty years, technological advances have rendered consumers particularly susceptible to risk related to globalization. Mary Douglas and Aaron Wildavsky explored the paradigm under the social sciences lens using both cultural theory and a critical approach to people's perception and interpretation of risk. To this end, "Research into risk perception based on a cultural model would try to discover what different characteristics of social life elicit different responses to danger" (Douglas and Wildavsky 1983: 8). They revealed that risk is a concept that is politically manipulated and socially construed. In light of this, the political exploitation of the concept of risk illustrates the Foucauldian notion of governmentality as a privileged means to better control the citizen through moral blame (Douglas 1994), which is sanctioned by greater state involvement and bureaucracy. Ulrich Beck furthered the argument, viewing these concepts as intrinsically linked to the individual's moral duty in the context of global sources of risk, such as climate change. In Beck's perspective, the individual's agency has potential adverse consequences for the entire community, which brings to the fore issues of accountability and socially acceptable levels of risk (Douglas and Wildavsky 1983). Cambodia is one of the most heavily mined and bombed areas in the history of modern warfare, and the ideas and practices of postconflict communities often reveal a discrepancy between the government's discourse on risk and local people's perceptions and interpretations, especially in cases where the individual is fined or sometimes jailed by the local police when he or she has recourse to live ordnance handling. For example, reusing the explosive contents for fishing and selling them to earn money are regular local activities that are outlawed by provincial subdecrees aimed at improving village safety.

Risk and the Victim Discourse of the Mine-Action and Development Sector

Despite more than twenty years of work on clearance of antipersonnel land mines and UXO in Cambodia, the scale of the contamination problem posed by explosive remnants of war (ERW) remains significant. It is assumed that the physical presence of UXO always endangers the economic life and social fabric of the rural communities most affected. International donor countries have therefore supported national demining endeavors as a means of fostering national reconstruction and development. However, this support has largely consisted of considerable levels of financial and technical assistance, which have brought with them a predominance of expert and foreign approaches at both rhetorical and practical levels. Drawing on the work of Michel Foucault in his book *The Anti-politics Machine*, James Ferguson argued that these expert and foreign views ignore the historical, political, and cultural realities of the target populations that development projects aim to help (Ferguson 1994). Consequently, such technical discourses can render the wider development work problematic and sometimes make some communities worse off by denying the abilities of subsistence farmers to use their own skills and resources to make their communities safer. Instead of merely ignoring the reality, such expert views may be tempted to construct a particular reality based on the village victim in order to justify external intervention and governmental control. For Ulrich Beck, "Risks are defined as the probabilities of physical harm due to given technological or other processes. Hence technical experts are given pole position to define agendas and impose bounding premises *a priori* on risk discourses" (Beck 1992: 4).

What makes matters worse for these villagers is the fact that deliberate exploitation of leftover armaments has been made an illegal and morally censured practice. Stimulated by the pervasive regional scrap-metal trade, the intentional searching out of bombs has become a common activity in many ethnic-minority villages, however (DiGregorio 1995; Moyes 2004; GICHD 2005c; Uk 2007; Baird and Shoemaker 2008; Schwenkel 2013). Such economically motivated forms of behavior have given rise to the deceptive idea that rural communities living in mine- and UXO-contaminated areas consist either of powerless victims waiting for external support (or a technical fix) or risk-addicted individuals who are in urgent need of being protected from themselves, especially in cases where technical efforts to render an area safe have been paradoxically followed by some local initiatives to put the antipersonnel land mines back (Bottomley 2003; Moyes 2004; Uk 2007).

In such a puzzling context, a critical examination of the various forces at play is a necessary step to further our understanding of the local survival strategies in officially classified high-risk areas. Because there is presently an extensive pool of literature on mine action and development, this chapter will not treat this particular theme as a major field of inquiry, nor will it examine

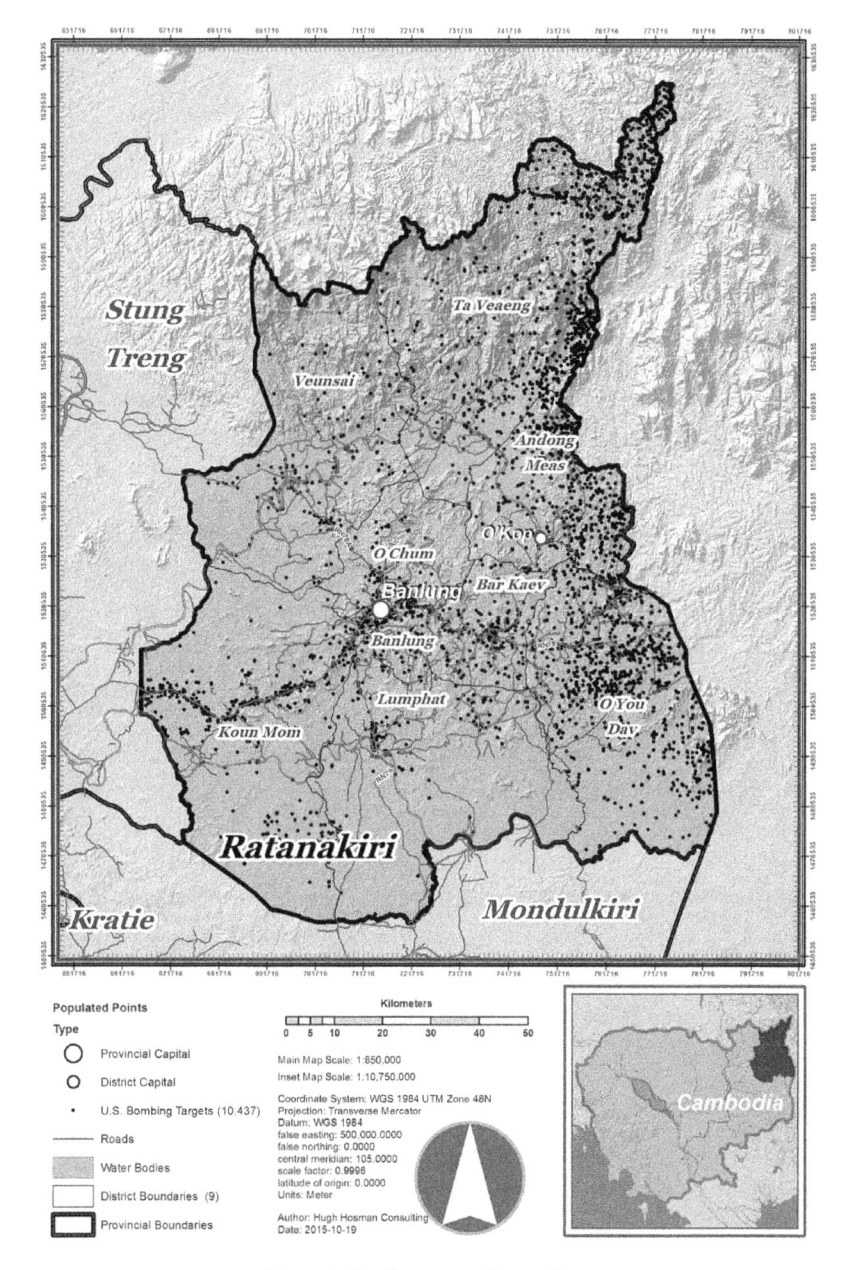

Figure 2. Bombing map of Ratanakiri.

84   Chapter 3

in great detail current tensions between communities and clearance agencies or national authorities. Its emphasis is more on the village and household levels, where social, economic, and political processes pertaining to local and intimate spheres permeate normative and individually endorsed dispositions for risk-related bodily practices.

Local Perceptions and Understanding of Risk

According to Jacques Dournes, life in the first part of the twentieth century was already fraught with everyday sources of risk in the forms of, for example, evil spirits, tigers, village feuds, foreign intrusions, and lack of rain (Dournes 1978). Some of these sources of risk may have persisted, changed, or disappeared, but the long-drawn-out conflicts have introduced new risks, and their single or combined effects may have a critical impact on a household's daily survival. The Jorai living in Leu engage in swidden cultivation, fishing, game hunting, and animal husbandry all year long. However, some men and young male adolescents also undertake bomb hunting to supplement their income all through the year. Because Southeast Asian peasants' lives are constantly under pressure from various sources of life uncertainty, the risk posed by the presence of land mines and UXO becomes one factor of vulnerability among many others. Villagers do not approach each source of risk in isolation but weigh one source of risk against another as part of their daily survival mechanism.

When I asked my informants about the Jorai translation of or an equivalent for "risk," they were at first puzzled by the question. After reflecting on it, they said that there was no direct translation for the concept, but that they used the Khmer expression *peuthoy peuthan* or its Jorai adaptation *peutak peutan*, both meaning "to go ahead." Others claimed that they used the Jorai terms *peumegn mang* or *peu teugom*, meaning "to go forward," thus conveying the idea that someone is heading for the potential source of danger. In examining these different attempts to define risk, it is important to note the absence of a direct translation of the term into both the Jorai and the Khmer languages. The closest Khmer expressions either draw from the concept of gambling, "to try one's luck," or indicate the absence of alternatives and hence the need to go ahead, "the readiness to go forward." Like the Euro-American definition, Leu villagers' conception of risk implies that the individual is an active agent who takes the decision to move in the direction of the hazard or uncertainty. In the context of subsistence farming, the concepts of risk, hazard, danger, and uncertainty can often be used interchangeably.

The local understanding of what constitutes a hazard and of which situations can be categorized as risky depends very much on the age, status, and gender of the informant. Furthermore, it is greatly shaped by time and by social, economic, and political contexts. In *Risk Revisited*, Pat Caplan reexamined the concept using a variety of social, cultural, and political backgrounds to get better insight into the ways people individually conceive of the various situations they see as being harmful (Caplan 2000). In Leu and other nearby postconflict Jorai villages, what may be considered a risky behavior at one time may not be at another because of a confluence of factors that may have rendered the household more or less vulnerable.

When village elders were asked about risks related to their livelihood, they identified being exposed to illness and thieves as the two major sources that they worried most about. Middle-aged and young male villagers identified the lack of cash, a risk that some women also emphasized. In all these cases, though, commonly identified at-risk situations showed that male heads of household were concerned that their direct exposure to a source of fatal risk would have severe implications for the survival of the entire household, which might heavily rely on them. Despite the fact that bomb hunting can potentially cause injuries or death, villagers who would set off hunting for ERW felt that they had a certain degree of control over the outcome of the activity because of personal experience (military background), habit (adjustment to a postconflict environment), skills (handling technique), or spirit protection, as in traditional game hunts, as I will show later (see figure 3). Most women, however, viewed illness and lack of food as the greatest threats to their livelihood because these sources of risk could directly affect their ability to look after their children. Among children aged between five and ten, the main source was ghostly appearances at night and encounters with strangers and foreigners (even the anthropologist). In their case, the impact of such sources of risk concerned their own safety rather than having wider repercussions.

Figure 3. Hunting for the bombs. Photo by author.

Local Attitudes and Responses to Sources of Risk

Postwar Economics

The international conflicts and civil wars affecting northeastern Cambodia have generated a range of new economic activities, the most significant of which is the recovery of ERW. Farmers who undertake activities of subsistence procurement have, since the hostilities, found themselves in the presence of a new sort of income-generation activity that, although unsafe, can grant them direct access to cash. At present the constant demand for metal, which is stimulated by countries like China, maintains the price of metal at a stable level (Moyes 2004; Russell 2013; Schwenkel 2013), while at the top (the source) of the supply chain, such markets are continually provided for by small villages like Leu and other bomb-hunting communities.

After the villagers' return to Leu, people found that the area was completely littered with debris of bombs and armaments. My research in different districts of Ratanakiri suggests that despite cultural variations, the local population invariably tried to remove the ERW in order to create a safer space to rebuild their homes and turn metal salvaging into an income-generating activity. Today, inhabitants of Leu say that there are no more visible bomb fragments in or near the village because most accessible items of debris have been foraged. Yet until my most recent visit in September 2014, villagers and the local blacksmith claimed that more could still be harvested in the forests and mountains.

Illustrating Pierre Bourdieu's social and behavioral notion of "habitus," (Bourdieu 1977: 53) persistent bomb hunters in particular have grown up living in a hazardous context in which they have regarded ERW as part of their rural normality. This adaptation to a hazardous landscape is the source of enduring learned and embodied dispositions for both individual and collective action. To this end, tampering with war scrap metal may constitute a habitus in itself. Whether to gain access to agricultural land or to reclaim metal for its economic value, interacting with UXO can be a key element of a person's survival strategy.

The Persistence of the Regional Scrap-Metal Trade

"After the end of US bombardment of Southeast Asia, a vigorous trade in war scrap metal emerged in the informal economies of Vietnam, Laos and Cambodia. With the expansion of a global market economy, the trade became increasingly transborder and transnational. Scrap metal from Vietnam travels to Laos, China and beyond; while metal detectors are often imported from abroad. After economic reform policies were launched in Vietnam in 1986, the industry grew significantly" (Schwenkel 2013: 144). From the perspective of the supply side, local villages constitute a major source of metal collection, and as such, they form the first link in the long chain that makes up the scrap-metal market. This metal is recovered from large and small bombs that have been generated by the succession of conflicts but largely by the US bombing of the country from 1964 to 1975. Steel and aluminum are the main metals derived from war scrap collection, the latter often salvaged from airplanes that have crashed in the mountains.

Collection starts at the household level, where, after recovery of bomb debris, a person will decide whether he or she wants to keep the metal for household use. If a villager decides to keep the metal, he or she may hand the fragment to the local blacksmith, who will refashion it into a knife for work in the *hwa*. A villager who decides to sell the fragment has two options. The first is sale of the metal to an itinerant scrap-metal dealer who frequently travels to the village and buys the metal at a fixed price of 500 riels per kilogram (12 US cents), which had remained unchanged when I returned to Leu in the fall of 2014. This price allows the dealer in turn to make a marginal gain when he resells it to a larger scrap dealer in the provincial town of Banlung or across the Vietnamese border near the neighboring district of O You Dav. Alternatively, the villager can travel to Bokeo, which is the nearest district town, or directly to Banlung to sell the salvaged metal for 600 to 800 riels per kilogram. In the latter case, the potential profit needs to be weighed against the cost of fuel incurred in making the journey. The further an individual metal collector can progress along the supply chain, the greater the return he or she stands to gain for the material.

Perceptions of the quality of the metal retrieved from bomb remnants vary. Tham, the village blacksmith, stated that a knife manufactured from bomb metal was less solid and more malleable than an industrial one sourced from the Banlung market. He added, however, that some people would favor it for this very reason because it was endlessly refashionable. One of the large scrap-metal dealers in Banlung argued that the metal derived from large bombs was the most valuable because of its thickness and solidity. He thus claimed that for this particular type of metal he was ready to offer a very good price (up to 1,000 riels per kilogram, or 25 US cents), provided that it was safe to handle (i.e., free from explosives).

Once the metal reaches a large scrap-metal dealer at the district or the provincial level, the dealers say that it is sent either to Vietnam or to Thailand via several other Cambodian provinces. At the border-crossing stage, the metal will still be in its original or raw form because Cambodia has no smelting facilities. Only once it has been transported abroad will it be refashioned into something else, at which point it will acquire additional value. Once smelted, the metal can be turned into construction materials that may be reexported to countries like China and Laos or even eventually find their way back into Cambodia.

Behind the Rationale of Bomb Hunting

At the village level, a member of the household, either an adult or a child, can effectively contribute to the collection of metal by becoming an intermittent or regular bomb hunter. In a context of subsistence livelihood, parenting in a risk-prone environment often contradicts Euro-American risk categories. In Leu, young children from the age of three start playing with their parents' knives, while older ones already know how to use them effectively to cut bamboo and wood for fuel. Young girls often imitate their mothers doing household chores when they are playing with their friends. While they are pretending to cook, using real fire is one of their favorite games, and they may occasionally be asked to help start cooking for the entire household's meal. A regular bomb hunter and a mother of three explained that from the age of seven onward, a child was able to dig using a shovel and hence was deemed capable of searching for bombs. Early exposure to potential sources of risks (cuts, burns, and explosions) enables very young persons to become active contributors to the household economy.

Villagers commented that salvaging bombs and bomb debris was a profitable activity despite regular accidents. Because of the constant price of metal, fueled by the regional demand, some people believed that it was a more profitable activity than farming. For Michael DiGregorio, who examined scavenging and junk buying in northern Vietnam, the activity was fully "integrated into agricultural cycles, provided small but important cash incomes, and exhibited a high degree of solidarity and exclusion" (DiGregorio 1995).

Some Jorai villages in Andong Meas district (literally "the golden well") have made bomb hunting a major source of income, comparable in importance to agriculture and gold mining. Some of my informants explained that to avoid being injured, people would look only for fragments and leave bombs that appeared intact or that had a fuse or explosive contents in them. By contrast, others who were former soldiers felt that they could dismantle the bombs in order to sell the metal and recover the explosives for use for fishing, hence finding in the activity a double economic incentive. In this particular case, if the probability of an accident is high and its consequences possibly fatal, the decision to take the risk is motivated by the belief that the expected reward will be great and thus worth the exposure. By the same token, a female regular bomb hunter from a neighbouring Jorai village told me, "Of course we are afraid of dying, but even if someone died, we know that there will still be the money from the selling of the metal." Bomb hunters are usually aware of the risk they take and so employ careful measures in order to protect themselves, either by filtering through the debris and collecting harmless parts or by offering prayers and sacrifices to the spirits.

A particular category of bomb hunters that is prevalent in a few Jorai villages in the area is young male adolescents. Nay, a young Jorai adult, told me that he used to go bomb hunting but had stopped since he began working in his orchard. He explained that he had never been afraid of the bombs even when accidents occurred. He commented instead that he was fascinated by them, wondering how there could be so much power in a bomb. According to yearly statistics on accidents resulting from ERW, the young male segment of the population is usually the most at risk, as recorded by the Cambodia Mine/ERW Victim Information System on monthly and yearly bases. Reasons for this go beyond mere economic incentives and can in part include the spellbinding power of the dangerous object and the adrenaline triggered by unearthing or dismantling a bomb, which makes it a singular activity.

In the course of my research in Leu, no ERW-related accident happened in the village. In January 2008, however, a bomb exploded in the Jorai bomb hunters' village of Plói Phdol Krom, which is located a few kilometers upstream from Leu. The accident caused severe injuries to three male adolescents, two of whom were transported urgently to the district hospital because they had been burned by the bomb's chemical contents. Interviewed a month later, one of the victims claimed that they had hit the bomb unintentionally while they were trying to dig up sweet potatoes. A rather different version of the event was offered by a village elder, who commented instead that the accident had been caused by the fact that the adolescents had been recklessly hitting the bomb to seek excitement. In such a case, an accident is not necessarily a strong-enough reason to deter future risk-taking behavior. Indeed, one victim said that he would not hesitate to return to bomb hunting despite having been recently injured.

Reminiscent of Tim Ingold's description of the hunted animal who intentionally offers himself to the hunter (2000: 13), in Leu and Bok villages, people explained that they often encountered bomb debris when they were preparing a rice field, cutting trees and vegetation for the creation of a fruit and vegetable orchard, or hunting or traveling through the forest. Bomb hunting was most often said to be an occasional or spontaneous pursuit that essentially presented itself while a villager was conducting another activity. Tham, the village blacksmith, contradicted such accounts, however. "It is not true!" he said. "Entire families depart at seven in the morning, sometimes leaving someone to stay at home as a 'facade,' in order to return with some metal later in the day." In order to confirm his statement, Tham suggested that I interview his brother, a frequent bomb hunter who had recently returned home with a large bomb fragment. When he was interviewed, Tham's brother showed embarrassment and claimed that it was the first time he had salvaged a bomb remnant, which he had come across by chance as he was walking through the forest.

Bomb hunting is not an activity that most people, especially frequent hunters, feel comfortable talking about. A certain anxiety is connected to the topic for various reasons. One reason is that, according to provincial subdecrees, the activity is classified as illegal, and hence it is often done secretly. This in turn could put the bomb hunter in a more dangerous situation since, in case of an accident, he might avoid the district hospital to prevent being reported to the district police. A related reason is the perceived competition between villagers and professional organizations that in turn collaborate with the local police. The consequence is that bomb searching is an underground activity in both literal and figurative senses. Other reasons stem from the shame of a recent accident, which temporarily casts a shadow over the activity and may be a source of increased anxiety for the entire community. Victims often explain their misfortune in terms of bad luck or the agency of malevolent spirits, which will then need to be collectively appeased.

The Bomb Hunter and the Protection of the Spirits

For Luyin Blen, living in Leu today is less dangerous than it used to be "because there are fewer bombs lying on the ground." He commented that people felt generally safer than when they had been rebuilding the village in the aftermath of the war, but some were still afraid that ill-disposed *yang* (spirits) might detonate the remaining hidden bombs. Because of the uncertainty of UXO salvaging (especially retrieval of a live bomb), the possibility that it might detonate is often understood as a direct influence of the unpredictable *yang*.

Shortly after the previously mentioned accident in Plói Phdol Krom, which did not prove fatal for any of the victims involved, the elders decided to erect a sacrifice post to offer food and drink to the spirits. Some people I interviewed explained that it was a "sacrifice of reparation" to the spirits who might have been offended (and hence might have caused the accident) and an opportunity for the families of the victims to ask for future protection. Because Plói Phdol Krom is a bomb-hunter village, where more than half its households search for metal all year long, the assistance of the spirits in the day-to-day activities of its inhabitants is a crucial component of their risk-management strategy.

Most Leu villagers believe that spirits play an important role in making bomb hunting safe and successful. Luyin Blen and Blim, two village elders from Leu, told me that bomb hunters in Leu often make sacrifices in anticipation of their hunt, and while they are doing so, "they ask their soul not to disappear and leave them. They would also ask the spirits to make the bombs weaker." The bomb hunter addresses his or her soul (*bŏngat*) directly, asking it to remain within his or her body and not leave him or her.[1] Luyin Blen and Blim both stressed to me that the spirits that the bomb hunters are addressing are village spirits or spirits dwelling in nature and hence are external to the bomb itself. In other words, most Leu villagers trust that because they have been made by humans, bombs have no spirits living in them, and therefore that it is the external village or nature-dwelling spirits that must be enlisted to counteract their destructive power.

Some villagers who have served in the army do not share this view of spirits being able to provide protection during bomb hunting, however. Their warfare experience, combined with the absence of ritual activities during the prolonged conflicts, makes them feel confident that they can carry on hunting for bombs by trusting their skills rather than the support of the spirits. Expounding this perspective on the spiritual dimension of bomb hunting, some of my informants recounted a case that occurred a few years ago. This involved Vinn, a regular bomb hunter from Plói Keul in O You Dav district, who used to sacrifice a chicken or a pig before dismantling

---

1. Villagers believe that the body and the soul are two distinct but interdependent entities that separate each time a person sleeps, dreams, or falls ill. But when the soul wanders away and finds itself too far astray from the body, it sometimes loses its way back, causing the person to pass away (Lafont 1963; Dournes 1978).

large bombs but was nevertheless killed when one of them exploded. Some people commented that he might not have satisfied the spirits, but others argued that Vinn's sacrifices were "a wasteful practice since he had lost both the sacrificed animals and his own life!"

According to Luyin Blen, "Because villagers see that some bombs explode while some do not, they assume that the *yang* must have been protecting them. If not, why do bombs not explode all the time?" Owing to the unpredictability of the outcome, some villagers presume that the influence of the spirits must be at play in making bomb hunting a risky activity. For Jacques Dournes, the Jorai's conception of the world is that all things are interrelated, and that one effect must find its causes somewhere since "discontinuity does not pertain to the rational thinking of the individual" (Dournes 1972: 9–11). In that sense, the local perception of bomb hunting is that it becomes a more predictable activity when one directly and effectively engages with its influencing factors (the spiritual agency). Luyin Blen described how a day before setting off to search for bombs, most people will want to *sein areak* (in Khmer), which consists of lighting incense and offering to the spirit a ricewine jar and a chicken placed on top of it. At this moment, the following prayers can be addressed to the *yang*: "Today I want to dig for bombs. I am asking the *yang* for protection and for safety for my family."

> Kâo rā nao dôw pó sói,
> Daih amāng yang Tui Vai lāng kâo,
> Nām Biai tdlai vā nā,
> Biai moak moai.

> I am on my way to collect metal,
> May the spirit protect me,
> Prevent accidents from happening,
> Allow me to be safe, with no illnesses.

If later during the night the person does not have a bad dream, which can be interpreted as a warning sent by the *yang*, then it is a good omen for the forthcoming expedition. Being a hunter in essence, the bomb hunter follows the same rules that apply to the ordinary game hunter. In the same way in which the hunter sets off looking for prey, the bomb hunter needs to decipher the signs that are sent to him or her by nature. Luyin Blen further described some of these as follows: "When setting off the following morning, if the white birds sing on his left side, then lots of bombs will be found. If they sing on his right-hand side, it means there won't be so much. But if the birds cry very loud, then you will have to turn around and return to the village because there will be an accident!"

Similar preventive actions are also practiced among Khmer bomb hunters and deminers. In the village of O'Chheukrom, in Sala Krao district, Pailin province, deminers' wives claim that they regularly offer food, drinks, and prayers to the spirits of the land who live in the area chosen for land mine clearance. They explain that the offering occurs before clearance to ask permission to work in the spirit's territory and at completion to thank him for his protection. Like the Trobrianders who turn to magic to gain protection against the uncertainties and dangers of fishing in an open sea (Malinowski 1922), bomb hunters and deminers in the most affected regions of the country have recourse to spiritual support to gain confidence and feel that they can influence or have a sense of control over what they may sometimes perceive as taking a chance.

The Social Life of War-Associated Objects

Retrieve, Recycle, and Reuse

More than two and a half million tons of bombs were dropped on Cambodia and the Lao PDR, and the Ho Chi Minh Trail is infamous for being one of the most heavily bombed areas in modern warfare. Since the end of the conflicts, these weapons have also offered local communities a new means of sustaining themselves, however. This section studies the Jorai commodity and material culture as a crucial element of the postconflict reconstruction process. As a means of rebuilding their livelihoods, villagers from Leu and nearby communities have transformed bombs and bomb parts into functional objects of everyday life. In transforming the hazardous into the safe, these *homo faber* have refashioned items originally manufactured to cause death into objects endowed with new life. In this context, UXO in parts or as a whole may be reused by the entire community (e.g., a cluster-bomb casing may be recycled as a school bell or as kitchen utensils to be shared among household members).

Like many postconflict communities, the village of Leu illustrates the case of a particular sort of material culture that has been generated by the war-torn environment. Villagers explained that they had kept aluminum retrieved from planes that had crashed into the northeastern mountains to make rice-cooking pans, plates, cutlery, smoking pipes, and decorative items such as jewelry and hair slides. In the last example, the salvaged material is both a way to increase the economic status of the household and a means for female aesthetic enhancement. In relation to this use of bomb material, one villager had mixed feelings about the US bombardment, saying that although planes and bombs had brought death to the area, they had simultaneously been the source of a new income-generation activity. Ethnic-minority villages in heavily bombed areas of the Lao PDR make this war-commodity consumption even more visible by integrating bomb parts into the vernacular architecture (e.g., cluster-bomb casings reused as house stilts and plant pots). In the Jorai communities in Andong Meas, the bulk of the salvaged material is instead sold to the local scrap-metal dealer, and the remainder is kept to be used for manufacture of tools and objects. In light of this, the process of collection, physical transformation, and reuse allows whole or parts of ERW to be imbued with a new social life.

The Biography of Formidable Things

Although explosive products were originally designed to have a straightforward trajectory, the local salvaging of these items may contribute to the anthropological discussion of the "cultural biography of things" (Kopytoff 1986: 64). The bomb as an unusual type of object can be regarded as the result of a precise manufacturing process, without any encoded intention to embark on a new social life. The object as a whole (or its constitutive material, which acts as a synecdoche) may, however, be integrated into a new life cycle through both the transformative process and the reuse of the object. In effect, the ways war-generated objects are produced originally implies the finality or closure of the act that initially sent them away. Their local recycling means instead that they are rerouted through different practical purposes, endowed with new meanings, and transformed into valued commodities or transactional items. In light of this, the initial intention for closure (destruction and death programmed during the original fabrication process) is transformed into the openness and wide circulation of its recycled parts.

According to Gábor Vargyas, "The fact that objects travel between different social contexts and that in this process they (may) change their value and meaning, is not new to anthropology." In Vietnam, Vargyas explored a similar theme in researching the integration of a recovered US soldier's dog tag into a Bru shamanic headdress in what he called a survival of "semiotic guerilla warfare." Drawing on the theoretical concept of "bricolage," he argued that the presence of such objects may stimulate local symbolic innovation in the sense that "new circumstances and new materials open up new forms of symbolic expression—along old ways. Taking the example of the soldier's dogtag and the plastic seat of a matchbox toy car . . . objects migrate between widely opposed, moreover hostile social realms . . . (along with) transformation of meaning and value they undergo during this process—demonstrating thus the Bru cycle that leads 'from opposition to de-fusion, from resistance to incorporation'" (Vargyas 2013: 1). In a similar way, in collecting, transforming, and reusing war-derived objects, Leu villagers have acted like the Bru bricoleurs from northern Vietnam, mixing "two apparently incompatible realities . . . on an apparently unsuitable scale," for instance, by turning the parts of a war-associated object into female personal adornments, thereby "erasing and subverting their original straight meaning" (Dick Hebdige quoted in Vargyas 2013).[2] As the originally ascribed meaning and function shift through time, places, and hands, the owner of the object (or its reproduction) continually builds its biography.

A corollary of the unexpected reuse of the salvaged object is the local industry of replicas of war remnants, such as American soldiers' dog tags, which seem to have authentic value for tourists only if they are produced in heavily bombed countries. In this context, the replica may eventually reverse its trajectory to the point of origin (via tourists returning to the producer country) where the originals were first manufactured and intended for a totally different purpose. I will further examine this particular line of inquiry critically in chapter 5, showing that the economy of war memorabilia can equally become an integrative part of the postconflict material culture that characterizes Leu and other nearby Jorai and ethnic-minority villages.

---

2. In a southern province of Laos, in the village of Ban Ken Kup, where the inhabitants identify themselves as Khamu (normally located in the north), children wear recycled bullets as pendants, which are filled with a blessed substance that is supposed to protect them against malevolent spirits.

The Belongings of the Foreign Dead

Like EWR, foreign soldiers' personal belongings can be appropriated, recycled, and reused. The appropriation of US soldiers' belongings is common in parts of Cambodia, Vietnam, and the Lao PDR, where specific objects are reused and worn by local collectors, both members of the dominant ethnic group and members of ethnic minorities. My informants mentioned that genuine war paraphernalia or dog tags that had been the property of a US soldier (often found by rivers) had to be ritually processed in order to ask the permission of the previous owner. In the case of these particular necklaces, some local communities of northeastern Cambodia and southeastern Laos (in Ban Ken Kup, for instance) have been reappropriating them to protect young children against malevolent spirits. Indeed, the power inherently associated with the foreigner (and thus encoded in his or her personal object) is often perceived as being capable of offsetting the malicious influences of the local spirits. One of the persons I worked with said that contrary to the ordinary scrap metal derived from bombs, people are reluctant to sell necklaces because they keep their children safe. At times when someone was ready to sell a salvaged dog tag, prices would reach the substantial amount of 50,000 or 60,000 Cambodian riels (up to 15 USD).

This perspective further illuminates the tenacity and creativity of postconflict Southeast Asian communities in demonstrating how the successful appropriation of the foreign object may be comparable to an act of virtual conquest. In this sense, its acquisition can be associated with bringing home a war trophy. In the same vein, a few former Jorai soldiers I worked with believed that possessing the objects of the dead foreigners was safe, mentioning, for instance, that the reuse of US soldiers' helmets was a common and useful practice at the time of the conflicts. With the exception of those former soldiers who had served under the Khmer Rouge and the Vietnamese-established regimes, most of my informants claimed that they would not risk the collection of belongings of dead foreigners because of their close association with the original owner and thus their nature as dangerous or treacherous objects.

A village elder from Tang village explained that one of his peers had once found the remains of a parachute previously owned by a US soldier and had brought it back to the village in order to reuse the material to make himself a shirt. A few days later the shirt caught fire while he was cooking. While narrating this episode, the victim was taunted by the other villagers because his act was viewed as foolish. Jorai villagers believe that the belongings of the dead can be repossessed only after asking permission from the soul of the dead, which they believe is still enclosed in his belongings. As I will discuss in chapter 4, in after death, a person is buried together with his or her personal effects, which are symbolically viewed as body parts and inseparable objects the deceased will take away into the afterlife.

A villager who repossesses objects without appropriate rituals addressed to the legitimate owner may be regarded as having committed a serious offense against the spirit of the dead. In fact, the appropriation of such objects is thoroughly imbued with questions of morality, remembrance, and legitimacy. The foreign spirit-empowered object therefore raises risk-related questions of personal and community safety. Indeed, taking the possessions of the deceased may be the equivalent of theft, an ill-fated act that may cause future misfortune. Male and female village elders explained that when they found bones that belonged to a foreigner, they usually said a prayer to the spirit and left the remains undisturbed.

Materiality and Agency

The preceding examples enable us to revisit Alfred Gell's theory of objects and agency, especially with respect to Strathern's concept of the "partible" (Strathern 1988: 324; 2004) and expression "distributed person" (Strathern 2005: 10). In *Art and Agency*, Gell drew on the example of Khmer Rouge soldiers' use of land mines as "a distributed extension" of their agency. Gell stated, "Their kind of agency would be unthinkable except in conjunction with the spatio-temporally expanded capacity for violence, which the possession of mines makes possible. Pol Pot's soldiers possessed (like all of us) what I shall later discuss as 'distributed personhood'. As agents, they were not just where their bodies were, but in many different places (and times) simultaneously. Those mines were components of their identities as human persons, just as much as their fingerprints or the litanies of hate and fear, which inspired their action" (Gell 1998: 21).

Gell's example of the Khmer Rouge land mines can be further expanded to encompass the ERW left by the intense aerial bombardment of the area.

As a warfare strategy, the US bombing acted in essentially the same fashion, enabling the distribution of personhood and intention across a large surface area. In this particular context, this combat technique illustrates the notion of fractal personhood as further examined by Marilyn Strathern, whereby "persons are imagined as entities with relations integral to them, they cannot be thought of in terms of whole numbers, whether as entire units or as parts of a whole. Persons act as though they have a fractal dimensionality: however much they are divided or multiplied, persons and relations remain in proportion to each other, always keep their scale" (Strathern 1993: 49). The collection and successful modification of the objects by villagers thus appear to be an ingenious way to reverse the encoded primary intention (death) and replace it with their own (supporting local livelihood). For Alfred Gell, "Any artefact, by virtue of being a manufactured thing, motivates an abduction which specifies the identity of the agent who made or originated it. Manufactured objects are 'caused' by their makers, just as smoke is caused by fire, hence manufactured objects are indexes of their makers. Although these indexes act as material entities whose makers attribute specific meanings, their re-appropriation by the user (or intended victim) reproduces the perfect 'abduction of agency'" (Gell 1998: 23). Over time, the succeeding users thus continually substitute their own personhood for the original, whose audacious abduction is at the beginning of the life cycle of formidable things. And the more users and the more abductions that are successively performed, the longer and more novel the life cycle of the object becomes.

As a historical object, cluster bombs or antipersonnel land mines can be equally invested with present time by undergoing a transformative process. The dismantling and use of a land mine, originally set to injure and kill, are ways to turn it into an object that will be adjusted to the political and economic situation of the present. It is in a sense a deliberate reprogramming of the object that encodes it with new intentions and new time frames (for instance, by switching from an antipersonnel to a personnel object). Failure to take control of it often results in the tragic death or injury of a person, which occasionally stresses the power of the violent past over the present. Indeed, the presence of ERW can be framed as the persistence of the past in its material form. Put somewhat differently, the continued presence of the objects can be viewed as a prolongation of the conflicts into the present day by expanding their spatiotemporal capacity.

The Presence of Foreign Bodies

When a stranger tragically dies away from his or her homeland, local villagers often assume that the stranger's ghost has lost its former mobility and thus has become trapped in the land where the stranger perished (Kwon 2008). As Georg Simmel pointed out: "The stranger is by nature 'no owner of soil'—soil not only in the physical, but also in the figurative sense of a life-substance which is fixed, if not in a point in space, at least in an ideal point of the social environment. Although in more intimate relations, he may develop all kinds of charms and significance, as long as he is considered a stranger in the eyes of the other, he is not an 'owner of soil'" (Wolff 1950: 403).

In times of death, the departed one, even if he or she is a very close relative or a kindhearted village member, is regarded as a potential source of threat to the entire community until the final abandonment of the grave (see chapter 4), when it is believed that the soul has safely traveled to its next life. As I will discuss in further detail in chapter 4, times of death are thus particularly risky periods when the entire village is temporarily rendered more exposed to various sources of hazard, with the malevolent spirits or *yang* being the most potent. Indeed, the proximity of death appears as a great source of risk that, when it strikes in the village, has the potential to contaminate all the villagers, children and adults alike. Local strategies that enable the villagers to protect themselves against the return of ghosts or the malicious influence of the *yang* consist, among other things, of rendering oneself impure. Most of the time, keeping oneself clean and pure from death is a means to keep the *yang* away. In the following case, making oneself extremely impure is the reverse strategy to keep the malevolent spirits at bay.

> Stricken by fear, I did everything I could to make myself impure in the eyes of the *yang*. Each time someone died somewhere, I would help carry the dead [the corpse is generally carried away by four men on top of their shoulders to the cemetery, where a coffin lies open; the corpse is taken to its final home a few days after death], holding him well above my head so that the liquid from the decaying body would trickle down my shoulders and breast. I did it seven times; later on I had this dream and heard someone say to me: "I am not staying with you anymore because you are impure." (Dournes 1978: 95)

In the case of a foreigner's death, the threat is locally perceived as even more potent because the villagers feel that they have very limited means or knowledge to protect themselves. In the words of Arnold van Gennep, "For a great many peoples a stranger is sacred, endowed with magico-religious powers, and supernaturally benevolent and malevolent" (Van Gennep 1960: 26). Such fear, which is widespread among ethnic-minority communities living in the highlands, is well illustrated in the literature of the French Mission in Vietnam. The following presents a colorful vignette describing the anxiety of the Bahnar when a French missionary suddenly fell severely ill while trying to build a Christian mission:

> Seeing him in such a state, the savages thought that he was going to pass away. They believe in ghosts and are terror stricken by them. A foreigner, as extraordinary as this one, who happened to die among them would undoubtedly make the most formidable of all ghosts. With this apprehension in mind, a great number of them came several times to conjure him not to hold it against them once he was dead:—we are very much afflicted by your illness. But if it takes you away, please have mercy on us and do not come back to torment us. (Simonnet 1977: 71).

The death of a foreigner thus appears as a complex situation in which villagers need to find practical ways to make their life safer. Wars that brought death to the local population and foreign soldiers alike have created a landscape that remains deeply entangled with displaced—or misplaced—objects and spirits from a distant land.

As with bomb hunting, people have occasionally taken the risk of contributing to the recovery of foreigners' remains despite the potential hazards this can present. However, helping the remains of the foreign soldiers find their way back to their real home is also a means for them to free their land of "an anomalous and disturbing presence" (Harrison 2008: 781). These practices may find their rational justification in economic incentives, but they can also be motivated by the desire to live in peace with the accepted presence of the stranger/foreigner or the genuine belief that the stranger has at last returned where he or she belongs.

Hunting for Foreign Bodies

In 1973, the US government set up a vast prisoner-of-war and missing-in-action (MIA) program in Southeast Asia in order to retrieve the remains of US soldiers who had disappeared during the conflicts of the 1960s and early 1970s.[3] In March 2008, the US ambassador to Cambodia announced that, in collaboration with the Cambodian government, the remains of twenty-nine MIA American servicemen had been found and repatriated. Nowadays, a remaining forty-nine are missing on Cambodian soil.

The American MIA program has been the subject of an extensive literature. According to some authors, it is closely associated with the fact that the Vietnam War is still an open wound in the American psyche (Lesinski 1998; Kwon 2008). In this regard, Hawley noted, "It indicates the failure of the United States to truly end the war in Vietnam: some of its warriors, after all, have failed to return home. Perhaps still more compelling, the absent body stands as the most material indication of the defeat that occurred in Southeast Asia, an ever-present reminder of the catastrophe that continues to afflict the American body politic" (Hawley 2005: 4).

Investigative and recovery missions have been undertaken in the region for more than twenty years. In this context, where the postconflict landscape remains imbued with unburied dead, ritual specialists acting as mediums to communicate with and find displaced individuals have sometimes established a lucrative and successful practice, especially in Vietnam (Kwon 2008). Alongside the extensive scrap-metal trade in the region, a parallel market in alleged US soldier remains has also emerged. This has stimulated such fraudulent practices as the production of fake remains and the manipulation of the local workforce through the pretense of financial rewards.[4]

---

3. A person can be listed as killed in action (KIA), killed in action/body not recovered (KIA/BNR), prisoner of war (POW), or missing in action (MIA). Of all these categories, MIA is the most nebulous, for the fate of the person cannot be readily determined. Listed as MIA are "active duty military personnel who are not present at their duty station due to apparent involuntary reasons and whose location is not known" (US Department of Defense, *U.S. Casualties*, 1985, quoted in Lesinski 1998: 2).

4. "Although the US has never waived standard entry requirements in exchange for human remains, some Vietnamese have gone to extraordinary lengths to procure remains for this purpose, including modifying the remains of Southeast Asian Mongoloids to make them resemble the larger, longer bones of Caucasoids. In one case, a set of remains obtained from the Viet boat people contained two human femurs. Analysis at CIL [the Central Identification Library based in

MIA missions typically employ a pool of ethnic-minority researchers, since their knowledge of the region and their access to local informants are valuable resources that can help better locate the remains. In this context, the multiple sources of hazard inherent in the MIA hunt (e.g., encountering malevolent spirits, injuries due to live ERW lying in sites of crashed planes) are rationally balanced against expected profits; hence a potentially risky situation can become a coveted opportunity as follows:

> A second difficulty, and still more troublesome from the standpoint of forensic science, is the extensive prior scavenging by humans of aircraft crash sites and other locations possibly containing the remains of unaccounted-for-soldiers. The reasons for such activity are numerous, but in a great number of cases stem from the awareness of Southeast Asian people of the strong desire of the US to repatriate the remains of its KIA (killed in action). Virtually all sites pertaining to unaccounted-for Americans have thus been extensively scavenged. Remains are then offered for sale either directly to the United States or to Vietnamese boat people by remains traders who convince them that possession of such remains will gain them automatic entry into the US. Aircraft crash sites present an additional bonanza because pieces of the downed aircraft can be sold as scrap metal. (Hawley 2005: 99)

Touch, one of my Khmer informants who had been part of such recovery missions, had operated in the mountains of the northeast provinces of Mondulkiri, Stung Treng, and Ratanakiri from 2003 to 2004, where he had conducted research in Andong Meas near Leu. For Touch, the MIA program was a profitable way for anyone involved to make a living. The following was the scale of wages, based on nationalities: (1) employed foreigners, 185 USD to 200 USD per day; (2) Khmers, 35 USD per day; (3) ethnic-minority workers, 10 USD per day in addition to the provision of food and drinks. Touch described how the missions always involved working closely with the local populations of Jorai, Tampuon, Kachok, Brao, Lao, or Vietnamese to gather precise information on the last recorded locations of the remains. Quite often local informants told the mission teams that once they had found the remains of a foreign soldier, they would take them away from the

---

Hawaii] revealed that both bones had been 'lengthened' through a process that included cutting them in half, inserting a two-inch-long steel bar lengthwise in the bone, and then reattaching the two ends" (Huckshorn and Larimer 1996: 256).

vicinity of the village into isolated areas such as the foot of the mountains. (I explore the rationale for this practice later.) In some cases, though, people would refuse to collaborate with the Americans because of their past tragic experience and would manifest their resentment by "refusing to talk to them."

My informant explained that when a village had helped successfully locate the bones of an MIA soldier, the US Embassy would reward the village with the sum of 100 USD for the inhabitants to carry out rituals, which involved animal sacrifices for the celebration of the bones being finally taken away from their land and returned to their rightful home. Asked whether the Khmer employees would also perform rituals when completing a mission, Touch responded, "No, we don't. We only use the money to buy beer and get drunk to celebrate. This is our ritual!"

Pou Ksor, a village elder from Leu, told me that he had participated in an MIA recovery mission ten years earlier. Essentially motivated by the financial rewards, which were then said to amount to 5,000 USD per body identified, Pou Ksor left Leu to cross the Vietnamese border and return to his family's native place in Kontum, where, according to him, "there are plenty of human remains and plane carcasses." Under the guidance of a Jorai military person who told him where to dig, he went alone and managed to retrieve body parts and objects attributed to nine different bodies (including teeth, hair, the bones of an arm and a leg, a dog tag, and shoe soles). He bemoaned the fact that it was difficult work and that despite spending three months in Vietnam conducting intensive searches, he ultimately did not get paid by the MIA program staff based in Banlung back in Ratanakiri province.[5] Pou Ksor regretted all the time and effort he had spent. At the same time, he felt that he had nonetheless helped the lost bodies find their way back home.

Searching for MIA remains is often associated with arduous and at times hazardous work in isolated areas. Pou Ksor, who had worked on his own, mentioned that some sites were difficult to access because of dense vegetation, which during the wet season becomes a breeding ground for mosquitoes that transmit malaria. Other potential sources of risk associated

---

5. Pou Ksor explained that it had been agreed beforehand with a Cambodian member of staff of the US Embassy in Phnom Penh that he would get paid for each and every item of remains that would help identify an MIA US serviceman.

with the postconflict landscape may also include the following: "Jet fuel sometimes lingers in the soil surrounding a downed aircraft, requiring searchers to climb out of the excavation pit periodically to rinse off their skin. Live ordnance in and around the excavation site, including unexploded bombs, shells, grenades, mines, and rockets, poses a special danger. . . . In Laos, the [recovery team] must make arrangements with the village shaman, including sacrifices and other offerings, to clear the ground of spirits prior to an excavation" (Hawley 2005: 97). The presence of the displaced spirits in such tragic circumstances and places is a powerful source of physical and psychological hazard. But according to Neil Sheehan "Other motives for disturbing a site are commendable. For example, local villagers may wish to give the dead a decent burial regardless of nationality or wartime circumstances" (Sheehan 1995: 82).

Guiding the Lost Bodies and Souls Home

Pou Ksor explained that when he returned to the village from Vietnam, he carefully hid the MIA remains that he had found in the forest "the same way as we do for our ancestors," but he stressed, "I did not bring them into Leu village because it is *kŏm* [taboo]."[6] In Beck's perspective, the individual's agency has potential adverse consequences for the entire community and thus raises questions of accountability and socially accepted levels of risk. In this case, the remains of the foreigners were treated in the same ways local remains would normally be when a person had been struck by a bad death, hence satisfying the need of the spirit of the foreign dead while keeping the rest of the community safe. As Pou Ksor described, "I hid them in the forest and returned to give them rice and fish to feed them, and I said to them:

> *Wā sòi, wā ia*: eat and drink.
> *Anām bìòi duā va*: do not harm me, do not make me sick.
> *Ih gloū, khul dai, plei lan: Ih glack, khol day, Pleuy Lan*: return to your country, return to your fathers, to your village.
> *Kâo pā glan: Kao pack ghlan*: I am showing you the way.

---

6. For an insightful examination of taboo and danger, see Valeri 2000.

Among all the villagers I worked with, no one showed any feeling of resentment toward the foreigner and former enemy. In a sense, helping find and send the remains back to the families abroad was widely perceived as a natural and moral obligation. In Pou Ksor's words, he was only a "guide" or an intermediary in the deceased's endeavor to "return home." As Simon Harrison described in his research on "returning effects of the battlefield dead," the role of the individual is likewise perceived as instrumental: "The donors and the recipients alike speak as if the artefacts worked their way home through chance personal connections to which they miraculously gave rise, as if animated by the life or spirit of the original owner or his family, or as if some providential agency has guided those involved in returning them" (Harrison 2008: 785–86). In a sense, local families who have lost traces of their relatives also hope that others will do the same things for the souls of their own disappeared kin. As Kwon wrote, "One man's ghost is another man's ancestor" (Kwon 2008: 99).

Similar sentiments have been illustrated in the local burial of foreign remains. Despite the potential risk in coming into close contact with unknown and foreign souls, some villagers have taken the initiative to offer the unburied dead a proper burial ceremony and have chosen an appropriate site to help them find peace. In this particular case, the soul of the stranger has fully become a part of the local landscape, sanctioned this time by the villagers' deliberate act of integration and acceptance. For Heonik Kwon, such local behavior and attitudes toward the remains are acts of liberation not only for the wandering soul, who can finally rest in peace, but also for the one who liberated that soul. Kwon's research on the ghosts of war in Vietnam brought to light illuminating accounts concerning the interaction between the foreign ghost and the reluctant or welcoming hosts. As shown in the following example, the host can be forced to make peace with the former enemy in a landscape where the displaced foreign spirits have gained their own right to exist.

The Vietnamese soldiers of a small military unit reported to their lieutenant that they had repeatedly witnessed the apparition of a foreign ghost at night, "a tall unarmed man whose torn uniform was soaked in mud." In defiance, the lieutenant, "ordering his men to watch him . . . urinated on the spot [where the foreign ghost had been seen]." Although the ghostly apparitions ceased immediately after the incident, the lieutenant became severely ill in the course of the following months. As the illness worsened, he decided to use the services of a ritual specialist who told him that the ghost had been deeply offended by his behavior, and therefore, reparation was needed. Under the guidance of the ritual specialist, the officer returned to the spot where the incident occurred and exhumed a skull with a bullet hole in it. After receiving confirmation that the skull was MIA remains, the lieutenant helped repatriate it to its homeland. After this, "the officer's recovery from a near mental breakdown was dramatic." As narrated by Kwon, the following happened:

> During our visit to the ritual specialist the officer said, "Vietnam defeated America. But that American officer nearly defeated me, an officer in the Vietnamese Army, long after the war's end. The bullet we shot through his head almost drove me insane." The man's relative, an elderly veteran, was not pleased to hear this remark. Studying his face with penetrating eyes, the elder said, "Nephew, one does not fight with the dead. American or Vietnamese, the dead should be respected. No one should deliberately urinate on their resting places." And the ritual specialist intervened: "Dead people don't fight. They are not really even angry. They simply want to be remembered. They want someone to know what they went through. I can't tell you the sorrow of that handsome young American. He was so handsome and tall. The man said, "Aunt, thank you, thank you. Forgive me, forgive me." I heard it all, all in his language. It was all too confusing. I told him, "It's all fine now. Go and rest." (Kwon 2008: 40)

Although the village elders of Leu said that they did not feel any resentment toward their former enemies, most of them thought of this as a time-bound issue. In fact, people consider that a long time has elapsed since the end of the conflicts, and their attitudes emphasize the fact that it is now time for each and every person to find peace. Peace is made either by helping the homeless foreign dead find a new home or by leading the way back to the original one (Harrison 2008; Kwon 2008).

The Missing Bodies Who Do Not Want to Be Found

Pou Ksor told me that in the course of his hunt for MIA remains, he had encountered former US soldiers who were still living in the villages where they had originally been taken prisoner but had since rebuilt their life. He recalled, "When I went to Kontum, I found a seventy-year-old American who could speak a bit of Jorai and did not want to return to his home country. He told me he did not want to be found. . . . There are some who live in other Jorai villages who have remained in contact with their children and get money sent to them. . . . One old man has his daughter send him money every month." As Pou Ksor explained, although these people were regarded as foes, they had since found a new home among the people whom they had once been fighting. Indeed, as time elapsed, they had become an ordinary feature of the postconflict social landscape.

Heonik Kwon's research on the ghosts generated by the Vietnam War has shown that some foreign ghosts have fully integrated into the pantheon of the local deities, hence turning the potentially malicious wandering soul of the former enemy into a benevolent genius loci. In this context, the foreign ghost has at last become "owner of the soil" contesting Simmel's definition of the stranger by fixing himself in the social environment and in the organic matter of the physical environment. The stranger hereby becomes the soil.

Moreover, as an interesting variation of Giorgio Agamben's *homo sacer* or the "man set apart," the dead stranger has to some extent maintained his or her ability to move between separate and opposite domains, for he or she can become both sacred and accursed. Agamben's use of the term *sacer* implies a double exclusion from the human law (*ius humanum*) and from the divine law (*ius divinum*), which subsequently renders him cursed and sacred at the same time (Agamben 1998: 82). This process of inversion is particularly powerful in appropriating and commanding the formidable other, as will be shown by the example of the manufacturing of the bombing plane in Leu (see chapter 5).

The repatriation of American bodies from Southeast Asia can be seen beyond their mere materiality as participating in the rebuilding of the general body politic as previously described by Hawley (2008). Resonating with Judith Butler's work on body matters, meanings, and values, this perspective allows us to see this exceptional program as part of a wider reconstruction or healing process (Butler 1993). In the same manner, as I will discuss in chapter 4, inhabitants of Leu and other neighboring villages have been searching for missing relatives in the hope of reconstituting the fragmented family genealogical order (Kwon 2006, 2008), as well as reintegrating the body parts of lost relatives within the collective social and historical body of the community.

This chapter has sought to investigate the ways a Jorai community in northeastern Cambodia is adjusting to and recovering from decades of regional and civil conflicts that have destroyed their human-made and natural environments. It is an ethnography of the ways Jorai villagers perceive and interact with a variety of hazards amid a familiar landscape that has been rendered potentially more dangerous to the individual's survival strategy. It entailed the study of local perceptions of a hostile environment and the survival strategies developed by subsistence farmers to achieve normality in socioeconomic relations and spiritual well-being. Despite the tragedy of the war, some of the most heavily UXO-affected villages in northeastern Cambodia, like Leu, have adjusted to a transformed landscape by very resourceful but sometimes dangerous means.

This chapter has endeavored to provide insight into the individual's conscious decision to take risk when the risk derived from the material or bodily presence of remnants of war is offset by another risk factor that may be locally perceived and interpreted as more potent. This approach allows a nuanced understanding of the survival mechanisms of the subsistence farmer and shows the extent of the individual's resilience in reframing dangerous challenges as opportunities. Postconflict healing by means of ritualistic performances and symbolic inversion can also constitute privileged means for the survivors to maintain the continuity of life despite the discontinuity brought by the violence of the conflicts. In regaining control of his destiny, this persistent *homo faber* or workingman tries to improve the course of life and the afterlife. After this exploration of issues surrounding material things, I will now turn to the spiritual risk-coping mechanisms of the villagers of Leu.

Chapter 4

Adjusting Rituals

This chapter deals with postconflict continuity and changes in relation to life and death. It describes how funerals constitute an essential feature of life in Leu and how caring for the dead weaves continuous threads connecting the living and the deceased in mutually beneficial webs. Its central focus is how long-drawn-out conflicts have interrupted and influenced funerals and propitiatory ceremonies, with a succession of wars producing new causes of bad death and postponing, if not taking away, the time to grieve.

In addition, this chapter seeks to explain the ways in which traditional rituals adapt to the disruption of war and how those injured in war are physically and morally reincorporated into the social body of the community. By drawing on the villagers' experience of the US bombing, it examines how the encounter with the dangerous object can be reenacted through the reproduction, representation, and display of weapons. It investigates to what extent the physical and psychological manipulation of the alien object of death, particularly the bombing plane, can become a privileged site for persons to reconcile themselves to their traumatic past.

Death and the Period after Death in Leu

A Funeral in the Village

It is February 2009, and Veam, a female village elder, has died peacefully after briefly suffering from lung failure. Veam had once been married, but after her husband left her, she lived with her sister in Leu and did not remarry. In accordance with the local custom, Veam's coffin has been displayed for three days beneath a temporary awning in front of the family's house. Beside it is a sacrifice post on top of which a westward-facing sculpted plane flies (figure 4). In the course of the past three days and nights, people have sat around the coffin to mourn and talk to the dead, drink, eat, sing, dance, and play the gongs. Tomorrow, the fourth day after the death, the coffin will be taken to its final resting place.

My informants explained that keeping the coffin in the village for three days before the burial is done to enable all the relatives to have time to gather and say farewell. It also gives them enough time to perform all the rituals that are deemed necessary for the dead to leave this world successfully. On this particular occasion, a cow and a buffalo were slaughtered at the foot of the sacrifice post to encourage the spirits to welcome the new dead among them. Leu villagers believe that the spirits can be fed only through the killing of the proffered animal, as if death (along with the circulation of blood) is a necessary condition to travel from this world to the other.

Pierre-Bernard Lafont argued that the Jorai sacrifice to the spirits aims to connect humans with the sacred and to ensure the circulation of energies. Indeed, an animal that died of natural causes (without blood spilling) is considered to have died for no reason and thus may not be consumed either by spirits or by humans (Lafont 1963). As I will discuss later, if the death of the human body liberates the soul to travel to the other world, animals and objects that accompany the dead also need to undergo a similar process through slaughtering and breaking, respectively, so that in the next world they become alive and consumable or usable again (Dournes 1978). As Pou Ksor, Veam's brother-in-law, commented, "If the sacrifices are not all well completed, the dead will be rejected from the other world" (see Bloch and Parry 1982).

In this regard, the dead rely on their kin, who will facilitate their transition from one world to the next through ritual actions. In a sense, the two

Figure 4. Plane flying for Veam's funeral, Leu village. Photo by author.

worlds coexist in a reciprocal and interdependent manner. Villagers try to secure for the departed ones a safe and happy place in the afterworld, while the latter can provide guidance and protection to their kin and descendants throughout their lives. This recalls the observation of Robert Hertz that such funerary requirements constitute the moral duties of the living toward their dead relatives because "the body of the deceased is not regarded like the carcass of some animal: specific care must be given to it and a correct burial; not merely for reasons of hygiene but out of moral obligation" (Hertz 1960: 27). In Leu, these practices are consistent with those performed in previous generations.

It is the fourth day after Veam's death. As the funeral cortege winds its way to the cemetery through secondary forest, village elders and younger villagers follow quietly to the sound of musical instruments and exclamations of mourning. Once the coffin is lowered into the ground, the relatives uncover the face of their departed kinswoman one last time. A village elder explains, "It allows us to remember her and see her in our dreams." But suddenly a man breaks free from the company, hurriedly confessing that "he cannot" because he does "not want to see the face of the dead." Seeing the face of the dead is often regarded as a duty for the family members, who are meant to remember their past relatives. In this regard, adults and children, as well as close friends, may want to fix the features of the departed in their memory as if engaged in a photographic process. For others who have no blood ties to the dead, like the man who ran off, remembering the face of the dead is more a matter of choice.

Making the Dead Body Complete

In line with Jorai customs, relatives have brought along Veam's personal belongings to place on top of her grave (Maître 1912; Lafont 1963; Dournes 1978). The objects that accompany the dead (in this case the woven mat she used to sleep on and the basket she always carried on her back) are said to be objects that she will take with her into the next life. The main intention is to turn the grave into a nice home so that the *bongat* (soul) will be content to remain in it rather than returning to the village as a wandering ghost (*atâo*) who misses her former life. This belief is also shared by the Dayak of Borneo, whose funerary practices show that "there is in fact a close tie between the container of the bones and the 'town of the dead': it is the soul or spiritual substance of the charnelhouse, and of the brilliant accessories around it, which after undergoing a transformation will form in the sky the home and the treasures of the deceased" (Hertz 1960: 60).

My informants explained further that the objects are placed on the grave to ensure that on arrival in the next life, the reincarnated person will already own essential objects and thus start his or her new existence well equipped. Wai, a Jorai convert to Christianity, commented that these objects are a way for the dead to pay their entrance fees into their new abode, a concept reminiscent of the Greek mythological tradition of putting coins on someone's eyelids to pay for his or her river journey into the underworld. According to Wai, the next realm is guarded by someone who, in exchange for the proffered objects, will grant his protection to the dead throughout their new life. This belief was echoed by Dournes's Jorai informants in highland Vietnam, who interpreted the offerings as payment to the old Hebrei, or the mythical "grandmother with large breasts," who takes the departed in her small boat across the Mlu-Mlia River so that he or she can start a new existence on the opposite shores.

Most Jorai living in Leu do not comment on the afterlife with any confidence. Their funerary rituals suggest, however, that they hold sufficient belief in the possibility of reincarnation that it is worthwhile to bring the personal belongings of the departed ones to the grave. For Lafont, the objects that are handed over to the dead are the most expensive ones, a sign, the author suggested, that the afterlife is regarded as having more value than the present. For the inhabitants of Leu, the amount and quality of the belongings depend on the patrimony of the dead and on how much the relatives can contribute without depriving themselves.

Whether for their practical or symbolic values, funerary objects—like animals, as we shall see later—are believed to be reunited with the reincarnated soul in the next life. This belief has parallels with some Scandinavian funerary practices: "According to the traditional religion of the mountain Sami of northern Scandinavia, people are allowed to keep everything, including their reindeer herds, in the afterlife, the main difference being that pastures are abundant there. This kind of notion explains why the Sami (and many other peoples) were buried with their favourite clothes on, with their tools and, in the case of some hierarchical societies, their favourite slaves. Notions of the afterlife, be they abstract or concrete, obviously give an impression of continuity and serve to demystify death" (Eriksen 2001: 214).

Objects left on burial sites (as well as the sophisticated beauty of the grave itself) often give a clear indication of the deceased's social status in the community and in the afterlife. This illustrates Hertz's observation that "by virtue of the axiom 'Rich below, rich above' . . . without doubt the soul of each of these objects is believed to follow the deceased; naturally, the living family exalts itself, in its dead, before the eyes of the strangers present" (Hertz 1960: 135). Such objects may include everyday items that were shared among the various members of the household, such as rice-wine jars, mats, and cooking pots, as well as specific items used exclusively by the dead, like clothing, mattresses, baskets, smoking pipes, musical instruments, knives, and crossbows (Maître 1912; Dournes 1978; Ngo Van Doanh 1991).

The objects placed on the grave can thus be seen as identity markers that enable the living to identify their dead. A renowned hunter, for instance, will have his crossbow hanging from the roof sheltering his grave. Similarly, a talented musician may be buried with his drum placed nearby. For Hertz, the "impure cloud [that] surrounds the deceased and pollutes everything it touches" requires that all the belongings of the dead be destroyed, for they can no longer be of use to the living (Hertz 1960: 38). In Leu, however, villagers do not destroy the objects for purity purposes. They claim instead that the presence of the deceased's personal objects at the funeral is essential (even if they will be eventually destroyed) in order to make the grave, and to some extent the dead, feel "complete."

In researching the care of the ancestors among the Toraja in Sulawesi, Elizabeth Coville noted the local practice of "putting the pieces of the body back together" as a means of "re-membering the dead" (Coville 2002: 84–85). For the Jorai, placing personal objects beside the deceased may be interpreted not only as a decorative practice or means of identification but also as a way of making the dead body complete again in order to start anew in the afterworld. In other words, personal objects can be regarded as body parts that allow the dead person to be literally and metaphorically remembered before she or he engages in the journey to the next world.

One villager explained to me that the graves of children follow another set of rules because they have died "immature" and hence incomplete. Leu villagers bring to the graves of their very young dead only food offerings, with no personal objects, decorations, or specific rituals. Robert Hertz described how the Olo Maanyan consider juvenile deaths similarly: "Indeed, since the children have not yet entered the visible society, there is no reason to exclude them from it slowly and painfully. As they have not really been separated from the world of the spirits, they return there directly, without any sacred energies needing to be called upon, and without a period of painful transition appearing necessary" (Hertz 1960: 84). The death of a child may thus cause less social disruption than the death of an adult and may induce less anxiety regarding the villagers' vulnerability vis-à-vis the malice of the spirits who took the child away. As Hertz noted: "It is as though, for the collective consciousness, there were no real death in this case" (ibid.).[1] Some of my informants commented, however, that back in their relatives' villages in Vietnam, people begin to treat the grave of the child the same way as an adult's at the time when the deceased would have attained adulthood had she or he still been alive.[2] In other instances, the death of a child (especially a boy) may inspire the parents to proceed with the ordinary ceremonies for an adult, especially when they have the financial means to do this.

On the occasion of Veam's funeral, relatives, friends, and fellow villagers have brought along bottled rice wine, fruits, vegetables, and cooked rice in addition to personal and communal objects. Village elders explained that from this day onward, the dead person will need to be fed regularly until the burial site is finally left to nature on *pojah*, the festive occasion of the abandonment of the grave (see double obsequies in Hertz 1960, in which the first interment is followed months later by the crafting of a beautiful grave, and Bloch and Parry 1982).[3] Once the coffin is buried, a temporary roof made of interwoven leaves is placed above the heap of soil while cooked rice is scattered in the direction of the south. The villagers said that the sprinkling of rice propitiates the spirits that are immediately around, especially the ones living in the south, to which the *bongat* (soul) is believed to fly.

Thereafter, Veam's personal belongings are torn apart and irremediably destroyed. As two village elders explained, the woven mat and carrying bas-

---

1. Siu, the village wood-carver, buried his father and his three-month-old child in the village cemetery. The two graves are very distinct: the father's grave bears all the edificial and decorative features of a sophisticated grave, while the baby's grave is almost unnoticeable because of its size and lack of decoration.

2. The age of maturity is often a source of divergent opinions, but most villagers believe that at fifteen years of age a person can be considered an adult, which in Leu is also the age when marriages can be contracted.

3. The timing of this abandonment may differ from one Jorai village to another and even from one family to another. Lafont (1963) recorded five years for the abandonment of the grave. According to Robert Hertz, "This abnormal postponement of a rite which is as necessary to the peace and the well-being of the survivors as it is to the salvation of the deceased, is explained by the magnitude of the feast which has to accompany this rite" (Hertz 1960: 31).

ket are damaged quite purposefully: "You have to destroy them, for otherwise they are not the objects of the dead, they themselves are apart. If they were new, they would be the objects of the living." As discussed previously, if placing the personal belongings on top of the grave acts as an identity marker (identifying their owner), then the breaking of the objects in turn can be seen as an identity maker (making dead).

The same funerary practices are also found in other ethnic-minority communities. My research in neighboring districts suggests that some Tampuon, Kreung, and Brao communities hold similar beliefs about the breaking of objects (*pôčah*) as a means of mirroring the decomposition of the dead body. However, one informant in a Brao cemetery thought that the breaking acted essentially as a deterrent to prevent thefts. For Jacques Dournes, the act of breaking made the object "inalienable," which meant that it could not be "reused, given, or stolen." Be it a coffin, a rice-wine jar, a gong, or a basket, it follows (*pötui*) the dead to be used another time. This successful passage is better rendered through the partible quality of the accompanying object, which, as earlier mentioned by the village elder, indicates only that the world of the dead acts in the opposite way to the world of the living (Dournes 1968, 1975).[4] The following account from Dournes illustrates the transition from life to death that is made possible only through the act of breaking and dismembering:

> A man saw his dead wife in a dream: she was among the dead, "over there." She said to him, "Go back! Don't stay with me! If you really want to stay, then burn our house down, break all our rice-wine jars and smash all our belongings—destroy everything. Only then will you be able to stay with me, and we will recover our house and possessions here." The man then wakes up and burns, breaks, and destroys everything. Thereupon, he drops stone dead and enters the underworld, where he is reunited with his possessions, which he can then use again. This gives rise to the custom of the *pötui:* "dispatching the goods of the deceased into the other world once they have been broken." (Dournes 1978: 205)

---

4. In studying the funerary rituals of the Olo Ngaju, Hertz mentioned their similar desire to transform or cleanse the objects that are contaminated by the deceased's "impure cloud": "His belongings may no longer be used for profane purposes; they must be destroyed or dedicated to the deceased, or at least stripped, by appropriate rites, of the harmful quality they have acquired" (Hertz 1960: 38).

In Leu, the Jorai interpretation associating the dead and the crushed objects seems to be stimulated by a desire to reproduce harmony through shapes and meanings, which may then enable the villagers to think about the dead as clearly belonging to another world.[5] According to the elders, the world of the living is viewed as a place where people and objects are characterized by what is relatively new, whole, and functional (e.g., the usable basket), while the world of the dead is seen as being eroded, fragmented, or incomplete and irremediably dysfunctional (from the perspective of everyday use by the living). If grave and body belong to the same continuum, accumulating objects for the making of a comfortable grave may also serve the purpose of making the dead body complete. To this end, personal belongings can be regarded as extensions of the body, which for purposes of consistency also needs to bear traces of decay. In crushing the objects, the villagers have in essence produced fragmented body parts to somehow bring the incomplete dead body to its full completion before starting a new life. As Hertz wrote: "Death is not a mere destruction but a transition: as it progresses so does the rebirth; while the old body falls to ruins, a new body takes shape, with which the soul—provided the necessary rites have been performed—will enter another existence, often superior to the previous one" (Hertz 1960: 48).

Ensuring Continuity in Life and Death

As Veam's burial nears its end, people are still crying, singing, laughing, and teasing one another by turns. During these four days of celebration, many have become extremely drunk. The funerary singing (*cok*), which is broken by sobbing, laments the loss of a relative and friend and praises her as having been a good lady who never hurt anyone, worked hard in the field, and stayed at home. Veam's funeral is conducted in such a way that there is little room for the dead to fall between the two realms of the living and the dead. This is done to prevent her becoming entrapped in a tragic space as a wandering ghost (*atâo*). Luyin Blen described her as follows: "She has never re-married,

---

5. By comparison, in Bali the breaking of objects indicates separation but also completion, "as Balinese always break objects when something has been completed, not just in death ceremonies, but also house-building ceremonies, marriage, etc." Leo Howe, personal communication, August 2010.

I guess she never found anyone she liked.... It's the way it is.... Or maybe it's because she was ugly, she was born with a big tummy.... This is an easy funeral since she was a very good lady. Veam has never hurt a human being or an animal. The spirits wouldn't make it difficult for her to enter the world of the dead. They will welcome her into the next world."

In the tone of Luyin Blen's voice, one can detect the confidence that this death is unproblematic in the sense that the spirits will accept the villagers' offerings (*pödong*) and that her good death (which occurred at home and at an old age) is unlikely to badly affect the life of the community. Although the villagers hope that the departed one will start a smooth journey to the next world, this transition is not without risk for both the dead and the living (Hertz 1960; Lafont 1963). Indeed, for the living, death usually renders their village more vulnerable to the influence of malevolent spirits that may want to cause illnesses and further sorrow. In light of this, the success of a funeral can also be viewed as an act of self-preservation on the part of fellow villagers.

A few months after the initial burial, Leu inhabitants and acquaintances from neighboring villages will celebrate the hundred days that follow Veam's death. This ceremony entails animal sacrifices and sharing of rice wine and meat among relatives and friends. Khmers celebrate a similar commemoration on the hundredth day after a death. However, a village elder commented that this ceremony forms an essential part of their Jorai tradition, which he described as "ritual actions that have been handed down from the past generations." For this village elder, the hundred-day ceremony is usually followed by the "village ceremony," which involves the offering of seven pigs, seven chickens, and seven jars of rice wine, a small amount of which will be placed in a spirit house in front of the village's main entrance. This ceremony enables the villagers to preserve the equilibrium of village life because the village may have become more vulnerable after the death of a member of the community. On this occasion, people invite the spirits to share food and call on their ancestors "not to forget the rain, help their children [descendants] learn and gain knowledge, and not be lost [in life]."

Funerals and rituals that serve to revitalize the village appear to work in the logic of a binary system. Because of the mutually supporting relations linking the world of the dead and the world of the living, they are occasions to readjust the balance of life and death and an opportunity to remind the ancestors that the living need their continual protection. Most people in Leu believe that the soul of the departed one "goes somewhere else." However, they also presume that some of their ancestors' souls have remained close to them by settling on the outskirts of the village in order to "protect people performing good deeds and punish the ones who infringe traditional laws."

Leu's cemetery is positioned along the river at the edge of the forest, near the site where the village was originally located before a series of inauspicious deaths forced it to move. People from the same family are often buried in the same grave unless they have died a bad death, in which case the victim will be buried farther from the remains of his or her kin or outside the village cemetery (*pösat*) in the forest. Dournes specified that only dead relatives who are directly related can share the same funerary roof (Dournes 1975). The village cemetery is thus a place where most of the ancestors are buried, and people said they that would continue to bury their relatives there until there was no more space left, at which point they would need to find another location. A few elders commented that this long-maintained tradition had started to erode, however. Not only had funerary rituals "already been shortened," but they had also been modified to resemble Khmer funerary practices. According to the elders, some families in this and other villages had unearthed the remains of their relatives in order to cremate them and place the ashes in Buddhist pagodas. For these members of the village's older generation, removing the remains was comparable to uprooting relatives from the continuity of family ancestry, thus breaking the mutually beneficial link that connects the living and the dead.

The idea of the burial place remaining unchangeable is also held by the Jorai highlanders of Vietnam: "The ancestors are part of the village, and the Jorai are attached to them much as the Hebrews are to the remains of Joseph; it is one of the elements that ties them to the land. Alive, the Jorai is not fond of the sylvan landscape; dead, he is buried with his family at the edge of the forest" (Dournes 1969: 106). Yet more than a physical connection that draw people closer to the remains of the ancestors, the local belief that each component of nature can become the privileged dwelling of an ancestor makes this attachment to the place more potent. As Dovert pointed out, "Admittedly the link to the land is not absent. Each place is 'inhabited' by the ancestors and by the spirits, which qualifies it in a symbolic and enduring manner, although not necessarily in the logic of an influence or an exclusive use. Therefore, for the *Jorai* the link to the original land imposes itself through its memory and the memory of the places inhabited successively, yet it is not a permanent control over the space" (Dovert 2005: 58).

As mentioned earlier, the Jorai of Leu regard the dense forest as an untamed area where the spirits can roam free. Consequently, the world of the dead is associated with the edge of the forested realm, an ambiguous place that is often within walking distance from the village but is still a space where things may happen beyond human control. All the village elders agreed that a Jorai's life is spent in a human-made open space outside the forest, but at death he or she should ultimately be buried in the shade of the forest canopy. This apparent contradiction can be explained by the fact that the villagers believe that the world of the dead is a complete inversion of the world of the living. As soon as one crosses the threshold of death, the world he or she knew is turned on its head, with fishes flying in the sky and birds swimming in rivers (Lafont 1963; Dournes 1968, 1975; Bourdier 2006). As two elders commented, "We don't know if it's true, some people may have lied, some people may have told the truth. But we know our great-great-grandfathers used to say so. . . . Because it is the world of the dead, it has to be totally different from our world!"

For Siu, the village wood-carver, this interpretation was supported by the fact that "at death a wife moves into her husband's grave. If she dies before him, then husband and wife will be buried separately." Most villagers believe that a husband usually precedes his wife in death. When a wife dies first, the case is interpreted as an anomaly, which is later expressed by the fact that the spouses are buried apart. But in what is locally comprehended as an ordinary death sequence (that is, when a wife outlives her husband), the Jorai tradition of matrilocal residence is inverted, for the wife is the one who will then move into her husband's "house" (*sang*).

The villagers' representation of what the afterworld may look like thus translates into some sort of continuity between life and death. The reassurance that the soul of the departed will embrace a new life and that personal items, animals, and future relatives will accompany her or him into the next world also enables them to maintain a sense of certainty, which is essential in their contemplation of what may happen to them after mortal life. But, as implied by comments quoted earlier, this assumption of continuity runs alongside a sense that the world of the dead is a perfect inversion of the land of the living. As if gazing through a looking glass, some village elders believe that the world after death is a parallel world governed by the same rules applied in reverse, whereby nighttime for the living becomes daytime for the dead. This conception works in the same way as a photographic slide. In its original position, the slide may show the inert and dismembered body buried in Leu cemetery, but when it is tilted at a 180-degree angle, it reveals the reconstituted body walking into his or her new existence.

According to Jacques Dournes, this inverted system of representation derives less from the desire to know what happens after death than from a need to reinforce the connection to the ancestors. It is a confirmation that the living find their raison d'être in their ancestors. In fact, for his Jorai informants, "the past is the future of the descendants." In other words, "The Jorai does not put anything aside for his children's future, he gives all he can to the dead and leaves the remaining to his parents-in-law; the generation that follows does not matter, it is only an extension" (Dournes 1972: 218). This idea resonates with Lafont's claim that all these practices suggest that the human being becomes worthwhile only after his or her death. This belief may in turn explain the visible discrepancies that one can observe between the sophisticated beauty of the final grave and the poverty of the everyday home, the cleanliness of the cemetery and the accumulated waste in the village, and the very beautiful attire placed inside the coffin and the tattered clothes worn by the living in Leu and other nearby Jorai villages (Dournes 1972: 218).

The Abandonment of the Grave

In multistage funerary rituals reminiscent of Indonesian death practices (Chambert-Loir and Reid 2002), the villagers' second burial or final abandonment of the grave (*pojah*) marks an important step in decisively separating the living from the dead. As the dead soul embarks on an important journey toward a new existence, mourning comes to an end. This usually takes place two years after the burial, sometimes even later if the family has taken additional time to redecorate the grave with a new roof and a sculpted fence (Lafont 1963).

The status of the family and, more important, the money they have saved since the initial burial are the main factors dictating the size of the festivities and the final beauty of the grave.[6] The temporary leafy roof is rebuilt in

---

6. With reference to Indonesian ritual practices, Hertz commented, "This feast [the final ceremony], which lasts for several days, sometimes even a month, is of extreme importance to the

wood, and the grave is surrounded by a fence (*krep*) adorned with effigies (*rup*) that are said to carry on the relatives' duties to mourn and care for their dead. The abandonment of the grave marks a crucial phase during which the dead person is supposed to depart for a new abode, thus leaving the world of the living in peace. It also means that the grave will not be visited (or cleaned) anymore, and that the entire edifice will be left to deteriorate. The decay that slowly spreads through the structure of the grave, the crushed personal items, and the funerary statues are visible signs that nature has taken over and that the dead person has traveled safely into the next world. Leu villagers agree that it is traditionally *kŏm* (taboo) for people to visit the grave after it has been abandoned unless they do so to bury a close relative nearby. Jacques Dournes interpreted this Jorai tradition as a rite of passage whereby, upon reaching maturity, the dead person has finally left to resume a new life:

> They believe that as long as the dead person has not been thus abandoned, he is held prisoner by the very spirit who caused him or her to die: in other words, he is on probation as if in some sort of purgatory. To this end, a ceremony of the abandonment of the grave is meant to pay a fee to the spirit of the dead person so that the latter can finally free the entrapped soul. The *bongat* [soul] will thus be able to fly away in the same manner in which the chicken that is being sacrificed for the occasion is tossed into the sky. Prayers that are said at this very moment inform the dead person that he is now left on his own, that he no longer belongs to the world of the living, and that he must leave the pleasures of human existence behind. (quoted in Goy et al. 2006: 97)

A New Cause of Bad Death

As described earlier, ordinary death or death attributed to natural causes, such as old age, requires a succession of rituals that necessitate the participation of the entire community. These rituals are inscribed in a specific time frame, starting with the display of the coffin in the village and culminating

---

natives: it requires elaborate preparations and expenses which often reduce the family of the deceased to extreme poverty" (Hertz 1960: 53).

in the abandonment of the grave. As in various societies in Southeast Asia, bad death resulting from an act of violence is conceived of as a direct threat to both the soul of the departed and the rest of the community (Lafont 1963; Bloch and Parry 1982; Ang 1986; Kwon 2006). Leu villagers often say that they are particularly afraid of violent deaths (*driang*). According to some of my informants, although a bad death immediately affects only the bereaved family, the entire village feels compelled to participate actively in facilitating the deceased's transition to her or his next existence in order to avoid the spread of such ominous influences from one family to another.

In April 2008, an elderly woman committed suicide in the village by hanging herself. My informants explained that she had been in pain for a long time and had decided to put an end to her suffering. This left her husband a widower. Five months later her husband died a natural death. Siu, who helped prepared the grave of the husband, explained that he could not be buried with his wife, and that the respective graves of the spouses needed to be separated by "at least seven meters." A number of people said that once someone died, "the closest to the dead," that is, the kin, become the most vulnerable to death, disease, and other suffering. In the case of the suicide, the wife not only died before her husband (thus disrupting local rules of gender life expectancy) but also died a bad death. In this instance, the closest to the dead woman was the husband because they were living alone and had no children. In the eyes of the villagers, the fact that the husband died shortly after his wife reinforced the idea that her death had adversely affected him. At the same time, the idea of a specified distance between the graves suggests that pollution can also occur after death, so burying the husband away from his wife was perceived as a way to grant him protection in the next life. Given the nature of her death and the poverty of the family, this woman's funeral was carried out simply and modestly, with no prospect of further rituals thereafter.

This case shows that the local concept of pollution is pervasive in both life and death. Bad death often needs to be dealt with more promptly, but with increased precautions, to prevent it from affecting both the living in the village and the ancestors' remains in the village cemetery. However, Siu explained that the ailing wife who committed suicide had nonetheless been buried inside the village cemetery because, since she had been suffering for a while, her fellow villagers were expecting her to die at any moment. In Leu, insanity, physical ailments, and long suffering often place people in a different social space, as if they are already inhabiting a different world. In such cases, the individual often becomes socially dead.

Leu villagers have different ideas about what can be defined as "violent death" (*driang*). One villager told me that despite the violence of her suicide, the unremitting illness affecting the woman made it impossible for her to lead an ordinary life. As a result, some villagers viewed her death with pity. Some of my informants observed that in the event of a violent death (e.g., a bomb accident), people usually leave the body buried with or wrapped in crushed bamboo in the forest rather than bringing it into the village. In this case, the use of broken bamboo in forest burials may be a simple substitute for personal belongings in order to help "re-member" the dead. They also explained how funerary rituals are performed outside the village boundaries to maintain a distance from the evil *yang* (spirit) that may have caused the violent death in the first place (Lafont 1963; Dournes 1978, on *malemort*; Gustafsson 2009). Van Gennep's concept of "liminality" or transition best characterizes the Jorai view of the forest here because it temporarily houses the impure body after its access to the village has been denied (Van Gennep 1960: 11). As we will see later, returning land mine survivors are given the same treatment and have to live in the forest for some time before being authorized to enter the village. In his ethnographic study of the massacres of Ha My and My Lai in central Vietnam, Heonik Kwon defined bad deaths as "dying in the street and outside," "dying accidentally," or "dying in violent circumstances" (Kwon 2006: 13). For the Jorai living in Leu, a victim of aerial bombings falls into all these categories.

Caring for the Unburied Dead

For the village elders, assuring a correct burial of the dead is perceived as an unquestionable responsibility. According to Luyin Blen, the buried bones of the ancestors are comparable to the sacred founding stone that is at the origin of the creation of the Jorai village, for at death, people are always buried unless the deceased is a *pötao* (king of fire or king of water), who is cremated and buried elsewhere because he transcends both the world of humans and that of the spirits. In light of this, the proximity of the cemetery to the village is often regarded as a tangible link that connects the villagers to their past and without which they would be deprived of their identity. War survivors in the village told me that at the time of intense conflicts, they were barely able to care for the dead. They added that during the Khmer Rouge period there was neither time nor political space for funerary rituals because all religious activities were banned.

In referring specifically to the event of the bombing, Leu villagers blamed their chaotic life in the forest for not having been able to carry out their duties because, as they put it, "it was impossible!" Some informants went on to describe how, when body parts were found, the remains were sometimes buried hastily for fear that the planes would spot those performing the death rituals. In other cases, corpses were simply left unburied because people feared losing their own lives, especially at the peak of the bombing. Villagers described returning in the aftermath of the wars to the places where their relatives were known to have died, and how even those whose relatives had disappeared without a trace would travel to the presumed site of death to fulfill their long-overdue duty by performing an "empty sacrifice" (*sein teute* in Khmer). Echoing Bloch and Parry's description of the skull and its crushing that is necessary to liberate the "breath of life" (Bloch and Parry 1982: 82), my informants said that this "emptiness" was due to the fact that the ritual was performed in the absence of the bones of the dead but in the hope that in some way it would still reach out to their souls and liberate them from their tragic conditions. As Hertz wrote: "The stay of the dead among the living is somewhat illegitimate and clandestine. It lives, as it were, marginally in the two worlds: if it ventures into the afterworld it is treated there like an intruder; here on earth it is an unfortunate guest whose proximity is dreaded. If it has no resting place it is doomed to wander incessantly, waiting anxiously for the feast which will put an end to its restlessness" (Hertz 1960: 36).

For some Leu villagers, finding the place of death meant that they could connect—or at least attempt to connect—with the departed because bodies and landscape had become enmeshed. This perspective resonates with Nicholas Saunders's comments on how the 2001 destruction of the World Trade Center resulted in the "act of dispersal represented by the fragmented and vaporised bodies of the dead" (Saunders 2003: 226), which thus turned the place itself into a memorial to their tragic loss. This example parallels Kwon's description of the massacre perpetuated in the village of Ha My by Republic of Korea marines, in which "the troops brought two D-7 bulldozers, which they used to flatten the houses, destroy the shallow graves, and obliterate the unburied bodies. This assault against the corpse is remembered as the most inhumane aspect of the incident, and it has complicated the process of family commemoration" (Kwon 2006: 46). In such circumstances, the process of reassembling body parts, personal items, and crushed objects to make the dead body complete is fraught with great difficulties.

In the "Dictionary of North American Jarai" one can find the following entry: *Črong pósat* means to prepare "a grave for someone who is known or presumed dead, but whose body is missing. The grave includes personal items belonging to the dead" (Lap 2009: 81). Although in the course of my research, none of my informants mentioned this practice, it remains interesting because it suggests that in the absence of the body of the dead, the bereaved family may try to perform an ordinary funeral for the missing person. In this case, placing personal belongings inside the grave makes up for the absence of the body, and the belongings are treated as body parts or objects that may find their way to their rightful owner in the afterworld.

In Leu, as well as in other neighboring Jorai villages, people said that because of the panic brought on by the aerial bombardment, they would just *kop tchaul* (bury and leave abandoned, in Khmer) the remains of dead relatives, thinking that they could organize an appropriate funeral in the future. However, a few people claimed that they were unable to care for the dead then or afterward because "it was too late!" Male and female village elders who shared this view described their inability to carry out their duties with thinly veiled guilt. Some people believed that it was indeed too late because the souls of their relatives were forever trapped between the world of the living and that of the dead. These souls then made themselves visible through dreams (*pleboh*) or ghostly forms at night (*atâo*).[7] One villager told me, "During the war there were so many dead bodies in the forest that the souls of the dead and the spirits came into your dreams."

My informants perceived dreams, like the forest, as a liminal space, an area locked between the world of the living and the dead where the latter can communicate with the living directly. In fact, dreams act as a singular

---

7. The idea of the roaming ghosts also affects the younger generation to a certain extent. Children approximately ten years old explained that they did not like walking on their own at night and tended to follow an adult very closely when they could. When they were asked what they saw, they responded that it was a white shadow that floated in the air and that often appeared at night.

128   Chapter 4

space that enables the soul of the living to drift away from the body to communicate with the gods, the spirits, and the souls of the dead (Lafont 1963; Dournes 1978). In this regard, the homeless dead who died a violent death (Van Gennep 1960; Chambert-Loir and Reid 2002) may find in dreams a means to contact relatives or strangers who might be able to help. The function of a dream is crucial in influencing decision making that can affect a community in multiple ways. As Elizabeth Coville pointed out, "Dreams are another common way in which the dead communicate directly with the living and foretell the future" (Coville 2002: 76). For example, dreams of one's future vocation, which part of the forest to clear, or where to resettle the village are all seen as messages sent from the spiritual domain, again underlining the interdependency between this world and the other.

Some of my informants said that the *pleboh bongat atâo* (dream of the soul of the dead) was essential for the living to be granted a second chance to care for the dead. Lagn, an older informant, told me that people were never too short of time or too late in fulfilling their moral obligations. According to him,

> When we sleep, it's like when we die because the spirits can talk to us and ask us to make sacrifices for them. . . . Someone who dies a violent death does not necessarily become a wandering ghost because you are too short of time to bury the corpse and perform the appropriate ritual . . . but I know some people who have said they have been haunted or directly affected by them.[8] They suffered from illnesses, they heard voices, which were confirmed by the barking dogs, because dogs can see the dead. . . . But these people can still do the same thing by calling the spirits of the dead and performing a ritual.

According to Lagn, the key to caring for the unburied dead resides in the ritualization of a belated act, which emphasizes the importance both of the intention and the meaning the individual brings to the action over the socially prescribed meaning of time. Like that of several village elders, Lagn's perception of the *sein teute* (empty sacrifice, in Khmer) exemplifies Humphrey and Laidlaw's archetypal actions of ritual whereby "meanings must be put into rituals to infuse its emptiness with spiritual significance. . . . The meanings should come from inside the self" (Humphrey and Laidlaw 1994: 2).

---

8. For greater insight into the angry ghost who manifests itself most violently, see (Gustafsson 2009).

Conversely, some villagers had a very acute sense of the emptiness of the act in both its physical form (the absence of the bones) and its cognitive form (the meaninglessness of the act caused by the time lag), thus illustrating the ways in which they conceived of such particular rituals as being "given," "external to themselves," and time bound (Humphrey and Laidlaw 1994: 5). The ritualized action that was thus extracted from its time frame (the time of death and the conventional sequence of traditional rituals) appeared of no use to them since the dead who had suffered from lack of burial and rituals were now thought of as being irreversibly lost. This view invites new perspectives, especially in light of Heonik Kwon's study of the villages of Ha My and My Lai in central Vietnam, which in 1968 both experienced massacres of civilians (Kwon 2006). Kwon's ethnography of commemoration practices by the surviving relatives and descendants shows that the time lag can actually become essential because it enables the dead children and infants to be reincorporated into the continuum of time through the rites performed a generation later by children who regard the dead as their uncles and aunts. Belated rituals can thus have the power to relocate the unburied dead in the vertical history of the family tree and, most important, liberate their souls, which enables them to leave their ghostly garbs and, at last, fully become ancestors.

Reflecting on this issue, Pou Ksor, one of the Leu village elders, claimed that it was indeed too late to perform the rituals and that there was nothing left for the survivors to do. On a later occasion, however, he explained that people still needed to do something for the dead, as well as for themselves. He recounted how, when the villagers resettled in Leu after the Vietnamese invasion of the country, the elders decided to organize a large propitiating ceremony for all the souls of the unburied dead and the awaiting spirits. On this occasion, all types of animals, including cows, buffaloes, and pigs, were offered. Pou Ksor called it the "ritual for the souls" and commented that on this particular day

> people made animal sacrifices because they pitied the dead. Something had to be done. . . . You prayed to the spirits of the dead and told them to go ahead and not be afraid to do so; we were also calling on ourselves to go ahead so that the war might be over and that it would not occur again. We prayed to the *preah* [god, in Khmer] in our house, and we prayed to the spirits who lived in the forest, in the mountain, in the water, and in the stone, asking them not

to be afraid and to care for our children and grandchildren. This was a single-day ritual that lasted from seven in the morning until late in the night.

Such a one-off ritual serves a double purpose. First, the ritual acts as a ceremony of reparation for the souls of the departed, as well as for the spirits and gods who may have felt neglected. It also acts as a healing process for the survivors, to ensure their spiritual well-being. In this case, the agent of the ritual—in other words, the person "for whom and through whom action is directed as it is" (Humphrey and Laidlaw 1994: 100)—enables the dead and the living to start anew, because both worlds have been greatly affected by the prolonged conflicts. An interesting feature of the incantation by Pou Ksor is the fact that the souls of the dead and the gods were perceived as being afraid and to some extent probably confused, a trait that was also shared by the village survivors. For Pou Ksor, the imagined feelings of the dead and spirits could be better conceived of as a mirrored version of our own; thus pitying the dead is also a way to pity ourselves. Some people in Leu therefore regarded this ritual as an important social, religious, and psychological event because it renewed the reciprocal obligations that the living had toward the spiritual domain and vice versa.

At times when retrieving the link between the living and the dead appears to be an essential component of the survival strategy for both individuals and the group, the possibility that meanings can be given to rituals rather than being encoded in them allows the survivors to come to terms with painful memories associated with unfulfilled hereditary obligations. Indeed, for Humphrey and Laidlaw, "Ritualisation can happen to anything. The view that ritualisation is a quality of actions, and not a class of events or institutions draws our attention to new aspects of ritual actions" (Humphrey and Laidlaw 1994: 3). In this regard, new causes of bad death, like dying from a bomb, and partial death, like losing a body part to a land mine, have introduced new aspects of rituals, as will be illustrated in the examples that follow.

Land Mine and Bomb Accidents

In 1995, a bomb explosion caused the death of six people from Leu and a neighboring village. People remembered this incident as being one of the most violent in a long time because there was a significant number of victims all at once. The bodies were never brought into the villages for the traditional display of the coffin. Leu villagers said that they nonetheless performed the traditional funerary rites by sacrificing animals for the souls of the dead and the spirits, sharing meat and rice wine. This time, however, the corpses were buried together away from the village cemetery in the depths of the forest.

Fatalities caused by salvaging explosive remnants of war, bombs, or land mines are examples of bad death that occasionally affect local communities living in this postconflict landscape. In Leu, as well as in surrounding Jorai villages located on the Ho Chi Minh Trail, bereaved relatives are placed in an ambiguous situation in which, on the one hand, they want the souls of departed kin to leave peacefully, and, on the other, they need to protect themselves because the violent death of their relatives could make them impure (*cölom*) (Hertz 1960; Lafont 1963). Today, however, views differ regarding the extent to which the funerary rituals for a violent death (*driang*) can be similar to the ones that are performed for an ordinary death. Although my informants agreed that there are geographic limitations regarding where the rituals and burial should take place, people who genuinely feel sorry for their dead relatives may want to try to maintain a sense of normality so that the dead are not left abandoned. Conversely, other villagers strongly believe that such graves need to be far away and abandoned immediately in order to prevent the malevolent spirit that caused the accident from following the dead into the village. My research in the area (especially in neighboring Jorai villages across the river) shows that such funerary practices are being frequently renegotiated as people's perceptions of what a violent death may be are subjected to varied individual interpretations.

My informants explained that upon returning from burying a victim of a bomb explosion, they have to perform a ritual that is intended to cleanse them from the pollution of having been near a bad death. Village elders, adults and children alike, need to have both their feet placed on top of the *dung* or *pok* (a large Jorai knife) before being washed with water mixed with chicken blood and rice wine. According to the village's traditional doctor,[9] every person needs

---

9. This villager does not like to be called *pöjau* or shaman, although he does perform exorcisms and cures illnesses from time to time. He insists that he knows very little and that the real shaman, who is occasionally solicited for important events, lives in another village in the commune.

to follow this purifying practice in order to ward off the evil spirits who are watching. At such moments, the village elder says the following words:

> Tah keumal hwick bad;
> Ngal Lei drah pouy, anouk, ya pai;
> Klach nay vo;
> Hwai tuam vach ta.

> [Sacrifice to the *areak*] No need to be afraid anymore;
> Clean our feet with blood from pig, chicken, and rice wine;
> Don't be sick [or, in this case, don't be like the dead];
> The same [accident] should not happen again.

Kluen, the village's traditional doctor, commented that this practice was directly inspired by an old ritual that was meant to cure people and ensure a good harvest. After a bomb accident, people need to protect themselves and ensure that life will resume in a safe and productive manner. Villagers therefore sacrifice pigs for the *yang* and mix chicken blood with water and rice wine so that no one will get "hot," which carries the meaning of "being ill." Survivors of a bomb or land mine accident also need to conform to specific rules in order to be fully reintegrated into the village. Pou Ksor said that when he returned from the UXO-contaminated northern province of Preah Vihear after a land mine accident, he was forced to spend a night outside Leu and leave a ten- to twenty-meter buffer zone between him and the boundary of the village. Likewise, in neighboring Bok, a former soldier who had lost a leg to a land mine accident explained that his return was also sanctioned by a temporary exclusion, thus giving enough space and time for the villagers to make the necessary sacrifices that would protect them. To some extent, one could argue that this practice is reminiscent of the double obsequies for the dead, whereby two different but complementary funerals are a prerequisite to ensure the dead peace and the promises of a better reincarnation.

Pou Ksor described how such sacrifices entail the slaughtering of a pig and the offering of rice-wine jars and cooked rice to the spirits living in the forest (*yang glai*). Such practices highlight the distinctive way in which incomplete bodies (hence polluted and polluting persons) are perceived locally. The return of the injured, and especially the disabled, is seen as a potent source of pollution because these persons are regarded as marked by death, taboo, and danger (Valeri 2000) or, as Luyin Blen described them, "as permanently connected with the war." On one occasion, Pou Ksor pondered, "I've got a dead soul. I am missing an eye, an arm." Two of my informants who belong to the postwar generation and are influenced by both Christian and Buddhist beliefs interpreted such physical disability as a direct result of a bad karma. This view resonates with the Khmer belief that a disabled person is impure because she or he is visibly affected by a sinful deed committed in the past. Pou Ksor, however, once narrated that at the time of the Khmer Rouge, an incident happened in 1975, which at that time, left him angry. He explained that he had been chosen to be a driver, but that at the last minute someone else had been designated instead. The person who replaced him was tasked to drive all the way to Tuol Sleng in Phnom Penh, the infamous S-21 detention center, never to return. Conscious of his lucky escape, Pou Ksor admitted, "I do have a bit of a good karma. I avoided Tuol Sleng, unlike some people in the villages who ended there."

In Leu, as well as in other villages in the commune where people have been physically impaired by the conflicts, the need to perform a ritual both to reintegrate the individual and to protect the villagers plays the same role as the cleansing practices that follow a funeral. Whether they are in direct response to the death of a person or to the incompleteness of a war victim (which may also be interpreted as the person's partial death), the ritual practices involved serve to restore the equilibrium of the energies that flow between the safety of the village and the uncertainty of the outside. As a village elder specified, "If the family had enough money, they should carry out the rituals twice: once in the forest and once inside the village. But first and foremost the ritual needs to be done outside for the spirits of the forest."

As mentioned previously, the village's inhabitants perceive it as a tame space cut out of the ominous influence of the forest. There are gradations in how tame physical space is felt to be, ranging from the village (the safest space) to the rice field or *hwa* (orchard) (a moderately safe space) to the dense forest (unsafe) (Dournes 1978). The following myth illuminates the idea that the village perimeter acts as a buffer zone stretching from the secure world of its inhabitants to the space beyond. It illustrates how the various distances between the village center and the outside work by degrees of physical inclusion or exclusion. In addition, this myth nicely brings together several themes discussed earlier, including the world of the dead as a reversed image of the world of the living, the breaking of the personal items, the second obsequies, and the importance of the buffalo sacrifice.

His father having died, a son builds a beautiful grave for the celebration of the abandonment of the grave. But for this he needs a buffalo. He decides then to take two copper bowls along in order to try to exchange them in the villages. Nobody wants to buy his bowls; he still has no buffalo. He next arrives in a place where a large number of people are preparing a grave. He has in fact entered the land of the dead, and his father is there as well. Father and son recognize each other:

"But it is my father who is here!"
"Where are you going to, child?"
"I am on my way to sell these bowls."
"In exchange for what?"
"In exchange for a buffalo, for the meal we will have on your grave, father!"
"You insolent pup, why do you insult me? It is for you and your mother, who have passed away, that I am preparing this grave!"

Father and son have an argument and accuse each other of being dead. The son then takes his father by the hand and tries to drag him out of there toward their village. The father becomes a buzzard, and the son carries the bird in his arms. As they draw close enough to the village to hear the voices of its inhabitants, the father turns into charcoal and then ashes. The son still holds him in his hands. As they are about to enter the village, the ashes turn into dew: the son can no longer hold it, it slips through his hands. He retraces his steps in a bid to find his father and bring him back to the village. At the third attempt, his father says to him: "Let it be, son! I am truly dead (*atâo*). If you really do care for me, destroy all our belongings in the house, break everything up, and come and join me with your mother!" After destroying everything, both son and mother fall dead. Only then are they able to cross to the other side and live together once again. (Dournes 1978: 203–4)

This story beautifully illustrates the binary opposition between the inside and the outside, the safe and the unsafe, the living and the dead. In light of this opposition, the separation between this world and the next is such that the living and the dead can meet only in a liminal space (such as dreams), inasmuch as the living are unwelcome in the afterworld and the dead have no place inside the village boundaries. This further exemplifies the Jorai saying that "the wind that blows in your world is not ours," meaning that the dead should henceforth remain with their companions in the realm of the deceased and not return to their village unless they are invited by their living relatives (Dournes 1975). In a sense, the gradual transformation undergone by the father from bird to dew as he approaches the village is a reversed illustration of the Jorai person's increased exposure to the multiple and unknown faces of the other described in chapter 1. The farther away the Jorai villager is from the village center, the more exposed he or she becomes to the unpredictable influences of nature, spirits, and strangers.

In a similar manner, the villagers' reintegration of those disabled in war is conducted in a gradual way as they are progressively inducted into the safest of all the places, the social space of the village, which functions as a large and complete organic body composed of all its inhabitants (Condominas 1980). This can explain why the village's war victims were left on the outskirts of their village but not quite within the depths of the forest, since the immediate area that surrounds the village—often a midcanopy forest—is regarded as an intermediate space. This compulsory stay in the environs of the village is thus a necessary step toward the full reintegration of the wounded into the village precincts.

Leu villagers believe that some spirits (*areak* or *yang*) are unpredictable and therefore unreliable, but if they are in doubt, they will often give them offerings to be granted their protection. Therefore, the ideal practice is for both spaces to be sanctioned by their own rituals, as if to maintain the balance of conflicting powers between the benevolent spirits dwelling inside and the ambiguous spirits living outside. This need to restore the sense of equilibrium is further underscored by the fact that before setting off on a long journey, villagers often ask their village spirits that their blessing might accompany them along the way. Luyin Blen commented that this traditional practice, originally based on the sacred stone that founded the village, had been and still is popular among bomb hunters.

Resymbolizing the Objects of Death

Introducing New Types of Warfare Sculptures

The Jorai cemetery (*pösat*) is often regarded as the art location par excellence, where all forms of artistic expression (sculpture, music, dances) are concentrated, especially at times of funerary rites (Dournes 1968, 1975; Ngo Van

Doanh 1991). Cambodian and Vietnamese Jorai are traditionally prolific wood-carvers, and one example of this wood-carving ability is illustrated in the way they decorate their cemetery. This type of sculpture was first documented by the French Christian missions in the 1850s in areas of central Vietnam adjacent to Ratanakiri province in Cambodia, where the Jorai, as well as other ethnic groups, followed the tradition of grave ornamentation (Maître 1912; Lafont 1963; Dournes 1968; Simonnet 1977; Goy and Coué 2006).

In the cemetery of Leu, village effigies that belong to the pantheon of funerary sculptures, such as the mourner (a crouching male with his chin resting on the palms of his hands), the peacock (the legendary surrogate mother of the Jorai and a symbol of beauty), the elephant (an animal associated with power and prestige), and the monkey (a popular dweller in the forest), now stand, however, alongside war-inspired carvings like the helicopter and bombing plane. In the case of grave decorations, planes appear in both sculpted and drawn forms. According to Siu, the talented wood-carver, the plane is a *damnang*, a substitute (in Khmer) for the traditional mourner who looks after the dead until his or her soul travels to the next world. As Joanna White noted in conducting her study of a selection of postconflict ethnic communities, "Fascinatingly, planes and helicopters have become part of their cultural iconography, represented in ritual decorations, drawings and weaving" (White 1995: 25).

Personal belongings act as identifiers of the grave's owner; roof drawings and sculptures can illustrate the former life of the dead person. A pregnant villager who died during childbirth can be represented by a woman with a large womb, while a man carrying an assault rifle on his shoulder can illustrate a soldier who died in combat. Many sculptures and illustrations may also be used for their symbolic value, however, in the sense that images of weaponry will enable the dead person to be well protected, strong, brave, and respected in his next life. Indeed, the decoration of the grave offers the opportunity to tell an imaginary story, which may become true in the next world. Like bringing personal objects to the grave, sculpting, drawing, and painting contribute in some way to the making or invention of someone's future identity. These good wishes for the dead translate either into three-dimensional representations, such as sculptures, or into two-dimensional drawings and paintings on traditional funerary monuments such as the *pösat atâo* (an edifice four to five meters high with a saddle-shaped roof line over it; see figure 5), which enable the family to foretell a better story in order to lead the dead toward a more fulfilling existence.

In this regard, war-associated ornaments on a ten-year-old boy's grave, for example, do not necessarily mean that the child was a soldier or had any connection with the war. It only means that his parents hope that in the next world the child will live a longer and happier life by being strong, valiant, and respected, male qualities that are suggested by the manipulation of symbols of warfare. Indeed, in *pósat atâo* villages, people think that only male graves will benefit from these types of illustrations because girls or women are believed not to need any of these particular human qualities. The depicted weaponry often includes knives, spears, crossbows, and, since the 1990s, hand grenades, assault rifles, rocket launchers, bombs, and planes. Such beliefs are not shared by every Jorai village in the commune, though, and people living in Phum Tang, which is located just across the river, insist that graves should not bear any war-related effigies since this may tragically affect the dead in his or her next life by being a bad omen of a violent death. Even if telling an imaginary story for the dead is a well-established practice in most local Jorai and other ethnic-minority cemeteries, the introduction of war-related effigies as characters, symbols, or mere aesthetic illustrations can remain subject to taboos, since their fundamental association with death may be perceived as insuperable.[10]

The people I worked with often said that in the aftermath of the war, the inhabitants of most villages were aware of the true nature of the planes, but they remained so fascinated by them that they started to make carved reproductions of them. In Leu, the association between the plane and the US bombardment that devastated the region more than thirty years ago remains strong, particularly among the adult segment of the population. In his study of human-made objects derived from and inspired by conflicts, Nicholas Saunders noted that the Vietnam War generated a plethora of "trench art" such as models of warfare equipment manufactured by soldiers for whom the American Huey helicopter gunship became "the definitive icon of technological war during the conflict" (Saunders 2003: 200). Furthermore, the

---

10. Among thirty villages spread in four districts that were visited, the majority of which are Jorai, 90% have used plane and other war-associated representations for sacred and more profane purposes.

fact that commercial air travel remains outside the experience of most Jorai people living in the area maintains the innate relationship among planes, bombing, and death in which the plane has ultimately become the sign (what announces death) and the symbol (the conception of death, not death itself). Indeed, for the older generation, a carved plane is often invested with personal experiential significance.

The Symbolic Appropriation of War-Related Objects

According to Siu, because planes and death are intimately connected, plane replicas are mostly made for funerary rites or for important propitiating purposes. People carve them for the traditional ritual of the buffalo sacrifice, in which the immolation of the animal appeases the spirits that have caused someone to fall sick or pays one's entrance fees into the next world (Condominas 1957; Lafont 1963; Dournes 1978). As he explained, "If there was no buffalo or cow to sacrifice, we would not make it; the plane is there only because we have such animals to offer the spirits." Because cows and buffaloes are the most valuable animals to be sacrificed, Leu villagers feel that it is only appropriate to have a plane placed on top of their sacrifice pole. Conversely, other ceremonies that entail the offering of a pig or a chicken will seldom necessitate the presence of a sculpted plane.[11] As recorded by Lafont in the course of his ethnographic study of the Jorai, "The sacrificial ceremony acts as a medium, a means to communicate with the sacred, which enables him to create a link, a communion between him and the invisible powers" (Lafont 1963: vi). This link and its inherent quality nonetheless depend on the animal that is offered because local people consider that the sacrifice of a chicken channels less power than the sacrifice of a buffalo, which has more chance to satisfy the demands of the spirits.

The buffalo sacrifice is a significant ritual that broadly marks important social events among the Jorai, as well as other highlanders in the Southeast Asian region (Lewis 1951; Condominas 1957; Lafont 1963; Simonnet 1977; Goy and Coué 2006). Paul Huard, a French scholar who documented similar ritual practices among the Mnong-Phnong across the Vietnamese

---

[11]. According to Lafont, the importance of animals, in descending order, is as follows: ox, buffalo, goat, castrated pig, large pig, small pig, and chicken (Lafont 1963).

border in the 1930s, explained that sacrifice posts are the tangible link among the divine, the officiating priest, and the soil (Goy and Coué 2006). The buffalo is attached to a post that is highly decorated and bears at its top the effigy of a male mourner or an animal. Since people's return to their village after the long-drawn-conflicts, however, sacrifice posts have started to feature more menacing sculptures like planes, helicopters, AK-47 assault rifles, crossbows, and swords. Leu villagers, as well as inhabitants of other ethnic-minority villages in neighboring districts (including some Tampuon, Kachok, Kraveth, Kreung, and Brao villages) now perpetuate this relatively new tradition of placing a carved plane above their ancestors' graves, on top of the sacrifice posts, in the middle of the rice field before planting, on the roof of the community house, or at the entrance of their village (see Ngo 1991).

In February 2009, a Jorai elder from Plói Leu Krong (formerly Leu) passed away. I was told that according to the funerary custom, a buffalo that belonged to the bereaved family was released in the forest so that people could "hunt" for it. After its release, the hunters had great difficulty capturing the animal, which meant that the village was being delayed in organizing the buffalo sacrifice that is necessary for the soul of the departed to be accepted into the next world.[12] In this context, the pursuit of the animal is more a semblance than a real hunt because people expect that the buffalo will offer itself to the hunters in order to accompany his owner in his journey to his new life. But after three days during which they were unable to capture the buffalo (which some villagers interpreted as an ominous sign), the hunters decided to borrow a gun from a policeman to kill the buffalo in order to speed up the preparations necessary for the ultimate burial. The idea of shooting the animal was perceived as an unusual departure from the local practice because the buffalo is supposed to be brought back alive before being slaughtered and finally burned at the sacrifice pole (*klay*). For my informants, the word *klay* refers to the fact that the animal has been brought to the sacrifice post and is now "out of human hands." In this case,

---

12. I was told that this is a tradition in most Jorai villages, including Leu. The animal is given a chance to be free and then is hunted by the villagers for the sacrificial ritual. According to a villager, the delay in finding it in this case was due to the fact that the animal refused to be caught, an indication of how difficult or demanding the spirits are in accepting the soul into the next world.

the animal was still trapped in the world of the living, and it was out of desperation that the family decided to kill it to avert the risk of being further delayed and losing the animal in the forest.

I was informed by the villagers that if there is a buffalo to sacrifice, there will be a plane effigy. However, without the buffalo, the village carvers felt that the sacrifice of another animal (especially of lesser economic and ritual value) would not warrant the special presence of a plane.

The attempt to bring a buffalo to the sacrifice pole ultimately remained unsuccessful, after which the villagers collectively decided to abandon the hunt. The family needed to carry on because the body had been exposed too long under the heat of the sun; as a result, other animals were offered to the spirits instead. Tim Ingold described that in the circumpolar North it is a common belief that the hunted animal offers itself, for "it belongs (like an object) to the dead and will be taken away too although given to the spirits." To this end, hunters strongly argue that "one should not kill an animal that does not consent to be taken." To kill without the animal's active connivance would be an act of violence that would carry the threat of equally violent retribution in the future (Ingold 2000: 121–22). In the same way, the absence of the buffalo in Plói Leu Krong was perceived by some elders as a major setback to the success of the funeral. Indeed, the village hunters complained that the buffalo had been spotted many times but refused to be caught, an indication that, in contrast to Veam's funeral previously described, the *yang* (spirits) were being more demanding in accepting this soul into their world (see Lewis 1951).

When Leu villagers celebrated Veam's funeral, a cow and a buffalo were offered to the spirits at the sacrifice post, which was decorated with a three-propeller plane. More than a mere element of aesthetic decoration, the carved plane played an important role in the funerary practices. People believe that because of its intrinsic power (*peutrang*), the plane can preside at the death of the animal while warding off evil spirits at the same time. As a village elder commented, "This is a bombing plane, the same as the ones that came to wage war on us! It is powerful, beautiful and it inspires fear!" An epitome of beauty and power, the plane has, in the aftermath of the wars, supplanted other more traditional icons. In some villages, two sculpted planes on top of the sacrifice pole are seen as being twice as powerful as one. For the village elders in Leu, the plane also has a mnemonic role because, on the one hand, it reminds people about their warfare experience, and, on the other, it tells the younger generation how their parents and grandparents were afraid of the bombing planes. As a villager put it, "[Planes] just look beautiful and it tells the children about the past and how we used to be so scared of them!"

This practice calls to mind the cargo-cult phenomenon observed in Melanesian societies in the southern Pacific, where encounters with foreigners, starting in the nineteenth century, and particularly during World War II, inspired local inhabitants to reproduce war-associated objects and modern goods (e.g., weapons, airplanes, airstrips, radios) and imitate foreign behaviors in an attempt to attract further "cargo" or material goods to be sent by the spirits who had "manufactured" these items for their usage (Worsley 1957; Lindstrom 1993; Kaplan 1995). The following observation refers to artistic object making in Oceania, but it also rings true in this postconflict Jorai village of Southeast Asia: "Whatever the particular understanding of fighting, art in this context is likely to be part of an experienced process, rather than an 'image' that we might productively understand as part of a system of collective representation" (Thomas 1995: 79).

Harnessing the Power of the Formidable Object

Michael Taussig reflected on the wooden figurines of the Indians of the Chocó that were used for traditional healing and observed that "the making and existence of the artifact that portrays something gives one power over that which is portrayed" (Taussig 1993: 13). Taussig calls it the "magic of mimesis" (ibid.) Likewise, the Jorai of Leu village have, by way of reproduction, adopted effigies that are historically connected with violent death, not only to gain protection from them but also, and more important, to channel their destructive power to serve local tutelary purposes. My informants explained that since the end of the Khmer Rouge regime, when people were finally able to resume their religious practices, the plane has become a favorite effigy, replacing the other images that were used in the past (e.g., birds like the turtledove or the ibis that is said to take the soul of the departed away; see Le Roux and Sellato 2006). Thoeun, who was born at the time of the deadliest US bombing in the early 1970s, described the function of the sculpted plane as follows: "The plane is there for the dead to fly away into the next world!" Of key importance here is that the plane not only physically takes the place of old effigies on top of the tallest pole (*klao*) that surrounds the grave but also takes over their designated role. In this case, the substitution is guided by its own logic because the plane appears to be a perfect replacement for the bird who leads the soul of the departed into its next life.

Today the villagers regard such representations as a symbol of omniscience since a plane flies high in the sky and can therefore warn the villagers against the evil spirits that may want to harm them (Paterson, n.d.). Similarly, people have replaced their traditional village spirit at the entrance of their village (often represented by a little house placed on its right-hand side) with a plane on top of a wooden post in order to safeguard it. What was once the cause of destruction and fear has therefore been inverted to take the role of a sentinel within the community. When the plane is placed on the rooftop of the communal house, it acts as an *areak* (spirit) that will not only protect the villagers but also take over the role of ancestors and advise them during their meetings. The presence of a plane thus becomes a source of protection, blessing, and advice for the living. The connection between the plane and the sky means that it is, in both literal and metaphorical senses, the perfect vehicle to communicate with the divine.

Images that are associated with death are usually *kŏm* (taboo) inside the village. Consequently, a person caught crossing a community with such sculptures can be subject to substantial fines. There is a minimum fine of 60,000 riels (15 USD) when villagers discover that a sculpture has crossed the boundaries of their village. However, my informants said that fines are often higher to cover the purchase of a pig that will be sacrificed in order to ward off evil spirits that may cause unexpected death. For Elizabeth Coville, who conducted research in Sulawesi, "Even gestures associated with death rituals (such as placing one's chin in one's palm while one's elbow is resting on a horizontal surface) are prohibited at times that are not associated with death" (Coville 2002: 76). In Leu, the act of carving such wood effigies is associated with the preparation of death rituals. According to my older informants, it is forbidden to carve such effigies inside the village, especially when someone has not yet died in the community where it is being made. Some Jorai believe that anyone who infringes this law will be struck down by lightning "unless the sculptures were made inside the cemetery where all the taboos are suspended and the flow of life brought to a halt" (Dournes 1968: 97). As an alternative, the wood-sculpting artisans of Leu choose the liminal space of the forest to undertake the carving process. The forest is also the place where the sculptures are left before and after completion. However, because of their power, beauty, and connection with the sky, the village elders have given their consent for plane replicas to be used in village rituals.

Alfred Gell argued that art objects mediate a technology in order to achieve specific ends (Gell 1998: 52). In this regard, the purposes and meanings of artistic objects aim at "accomplishment and power rather than mere beauty," which for Nicholas Thomas is conducive to a richer understanding of indigenous notions of power and the empowerment of material forms (Pinney and Thomas 2001: 9). For Jacques Dournes, the making of such effigies also fulfills a practical purpose rather than an aesthetic one because sculptures representing planes, birds, persons, and everyday objects are made to serve a function. Like their makers, such wooden representations act as true agents endowed with intention and causality (Gell 1998). In light of this, they can become "personnel de service pour les défunts," or servants of the dead who accompany (*pötui*) them into the next chapter of their life (Dournes 1968: 113).[13]

Whether war-associated sculptures function as servants of, substitutes for, or vessels of power, their local use is often a matter of doing or redoing, which, according to Gell, fits into this system of actions intended to change the world. In furthering Gell's argument, however, it should be noted that the appropriation, manipulation, and display of the formidable objects are all forms of praxis that not only produce meaning but can also become meaningful actions as they are being performed by the artisan, who may find in sculpting a way to heal some of his or her war traumas (e.g., the anxiety caused by the bombing plane). In this regard, the crafting of warfare objects is also a creative psychological process that enables their maker to harness their intrinsic power for positive purposes, thus turning them into signs of life. Sculpted planes in local villages, cemeteries, or rice fields may

---

13. Dournes offered a further hypothesis, inferring on the basis of a few Jorai mythical stories that such effigies could be substitutes for human victims that may have once been sacrificed in reparation for social and moral crimes in the village (Dournes 1968). This hypothesis was supported by Ngo Van Doanh (1991), who conducted research on Jorai and Bahnar graves.

be regarded by both makers and recipients as war trophies in their own right.

This chapter has examined the ways which a traumatic event has affected the ritual practices of Leu village and how this particular episode of intensive aerial bombardment prompted a reinforcement of local survival strategies. Leu villagers' coping abilities include, but are by no means limited to, physical resilience. Despite the violence of the destruction, the villagers' ritual performances show that both continuity and change exist in response to traumatic experience, whereby death-dealing implements enable traditional practices to remain the same, albeit adjustable, in order to respond to new causes of bad death. At the same time, these village practices facilitate the reintegration of the physically injured into the social fabric of the community and the insertion of the dead into collective history and memory. Although new causes of death have created a divide between those villagers who assume that it is too late to care for the unburied dead and those who believe there is always a given or chosen time to care for them, village rituals have succeeded in mixing the old with the new so that the ancestors may continue to bestow the blessing of fertility on the living.

Furthermore, the encounter with the dangerous object can be reenacted through the reproduction and representation of planes and weaponry, and this chapter has argued that this appropriation can become a privileged means for people to reconcile themselves to their violent past. To this end, the meanings conveyed by a tangible object can be subject to new interpretations and positive inversion by survivors as they reconceptualize violent death to create a life-reaffirming experience. The following chapter brings Gell's idea that art is about "doing" a step further since art not only contains a "special kind of technology that captivates and ensnares others in the intentionalities of its producers" (Pinney and Thomas 2001: 1), but also is first and foremost a technology that enchants its own maker.

Chapter 5

AESTHETIC FORMS OF MEMORY

There are different ways to preserve memory, such as archives, libraries, museums, and memorials. In Leu, as in many ethnic-minority villages in Ratanakiri province, the traditional repository of memory used to be the village elders, thus resonating with the words of the Malian writer and anthropologist Amadou Hampâté Bâ: "In Africa a dying old man is a library on fire."

The objective of this chapter is less to add to the vast existing literature on memory established by Ricoeur (2004), Connerton (1989), Halbwachs (1992), and Bloch (1998) (to name only a few) than to look at alternative vessels of memory created through sculpting, painting, carving, and weaving. Particular attention will be paid to the role of the craftsperson as a conscious, dedicated, and skillful individual who does not simply create but creates in a beautiful manner (Sennett 2008).

In reproducing work and seeking inspiration from earlier times, the technique of the craftsperson becomes the means whereby memories of the past, perceptions of the present, and predictions of the future are given form aesthetically. Drawing on Aristotle's definition of memory as the ability of the mind to store and retrieve sensations, thoughts, and knowledge of the past, the following ethnographic examples illustrate how artistic and visual channels of expression can treat the past as, to borrow Jürgen Habermas's expression, an "unfinished project" (Habermas 1996: 38).[1]

This chapter also argues that objects derived from craftsmanship, as well as the act of crafting itself, can open new perspectives on the ways postconflict villages interact with their past. The first two case studies concern Jorai communities where local craftsmanship produces objects that remain deeply imbued with the history of warfare in the region. The two cases that follow examine two postconflict Tampuon villages and elaborate the main theoretical argument that object making and object makers can both become sites for the manufacture of memory. The purpose is to map out and reflect on the wide diversity of object design, making, and ornamentation via which villagers respond to echoes from the past, voices of the present, and whispers of the future.

All four of the cases profiled feature the production of what has been termed "trench art," which can be defined as "any item made by soldiers, prisoners of war and civilians, from war matériel directly, or any other material, as long as it and they are associated temporally and/or spatially with armed conflict or its consequences" (Saunders 2003: 11). Although the memory objects described in this chapter originate neither from parts nor from whole physical remnants of war, they can be considered a meaningful manifestation of trench art. All of them recall Aristotle's wax tablets in the way in which they bear the visual prints of warfare episodes that have marked the lives of the inhabitants of this area.

Leu Village: Sculpting and Carving a Better Object

The Mnemonic Functions of Sculpting

Funerary statuary in Leu village encompasses a wide range of old and relatively new forms of traditional sculptures, which include animal and human

---

1. In Leu village, my informants found it difficult to conceptualize the Euro-American notion of "art" (see Gell 1998). In a sense, each and every object that is produced by what we would consider artistic means (e.g., sculpting, carving, painting, drawing, weaving) has first and foremost a functional and practical purpose. I use the term "artistic" to refer to this set of practices but will try, whenever possible, to avoid using the word "art" on its own because its Euro-American definition has little relevance for my informants.

effigies, as well as war-inspired items. The village wood-carver Siu's sculpting of elephants (either entirely or metonymically through representations of the tusks) is a skill that has been passed down through the generations. Formerly a mode of transportation and a sign of high social status, the elephant remains a symbol of wealth and a particular aesthetic motif in the ornamentation of burial sites (Roux 1929; Lafont 1963; Dournes 1968; Goy and Coué 2006). Inhabitants of Leu told me that since the end of the Khmer Rouge regime and the US bombardment, the presence of elephants has declined. They speculated that, faced with a severe reduction in their natural habitat, the remaining herds must have migrated across the Lao border.

Siu recalled that "the Jorai owned elephants in the past. My grandfather used to have an elephant in his village and traveled on it, but I haven't seen many ever since. . . . We can't find them anymore. . . . We sculpt them for the younger generation to know what elephants look like; otherwise, [children] will never know." From Siu's perspective, sculpting an elephant fulfills two main functions: first, ensuring that the grave is beautiful, and second, teaching children how to identify an animal most of them have never seen. In addition, the wood-carver considered sculpting a way of safeguarding and passing on the skill, commenting that "in some cemeteries people sculpt only the tusks because they don't know how to make an entire elephant anymore!" Siu explained that in Leu, sculpting technique derives either from direct teaching (transmitted from father to son) or from imitating sculptures seen in other Jorai or nearby Tampuon village cemeteries.

By leaving iconographical traces, Siu felt that he was preserving the Jorai tradition of elephant carving, perpetuating a skill and a form of knowledge that might otherwise disappear. Indeed, the act of carving enables the wood-carver to maintain the existence of the elephants among the villagers, bringing them to life at the time of a death in the village. For some village elders, a funerary effigy shaped like an elephant fulfills a fourth function, that of wishing the dead wealth in the afterlife.[2] The village cemetery functions as a place of remembrance both of departed relatives and of a long-gone lifestyle, until such time as nature reclaims the graves and their

---

2. If the objects gathered around the graves are the ones that the dead will bring into the next life, then we can infer that the elephant may be the vehicle that will take the dead into his or her new home.

ornaments. Through this process of erosion, nature gradually washes away the memory of the deceased, as well as the memory of the old traditions.

Plane carving for grave-decoration purposes can be regarded as fulfilling similar mnemonic functions. Some of my informants viewed the presence of a sculpted plane as a way to remember the deceased as a former soldier or "a person who was very quick and efficient in gathering food and weapons." The plane effigy thus represents past experiences of warfare and provides a memorial to the individual while facilitating a wider process of collective remembrance.

After the US bombardment and the United Nations Transitional Authority in Cambodia (UNTAC) intervention to support Cambodia's reconstruction between 1992 and 1993, villagers in Leu were keen on creating three-dimensional and two-dimensional representations of the planes they had seen. The people I worked with told me that they had not seen a plane since the UNTAC period ended fifteen years earlier. Most of the village's youngest inhabitants have never seen a real plane before. This does not necessarily prevent them from carving, drawing, or imagining planes, however. For Wai, who was born in the early 1980s, a sculpted plane "is something the sculptor has imagined. We imagine from what other people—old people—have told us. I don't know why we do that, but as far as I can remember, I have always seen this. The plane is there because it looks like it is where it needs to be. . . . It has landed for the funeral!" Wai's comment underlines the fact that the capacity to reproduce an object does not need to be sanctioned by empirical experience (seeing the object) but can be stimulated by memory tellers or local wooden sculptures, as well as television, newspapers, toys, printed t-shirts, and other sources of visual stimulation.

Beyond their symbolic and aesthetic meanings, the plane effigies featuring in ceremonies to propitiate spirits also convey a particular memory of past perceptions and behavior. According to a village elder, "The planes remind people about their foolishness. . . . Now we laugh at the thought that we were once so scared of them and that we were all running to hide from the flying spirits. . . . [The sculptures] tell our children about our experience of the past." Seen from this perspective, the plane acts as an open window on the villagers' collective history, through which people can contemplate events related to their own experience.

Most village elders and middle-aged individuals I worked with did not feel any ill will toward the Americans. Some felt that they had no or very little power over the course of the conflicts and that as time passed, any resentment became irrelevant. Despite seeing the US bombardment as particularly harrowing, some village elders nonetheless said that they now viewed their past belief in the planes being "flying gods" as a rare comic element amid otherwise traumatic memories of the period.

According to Paul Ricoeur, forgetting and forgiving are two crucial and interdependent components of the ethics of memory (Ricoeur 2004: 493–506). For the villagers living in Leu, though, the presence of a sculpted plane during rituals often acts as a mirror that triggers collective remembering, as well as the contemplation of the self in the past. For the village elders, remembering and laughing at one's past mistake can also lead to forgiveness. In this context, the process of forgiving oneself and others relies more on the act of remembering than on forgetting. For the same village elders, the fear that they felt when they first saw the bombing planes today makes way for an appreciation of the fascination that this same image inspires among the youngest inhabitants of the village. As one of them put it, "When the animal is killed at the foot of the sacrifice pole, the plane at its top shakes and moves to the great delight of the children." Each time a plane features in a village ritual, the flying sculpture comes to life, engendering a range of emotions among its inhabitants.

Sculpting and Carving a Better Plane

Having been taught the secrets of wood-carving by his father, Siu is regarded by his fellow villagers as one of the most skillful craftspersons in the area. Whether he is producing wood sculptures, knives, or house parts, Siu is perceived to have a special connection with his material, which seems naturally to flow through the deft movements of his sculpting knives. My hours of observation during several months of working with Siu led me to conclude that his ability equally to tame wood, bamboo, and water reeds so as to coincide exactly with the shape of his imagined object is stimulated not only by his apparent passion to make but also his passion to make beautifully. In many instances, he refashioned objects started by others, drawing on his aptitude for turning the object into the object they had in mind.

In December 2007, Siu completed a wooden effigy of a helicopter. Because it had three propellers, a Khmer visitor commented that this effigy could not be a true representation of a real aircraft. Unperturbed, Siu replied with undisguised pride, "This plane is awesome, powerful, more so than the ones that flew here before." One of the most interesting issues raised by this comment is Siu's inference that there is more to sculpting than the mere illustrative reproduction of an object. In the eyes of the external beholder, the plane was not and could not possibly be real, given the incongruity in its engineering. For Siu, conversely, the plane was even more real because it illustrated perfectly his idea of what a plane should be.

In considering the sculpting of a plane, one can infer that the material used (wood) is a tactile medium that can shape the very idea of the plane. From this perspective, which emphasizes the relationship between the maker and the object, the actual material that is shaped is less the tangible, palpable, and possibly destructible log than the virtual material in which the idea of the plane itself is made. To borrow Dorinne Kondo's expression, the attentive sculpting of the effigy thus demonstrates how "crafting a beautiful object" can become synonymous with "crafting a better idea of the object" (Kondo 1990: 241).

As I will demonstrate further in the following case studies, crafting the plane allows the individual to reconstruct the idea of a plane (what a plane should be, not what it was in the past or what it is today) and thus to gain control over the object and its inherent powers. By harnessing such powers through craftsmanship, the wood-carver can attribute new meanings to the object. Encoded with renewed ideas and values, the plane can eventually be invested with a guardianship duty to care for the living and the dead or simply remain a symbol of power and beauty. All of this poses the interesting question whether carving and adapting such images might be a means of taming the dangerous object so as to shift the status of the carver from one of victim (Siu's father died during the protracted conflicts) to that of master and controller. The next case study explores this idea further.

Carving an Imaginary Story

Smoking a pipe is a very common habit in Leu, as well as in neighboring villages. Regardless of gender and age, people invariably smoke several times a day. Children sometimes take up pipe smoking before they are four years old. According to Siu, wealthier villages used to use a special kind of smoking pipe called the *aagn gnogn* or *aagn prieuw*. Since the wars, however, the knowledge of how to make these pipes has largely been lost. The pipe form that is still in widespread usage is the *tagn vach*, which is owned by adults (especially women) and children alike and is generally made of bamboo or recycled aluminum salvaged from war debris. Some people in the village are said to be able to make the pipes, but few know how to carve them beautifully. Siu told me that he sometimes carves smoking pipes on request. He explained that there are geometrical motifs that are habitually found in the more common pipes, but that new designs are now integrated in order to enhance the decoration. He pointed out that each design has its own meaning, as well as posing its own set of challenges for the carver. Upon completing the structure of a bamboo *tagn vach* that I commissioned for the Cambridge Museum of Archaeology and Anthropology, Siu started the subtle carving process while simultaneously giving the following commentary (see figure 5).

> The first row of designs depicts *hlăt* [caterpillar]. It illustrates little teeth placed on the top and bottom lines of the bowl of the pipe. *Hlăt* is a small worm-like insect that eats grasses and leaves. . . . It is as green as a bamboo stick that has been freshly cut. . . . This particular motif illustrates the marking we can see on its body.
>
> The second row represents *la hot*, the leaf of a medicinal plant, which is often eaten by the *hlăt*. It is shaped like drops placed horizontally, with the pointed part facing left and the rounder tip oriented toward the right. *La hot* is a substitute tobacco that is commonly cultivated by villagers who like to smoke. On the pipe a row of *la hot* leaves is carved between two parallel lines of *hlăt*, meaning that the plant is being eaten by the insect from each side. Pipe carvings can include two rows of *hlăt*, at the top and at the bottom of the pipe, since sometimes the insect eats every single leaf of the plant. The space in the middle of the pipe bowl is generally reserved for an image of a tobacco leaf.
>
> The next row illustrates *la khda*, another type of leaf, which grows on the *waa* plant. *La khda* is a very acidic leaf and acts as an efficient pest repellent. Villagers use a pestle and mortar to crush the leaves and add water to the mixture, which they then pour onto *la hot* plants to protect them from parasites like the *let*. *La khda* is represented by a parallelogram placed inside a rectangle of checked motifs reminiscent of a spiderweb.
>
> The following illustration shows the *pŏke* (the gecko). The *pŏke* eats the *hlăt* and makes a very distinctive sound at night. . . . The last carving depicts the *sepol* [the plane], which is the one that ultimately kills the gecko.

152   Chapter 5

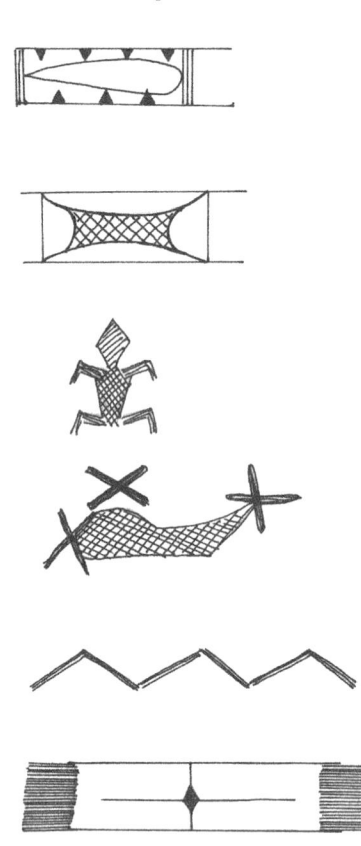

Figure 5. Author's reproduction of carved motifs on Siu's bamboo pipe representing: a caterpillar eating a tobacco leaf; acidic leaves planted by the villagers to prevent pests from eating the tobacco leaves; a gecko preying on the caterpillar; and a bombing plane targeting them all.

The designs that Siu carved also depict the body of the *hlăt* as long zigzag lines running along the stem of the pipe. Alongside, one finds the carving of a Jorai traditional comb with which to brush the hair and remove lice from the head (the fine teeth of the comb enable the person to trap the lice between them). The comb is represented as a rectangle with a cross in the middle; on each side of it is a succession of thin parallel lines (the teeth of the comb). Siu pointed out that "combing hair and smoking are two main Jorai social activities; people always carry their comb and pipe together; they are inseparable individual belongings [*dra gónam*]."

For Siu, his carving told the following story: "The plane eats the gecko, who has eaten the *hlăt*, who in turn has eaten the *la hot* leaves despite the *la khda* repellent.... In conclusion the plane is the most powerful because it kills everyone with a bomb!" The subtle carvings of the *tagn vach* bamboo pipe depict both traditional items and more modern ones, and the most interesting effects are derived from the association of the objects and the meanings produced. The main thrust of the story is that of an imaginary food chain in which the smaller elements are successively absorbed by the larger: the smoking leaf that is protected by other leaves is eaten by the caterpillar, while the gecko eats the caterpillar but in turn is "eaten" by the formidable plane. This tale of successive absorption can be summarized as follows:

Plane (*sepol*) > **gecko** (*pŏķe*) > **herbicide** (*la ķhda*) > **caterpillar** (*hlăt*) > **tobacco leaf** (*la hot*).

The carving of the smoking pipe appears here as an alternative system of inscription that enables the craftsperson to manipulate and mix together various elements of the past and present to create a story line. The carved motifs are based on a linear narrative composed of a beginning, a middle, and an end, which turns the pipe into a visual and discursive storytelling object. This story eventually concludes with a Jorai illustration of the Darwinian law of survival that lets the strongest live and the weakest die.

The Funerary Monument: A Distinctive Site of Memory

Peuho is a Jorai village located southeast of Leu in the neighboring district of O You Dav, only a few miles from the Vietnamese border. People in Peuho live a life of subsistence activities, notably farming and collecting remnants of war for sale across the border. In the village cemetery, one cannot fail to notice a *pósat atâo*, a tall funerary monument, with a roof shaped like a saddle, which, although almost completely covered by the vegetation, still reveals colorful excerpts from everyday life underneath a large flying plane. The construction of a *pósat atâo* marks the second burial of the dead, when, thanks to the care of his or her surviving kin, the deceased is finally ready and well equipped to commence the journey into the next life.[3]

---

3. Immediately after the death and before the first burial, the inhabitants of Peuho keep watch over the deceased for a few days and make a series of sacrifices involving buffaloes, pigs, and chickens.

Figure 6. Beuragn reproducing a *pósat atâo* on paper. Photo by author.

Keulagn Beuragn is the old painter who decorated the *pósat atâo* in Peuho after the death of a young boy a few years ago. He explained that nobody had ever taught him how to paint, because "one needs to see and naturally know how to do it." Beuragn regarded his aptitude for painting as more than a skill that could be passed on through the generations (like sculpting in Leu); it was a gift given by the *yang* (spirits). In his view, the craftsman who is dedicated to his work is an initiate who has been chosen by the spirits to fulfill specific duties. As a result, trying to teach someone how to paint would be *kanm* (taboo). In lieu of payment, the funerary painter receives a gift in exchange for his artistic work. Just as he sees his skill as a gift donated by the *yang*, his painting for other villagers is in turn considered a gift to them. These gifts from the villagers include live animals or cooking utensils (e.g., a saucepan). For the painting of the child's *pósat atâo*, Beuragn said that he had been rewarded with a chicken and cooked food.

The *pósat atâo* is an edifice four meters high with four sides, the largest sides being the ones on the front and on the back (Maître 1912). It takes two to three days to fully decorate it. During this time, the act of painting is guided by a series of taboos that isolate the painter in a variety of ways. Beuragn explained that in the course of this decorating period, the painter is not allowed to return to the village because he is considered polluted by his proximity to death. He is thus compelled to live temporarily outside the village boundaries in a small hut where he sleeps and eats until the end of his work. This physical exclusion seems to reflect the fact that the painter is socially considered dead. Only at the completion of what Beuragn described as "risky" work can he reintegrate into the social collectivity of the village (Bloch and Parry 1982).

A further taboo is associated with naming the person who did the painting: "If some villagers returned from a day's work in the field, saw the decoration, and asked who created it, it is *kanm* [taboo] to say the name of the person who painted it." For Beuragn, declaring his identity before the completion of the work could place him in a hazardous situation whereby he could be directly affected by the death (i.e., by becoming ill). In other words, preserving the anonymity of the painter is a way to guarantee his safety so that the evil *yang* find it difficult to identify him and harm him.

An additional proscription relates to the maturity of the painter, who needs to be at least sixty years of age. According to Beuragn, it is traditionally taboo for anyone under sixty to try to decorate a *pósat atâo*, especially children, since they are considered more vulnerable to the malevolent spirits.

Partly because of the costs and labor entailed, most people in Peuho believe that it is not necessary to build a *pósat atâo* for a child. Villagers tend to ornament the grave of a child only at the point when the deceased would have reached the age of fifteen and thus would have attained adulthood. A villager commented, "In the past, people used to build these funerary monuments all the time.... They were richly decorated with images of women winnowing, people using mortar and pestle.... But today fewer and fewer people can afford them." But in the preceding case, where the bereaved family was relatively affluent and very fond of their child, the head of the household decided to build a *pósat atâo* on top of his son's grave and asked Beuragn to decorate it. The latter explained that in this case a child's grave

156   Chapter 5

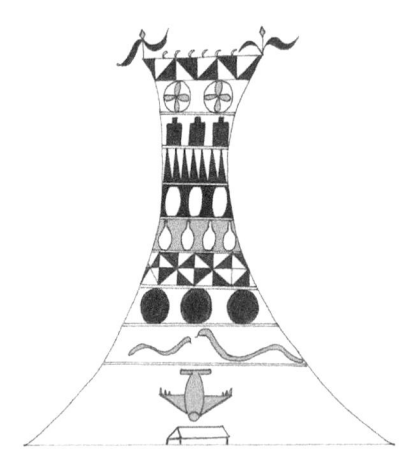

Figure 7. Author's reproduction of Beuragn's illustration of a *pósat atâo*, Plói Peuho, O You Dav district, Ratanakiri.

should look identical to an adult's. In the words of the painter, the most important consideration is that "it needs to be as beautiful as a temple" so that the dead will like his new home.

Beuragn's typical *pósat atâo* decoration combines motifs of flowers, items of everyday life, warfare objects, and celestial bodies. The painter agreed to produce a sample of his decorative skills for the anthropologist; the fine result is shown in figure 7. According to Beuragn, it is not *kanm* (taboo) to make a reproduction of a *pósat atâo* on paper; his only concern was that his drawings might not do justice to the real painting of the edifice because the format is considerably smaller (two A3 size sheets of paper taped together).

The painter starts by decorating the top of the *pósat atâo* and then works his way down. Beuragn commented that he always imagined the motifs that he wanted to create first (his favorite motif being the stars) and drew them using a succession of horizontal rows. There is no order that specifies which motif should come first, and the *pósat atâo* painter is quite free to decorate it in accordance with his own designs and choice of colors (Beuragn used a mixture of black, blue, and red dyes extracted from crushed stones and flowers). The drawing took a day to produce and shows the following:

On the top corners of the edifice are flowers "with heavenly hands."
Rows 1 and 2: flowers (or row 2 can also feature elephant trunks).
Row 3: hand grenades.

Row 4: orchids growing on trees.
Row 5: lighter sheaths (for a lighter composed of two stones to rub against one another).
Row 6: water gourds.
Row 7: two fighting snakes, with one about to eat the other.
At the bottom: a bombing plane over a house.

This example of a *pósat atâo* decoration shows an interesting mixture of flowers and objects. For the painter, the act of painting and knowing which images should come first, and in which color they should be depicted, is a spontaneous process. An important factor, though, is the relative symmetry with which the objects are placed. In this example, the shapes in the row of hand grenades are reminiscent of the row of water gourds; similarly, the two flowers "with heavenly hands" at the top visually echo the fighting snakes. Flowers are recurrent and particularly praised *pósat atâo* funerary motifs, while the human-made objects depicted include not only water gourds and lighter sheaths but also hand grenades. An intriguing feature is the last row depicting two snakes fighting each other, which in the words of the artist shows the largest "about to eat the other." For the painter, the snakes act as a beautiful allegory of the war, in which "one has to become the winner." In a sense, this last row announces the warfare theme, which, as he commented, often fills in the entire bottom space.

The last drawing, on the large panel at the base of the monument, thus features a warfare scene, which depicts a bombing plane about to destroy a house. Beuragn did not clearly remember when he started to draw war-associated objects, but he acknowledged that since the protracted conflicts in the region, grave decorators have progressively incorporated images of war that they remember. He clarified, however, that "if the cause of death is natural, then the *pósat atâo* will not be decorated with much warfare imagery." Conversely, if someone has died from the war or as a result of some other form of violence, the edifice will feature a lot of planes, knives, grenades, and assault rifles because "it is for other people to know the cause of death."

In the case of the boy's grave described earlier, Beuragn recalled that because the boy died from a long illness in the period after the UNTAC military presence in northeastern Cambodia, the edifice was decorated with a few weapons mixed together with images of everyday life. The painter asserted that the objects that were depicted were "not for the dead to take along into the afterlife" (as proffered objects placed on the grave would be) but only visual enhancements to turn the *pósat atâo* into a beautiful edifice. For Beuragn, war-inspired themes like hand grenades or flying bombing planes have now become established aesthetic motifs.

While he was drawing and coloring the plane in the bottom part of the virtual *pósat atâo*, Beuragn recalled that bombings in the area started from 6:00 a.m. to 7.00 a.m. and lasted until 4.00 p.m. Each plane that flew over the village used to drop four bombs. Another village elder, who was observing the drawing, added that since the bombing event, people in Peuho and other Jorai villages along the border have been singing songs that narrate the history of the bombardment. Most of these songs are revived in the first few months of the year, when the work in the *hwa* (fruit and vegetable orchard) is very limited and when various celebrations and rituals to the *yang* (spirits) take place.

The large panel at the base of the *pósat atâo* is a distinctive space that enables the family to tell the past story of the dead person or the imaginary story of his future life. When Beuragn was working in the village cemetery, he often left this particular space provisionally empty so that the bereaved family could decide which motifs they wanted, although he said that he was often free to illustrate the entire *pósat atâo* in accordance with his own inspiration. He commented, however, that these days not very many people wanted to have many planes and bombs since they preferred images that conveyed a sense of natural peace, especially if the deceased person had suffered for a long time before passing away. Such serene representations often involve trees and flowers, flying birds, or the long-established motif of two persons drinking at the rice-wine jar.

According to Beuragn, some people believe that commissioning an impression of beauty and peace is a way to conjure a future existence that may be free of violence. Painting the impression of tranquility on the wooden structure of the *pósat atâo* is therefore comparable to writing the future of the dead soul. In this case, the painter acts as a scribe who not only records the memory of the past but also tells the memory of the future. Functioning as a large-scale vista, the *pósat atâo* offers visions of the past, the present, and the future simultaneously.

Mek: Sculpting Dream-Inspired Objects and Carving Dreams

Dreaming the Sculptures

The village of Mek is located forty-five minutes away from Leu on a dirt road that links the provincial capital of Banlung to the northeastern tip of the province via the town of Bokeo. Mek is a Tampuon ethnic-minority village where men and women have mastered the technique of wood sculpture and water-gourd carving, respectively. In March 2008, the village was affected by a flu epidemic that caused an unusually large number of families to fall ill. Mek was consequently closed off for five days by a barricade placed across the entrance to prevent people from entering and leaving the village precincts. I was told that during this self-imposed quarantine, the villagers had been performing rituals to appease the spirits. One of them commented, "There are a lot of spirits in the Tampuon pantheon, so we perform rituals for every occasion, like village settlements, rice cultivations. . . . For the flu outbreak, people have sacrificed animals and offered white rice and black rice, white meat and black meat."

In such instances where the life of a village is threatened by unusual illnesses, the villagers need to find an effective way to restore physical and spiritual equilibrium. Making offerings in the form of foods of two contrasting colors placed in the spirit house may allow them to readjust the balance of powers that conditions their day-to-day life. To ensure further protection for the village, wood sculptors placed a sophisticated grouping of warfare effigies on top of the spirit house at the village entrance. A few weeks later, when I returned to visit Mek, a villager said, "The rituals have been successful in eradicating the flu."

One of my informants commented that the wooden sculptures at the village entrance were expressly intended to frighten malevolent spirits and prevent them from entering. All the sculptures—a plane, a helicopter, a man holding a crossbow, an AK-47 assault rifle, and a spear—invoked a war theme. Piled on top of one another on the roof of the spirit house, they appeared to be arranged so as to channel the combined power derived from their entanglement. The villager further commented that the sculptures were made by "mature" persons only because "young people do not know how to."

In contrast to Leu, where sculpting skills can be taught by one generation to the next, sculpting in Mek (like painting in Plói Peuho) appears to be limited exclusively to a few experienced people who have acquired the ability naturally. As a result, only three or four mature male individuals were considered capable of producing such fine craftwork. The villager added that the form of the effigies was decided when one of the sculptors had a dream. He reported that at the time of the flu outbreak, one of the mature craftsmen had a violent dream featuring "lots of flying helicopters and gunshots." This dream was then interpreted as a message sent by the tutelary spirits, indicating the kind of sculptures that needed to be made. Consequently, the general theme of warfare was manifested in three-dimensional form to fulfill three major functions: (1) reproduce the dream itself, (2) ward off evil spirits with the power embodied in the effigies, and (3) discourage people who might want to enter the village during the period of quarantine. A younger villager explained that the reproduction of formidable objects was the product of both the memory of the dream and the memory of the past conflicts that the mature craftsman had witnessed.

In this case, not only does the maturity of the sculptor facilitate his ability to turn wood into compelling objects, but his experience of the wars may also be perceived by fellow villagers as a process that has crafted the individual himself. For my informant, the making of new (helicopter and assault rifle) and traditional weapons (spear and crossbow) stemmed from a desire to render in beautiful form intimidating, effective, and resonant objects that are grounded in the older villagers' knowledge of warfare.

Within this sphere of influences, sculpting underscores a strong connection with the world of the spirits. In a sense, it may be perceived as a gift to translate the messages of the spirits into symbolically meaningful and tangible representations. The wood sculptors of Mek are thus key mediators who actively contribute to the defense of the entire village. It is by imbuing the sculptures with messages (and thereby power) sent from the spirit world to protect the living that the craftsmen can preserve their singular social space and likely their moral authority. Dreams initiated by the spirits and channeled via individuals can inspire sculptors to achieve a certain outcome; the following example will show how the female segment of the population can conversely craft their own dreams while carving water gourds.

Carving Transmitted and Imagined Memories

In the dusty village of Mek, the beginning of the dry season announces the time when women carve water gourds (see figure 8). Originating from the same Cucurbitaceae family as melons, cucumbers, pumpkins, and squash, the gourds are harvested, emptied of their pulp and seeds, and dried for a month before being carved. According to local craftswomen, the crafting process takes an entire day. Water gourds are common objects used by all members of the household for collecting, storing, and transporting water for a day's work in the fields. They can also be produced and carved for sale, moreover, as more and more tourists come to observe and buy the handicrafts of the young women who are known to be particularly clever with their hands.

Sculpting wood concerns male villagers only, but water-gourd carving is the exclusive domain of females. In contrast to wood sculpting, carving is not limited to a few mature women in the village. As soon as a girl knows how to handle a knife, she will often try her hand at carving bamboo or smaller gourds. As in Leu, where a father teaches his son how to sculpt wood, gourd carving in Mek is a skill that is passed on from mother to daughter through the generations. Today women decorate other personal objects in a similar manner; smoking pipes also offer a canvas, albeit much smaller, on which they can demonstrate their skills.

Water gourds are most commonly adorned with traditional motifs illustrating scenes of daily life (people working or performing rituals), indigenous animals (elephants and tigers), and villagers' livestock (e.g., pigs, chickens), as well as modern and technological objects (e.g., radios, trucks, helicopters, planes). I was told that the modern objects are mostly patterns and images that were taught to the gourd carvers or inspired by things they had seen. A male villager commented, however, that none of the young women had ever seen a plane, nor had any of them been to the provincial town of Banlung, where planes sometimes land. Yet all knew how to reproduce images taught to them by their mothers and grandmothers or copied from their peers.

As the male villager put it, "It is like learning how to write—you only need to imitate." This comment was substantiated by the fact that one of the young women seemed puzzled when she was asked where the warfare motifs originated. It was as if, having inherited them from their original designers (their elders), it was not for them to explain their origin any more. Others

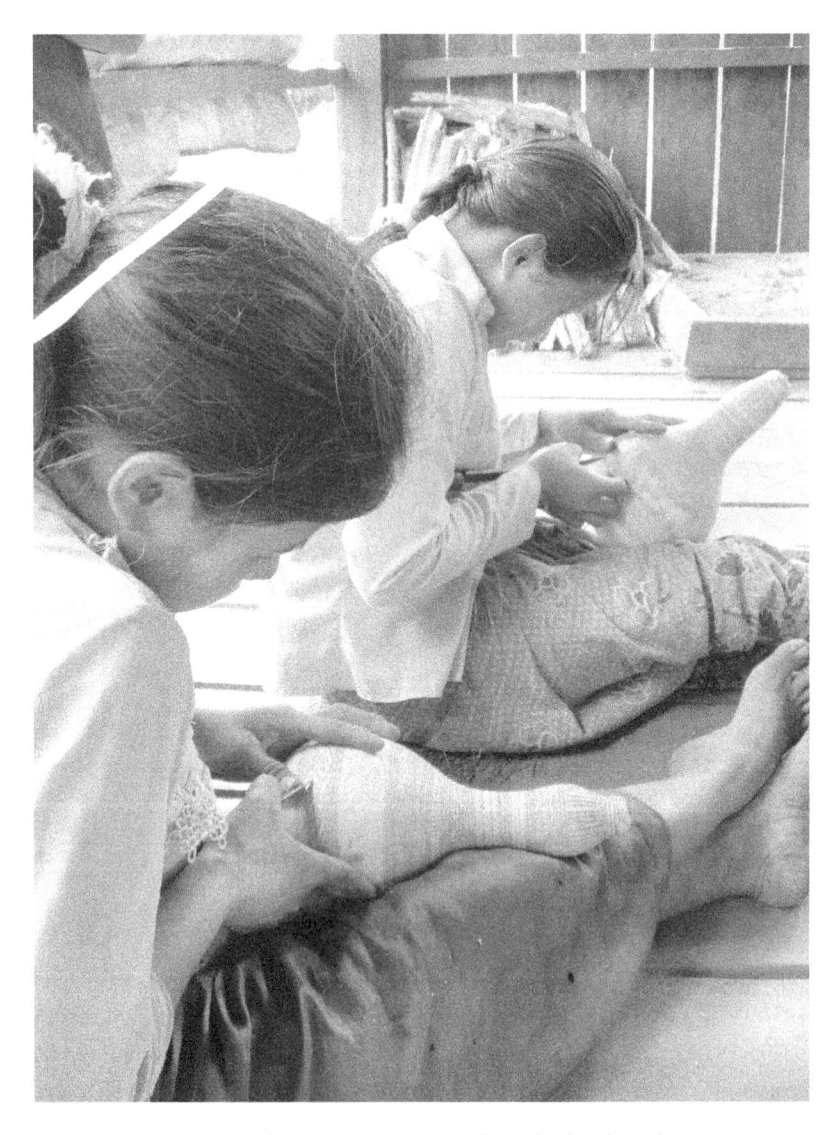

Figure 8. Girls carving water gourds, Plói Mek. Photo by author.

recalled having seen similar illustrations on their mothers' craftwork and regarded them as long-established motifs.

As with the sculpting of a plane effigy in Leu, the ability to produce is independent of empirical experience or seeing the object firsthand. In the context of water-gourd carving, some craftswomen may be engaging in a vicarious form of experience because others in the past have already seen the depicted objects. In this sense, the process is comparable to seeing through the eyes that have already seen, thus making tangible the link that connects the generations.

The artistic translation of war-associated subjects constitutes both a historical and an aesthetic theme in the way they are incorporated, rendered visible, and preserved. Acting like a manuscript, hand-carved water gourds convey the impressions of multiple witnesses connected through consecutive time threads. In a sense, it is not far removed from the medieval techniques of printing, which were essentially based on the reproduction of texts previously copied and recopied by earlier generations of scribes. In this regard, the individual female water-gourd carver constitutes only a single link in a long-established and extended chain of thoughts and image transmissions.

The richness and variety of some of the handmade carvings can turn the water gourds into evocative objects, offering a kaleidoscope of images. Thus carved, the gourd acts as a double recipient: one that holds water in its interior space while collecting visions of the past, the present, and possibly the future on its outside shell. Engaged in a singular form of scriptural process, the women of Mek use the external shell of the gourds to capture images, thus perpetuating a tradition of memory recording and telling. Most notable in this context is how young craftswomen complement the predominantly male role of storytelling. Through the recording act of carving stories and histories, the young ladies of Mek, like their mothers before them, are silent but visually eloquent storytellers.

The decoration of the gourds in Mek brings to mind the extensive use of fabric weaving by the Hmong ethnic-minority group living in Southeast Asia as a means of telling the stories of their lives and experiences "Traditionally," Susanne Bessac wrote, "the Hmong had no written language, using oral testimony and material culture to perpetuate their beliefs, culture and history. A complex mix of appliqué, cross-stitching, batik and embroidery, the *pa ndau*, or 'flower-clot' played a large role in this cultural transmission" (quoted in Saunders 2003: 219). After the Vietnam War, Hmong

164   Chapter 5

women began depicting their wartime experiences and their daily life in refugee camps in Thailand, using their crafts.

Terry Satsuki Milhaupt, a textile historian, researched the uses and meanings of the kimono all the way back to the seventeenth century, from clothing made for firefighters and courtesans to their Western fashionable adaptation. Japanese kimonos made during World War II incorporated warplanes, tanks, soldiers, AK-47 machine guns, bombs, and swastikas into the weaving pattern and even into childrens' outfits. According to the author, this traditional garment served as a "tableau" whereby specific events and effects of modernity could be reproduced (Milhaupt 2014).

In Mek, carving is likewise a technique of reproduction that fulfills an important role in helping preserve the visions of the past and the present. As in sculpting planes in Leu or painting weapons in Peuho, modern objects (e.g., planes, radios, trucks) are now fully part of the village water-gourd iconography. In this case, the carved object can be conceptually framed as Stendhal's "mirror that you carry along a path" (Stendhal 1854: 74). However, like every mirror, the water gourd may distort as much as it may offer a faithful reflection. Some illustrations of planes and helicopters seem to bear traces of the successive process of copying (and forgetting), with some images depicting hybrid vehicles that resemble a cross between a truck and a plane. Such a plane may transport people on its roof and be piloted by a driver poised behind a steering wheel while drawing on a cigarette.

One can infer that in such cases, the original depiction has already been greatly influenced by what may have been seen, heard, and eventually imagined as the image has been passed from one craftswoman to another. Like Siu, the wood-carver from Leu, the craftswoman may also have intentionally let her imagination and her experience (seeing crowded trucks along the main road) shape her idea of a plane or simply have created a "better" plane. Furthermore, the fact that most of these women, in contrast to their elders, have not experienced the war may have already generated differences in the meanings assigned to the image appearing on the surface of the water gourd. Ultimately, such illustrations remain the direct product of their maker's creativity, vision, and aesthetic sense. In other words, it is not the mere reproduction of the object that is most relevant, but how the object is remembered, translated, forgotten, and reimagined or simply wanted.

Representations are essential to the process of memory, whether it is the personal work of an individual or the product of collective remembering. In this sense, passing on the experience of the war appears less relevant than passing on a particular narration of the war. In Plói Mek, as well as other villages, members of the postconflict generation use their own understanding, imagination, and means of representation to tell their version of the conflicts. As Aletta Biersack persuasively argued, "In the interpretive mode, re-narration requires coming to terms with the events *as narrated*; and understanding and explanation become alike windows on historical consciousness" (Biersack 1991: 20). But as the inheritance of the past is handed on from generation to generation, the understanding of the event itself evolves through time as a dynamic entity.

The preceding has examined the use of war-related iconography in the decoration of objects that are now made as much for sale to outsiders as for everyday use. The following section examines an example of the role of the tourism market in greater detail. It will serve to show how the manufacture of local memory can also become an income-generating activity as memory makers provide for memory consumers in search of war memorabilia, as well as for themselves.

Laom Village: Weaving and Manufacturing Memories

The Tampuon village of Laom is located on the outskirts of the provincial town of Banlung in the district of Yeak Laom, on the northern road leading to Andong Meas and Bokeo districts. Large portions of the communal land have already been sold to Khmer land prospectors who often turn the fields into plantations, a trend that is increasingly widespread in Ratanakiri and often brings with it disputes between ethnic minorities and Khmer investors.

Laom is substantially exposed to the nearby hustle and bustle of Banlung, and there are signs that the attachment to customary practices still highly visible in other villages is weakening. One example is the abandonment of the practice of grave ornamentation, which Laom's inhabitants say is too costly and time consuming to maintain. A few women in the village have kept up the tradition of fabric weaving, however. This was previously a crucial means of commodity transactions between households and villages (e.g., a large woven piece of fabric was exchangeable for a bag of rice), but it is now primarily oriented toward the external market that caters for Khmer and especially foreign tourists.[4]

One of the most skillful fabric weavers in Laom, Sing, like other women living on the outskirts of Banlung, has seen the changing economic landscape bring with it new opportunities to further the production of village handcrafts. A mature craftswoman, Sing teaches her seven daughters how to weave old traditional patterns together with images of high-technology weapons. She told me that her mother and grandmother used to weave, and now it was her turn to transmit these skills to her own daughters. As in Plói Mek, where water-gourd carving is an exclusively female domain, fabric weaving in Plói Laom is passed on from mothers to daughters.

Integrating New Weaving Patterns

Sing's personal craftwork represents some of the richest and most colorful fabric designs produced in the village and the surrounding area (see figure 9). As she proudly pointed out, her next-door neighbor, who is also a weaver, often ended up buying the fabric that Sing made. In Sing's view, "She doesn't know how to make beautiful ones!" According to Sing, her designs are also being sought out and copied in other villages.

Sing explained that she generally uses blue, red, and white threads because they constitute the village's traditional fabric colors, but that she sometimes weaves with other tones, such as pink, green, and black, to diversify her products or simply provide for a special order. The fabrics are generally of two sizes; the larger ones, which are for use as skirts, vary in price between 10 and 25 USD. The skirts are dominated by broad horizontal bands of color interspersed with narrower ones in contrasting shades. Their most striking feature, however, is a third type of band that Sing incorporates. These are galleries of icon-like motifs that juxtapose everyday household objects to darker themes of war.

---

4. Like the *arpilleras* from Peru and Chile (hand embroidered and colorful textile pictures that often contained hidden messages sent out during times of political hardships) or the "story cloth" manufactured by the Hmong in Southeast Asia, textile weaving featuring war themes is a key source of income generation, especially for refugees (Saunders 2003: 218–19).

Figure 9. Sing wearing some of her creations, posing with her husband and son.
Photo by author.

Sing explained that she makes her own fabric designs by using traditional motifs (taught by her mother), as well as new ones inspired by things she has seen (e.g., planes). She added that she also weaves images of war-related objects she has never seen but has only heard of from her husband and fellow villagers. For instance, she explained that the hand grenade, one of her favorite motifs, is one of many images that her husband once described to her and drew on paper so that she could reproduce them on her loom. Although this was an object she had never set eyes on, she said that she had heard a lot about it and even knew details of how the grenade functions.

Sing recalled that she had gotten used to seeing planes, guns, and assault rifles in the past. If she was in doubt about their exact shapes, she usually asked her husband for advice. Her husband claimed that these objects were deeply etched in his memory because explosive items had been left lying on the ground during the US bombardment of the region. Today these warfare motifs form an intrinsic part of Sing's weaving style, alongside long-established Tampuon iconography like landscapes (hills and mountains), insects and animals (spiders, lizards, dogs), everyday objects (ladders), and ritual objects (urns, Tampuon *pósat atâo*).

By means of remembrance, visual representation, and association of ideas, Sing manages to weave large pieces of fabric into illustrated patterns, giving shape, color, and texture to her and her husband's memories. Another factor in her choice of imagery, however, is external demand, not least because Sing now supplies Khmer retailers in Banlung who market war-related souvenirs to foreign tourists. Sing claimed that one of these vendors asked her to teach weavers from four or five other villages how to weave warfare images in order to increase overall local production. "[War designs] are very popular with tourists!" she noted before asking me if I wanted to place an order and whether I could draw the warfare images I would like her to weave.

Looking at a series of fabrics completed by Sing, one cannot fail to notice that some warfare motifs are quite sketchy. She brushed this off lightheartedly: "It's quite new to me, so I am still learning!" Sing went on to explain, however, that some of the less well-defined war icons were the product of her daughters' tentative efforts to help her meet the increased demand and simultaneously add new images to their own weaving portfolios. Interestingly, even a single piece of Sing's fabric reveals the various pairs of hands at work, with a spectrum of levels of mastery of the warfare images.

Although Sing is quite keen on weaving motifs that resemble the shape of the original object, she also appears to enjoy working and reworking them as if they are malleable substances. On the one hand, objects such as planes and bombs are evoked using a minimum of lines, as though they are reduced to their elemental form. On the other, objects like the traditional Tampuon graves (*pósat atâo*) are depicted at a more sophisticated level of detail. Sing commented that her motifs are spontaneously woven one after another, independent of any desire to produce a particular story line (with a beginning, a middle, and an end). Extracting images sourced from different times and domains and placing them side by side enables her to tell any tale. Her main objective is to turn the fabric into a fine visual and discursive object that can lend itself to an infinite number of interpretations.

Memory Makers and Memory Consumers

In reference to the Jorai tradition of fabric weaving, Jacques Dournes wrote that woven fabric was comparable to a text. The work of reproduction involved in weaving underlines its textual and recording functions. Well aware of foreigners' fascination with warfare imagery, Sing appears to have specialized in the production of conflict-associated motifs, although she claimed that she started to weave weapons long before today's influx of tourists. According to Jean Michaud, tourism, "the new gold rush in the massif," can be either a curse or a blessing for ethnic minorities (Michaud 2006: 18). For Sing, the current market for war memorabilia (and especially for things related to the regional conflict of the 1970s) seems to have further stimulated her exploration of the domain of warfare iconography, which she likes to mix with traditional motifs, patterns, and colors.

What is worth noting here is that Sing is not just transmitting the memory of the past, as it might have been transmitted from mother to daughter, but is willing to tell stories and histories that are outside her own experience. In other words, by complying with the external demand for a particular set of illustrations, the craftswoman becomes a tool, albeit an essential one, in the fabrication of memory—or stories—which can be perceived as driven by the tourists' quest for war memorabilia. Within this fabrication process,

170   Chapter 5

the memory makers (the craftswomen) may indeed fulfill the needs of memory consumers (the tourists). This idea can be summarized as follows:

> Local memory object > foreign souvenir object.

However, as Wolf Kansteiner pointed out, in the history of collective memory, memory makers can sometimes become their own consumers, whether they are the craftspersons (who weave or carve) or the buyers (in search of a specific story) (Kansteiner 2002: 193–97). Illustrative of Paul Connerton's distinction between types of memory, Sing gave the impression that the informed knowledge she has of the hand grenade (cognitive memory) is part of her personal experience (personal memory).

> There is, first, a class of *personal* memory claims. These refer to those acts of remembering that take as their object one's life history. We speak of them as personal memories because they are located in and refer to a personal past. . . . A second group of memory claims—cognitive memory claims—covers uses of "remember" where we may be said to remember the meaning of words, or lines of verses. . . . What this type of remembering requires, is not that the object of memory be something that is past, but that the person who remembers that thing must have met, experienced or learned of it in the past. (Connerton 1989: 22)

Through the knowledge gained from the repetitive act of aesthetic representation (copying), cognitive memory and personal memory have eventually collapsed into each other, thus giving the craftswoman a firsthand, albeit virtual, experience of the object.

It is clear that in asking me to draw images of weapons, Sing was anticipating adding additional warfare icons to her portfolio. She may also have felt, however, that she could incorporate someone else's memories through the repetitive and learning process of weaving, which would in turn allow her to know—and to some extent experience—the object. This recalls Mary Carruthers's examination of the role of memory in knowledge transmission and preservation in medieval scholarship and her notion of "making one's own" that underlines the fact that something can be made "familiar" only by "making it a part of one's experience." With reference to medieval scholars who read and memorized texts and illuminations, Carruthers drew attention to the fact that "'efficere tibi illas familiares,' Augustine's admonition to

Francesco, does not mean 'familiar' in the modern sense. *Familiaris* is rather a synonym of *domesticus*, that is, to make something familiar by making it a part of your own experience" (Carruthers 1990: 204–5). One could thus surmise that the act of weaving provides a continuum that enables makers to digest transmitted knowledge in order to become consumers, and vice versa. As a result of the market dynamics of supply and demand, memory makers and memory consumers thus become interchangeable.

Searching for Authenticity

The tourist industry in Ratanakiri has steadily been increasing since 2005 and is likely to develop further with the expansion of the infrastructure linking Cambodia, the Lao PDR, and Vietnam. Although commercial flights between the capital city of Phnom Penh and the town of Banlung have been discontinued for more than ten years, road transportation systems are benefiting from aid-funded development projects, and more and more vehicles travel daily between the two towns; the journey takes only nine to twelve hours during the dry season. Travel agencies advertise the two northeastern provinces of Ratanakiri and Mondulkiri as a destination for ecotourism, marketing their national parks and ethnic-minority villages as singular environmental and cultural attractions that remain relatively unscathed by mass tourism, which, for instance, targets world heritage site like Angkor Wat in the northwestern province of Siem Reap.

Numerous young, ambitious, and self-employed Khmer tourist guides are now based in northeastern Cambodia. The touristic itineraries they devise include the "discovery" of local handicrafts, as well as ethnic-minority cemeteries beautifully decorated with war-inspired ornaments. Those people I met who showed a particular interest in going with Khmer guides to visit these places and acquiring war memorabilia included retired US soldiers who had previously worked in the region during the Vietnam War (often training Jorai special forces), UXO and mine-action experts, former military personnel deployed in the area at the time of UNTAC (from 1992 to 1993), and young backpackers in search of unusual souvenirs to take back home.

For each of these categories of memory consumers, the objects in question mediate a different relationship between the individual and the illustrated episodes of the war (Saunders 2003). In all cases, however, it is the memories, images, and story lines conveyed, rather than the object or receptacle itself (be it a water gourd or a piece of fabric), that are the main source of attraction and hence the real object of commodification. In keeping with Appadurai's "social life" (Appadurai 1986: 13) or Kopytoff's "biography of things" (Kopytoff 1986: 66) the illustrated memories of past and present craftswomen show that intangible things can also generate their own biography as they become someone else's possession.

The Soviet occupation of Afghanistan from 1979 to 1989 prompted a similar incorporation of war-inspired motifs into the designs of the carpets woven by Afghan women. According to Jack Lee, "The images of war often . . . evolved from traditional natural forms: helicopters from chickens, hand grenades from the floral *boteh* or Paisley motif," and these conflict-themed rugs became known as *qalin-e jangi* (fight-carpets) and *qalin-e jihad* (war carpets) (Lee, quoted in Saunders 2003: 202). As their popularity increased, the rugs circulated back to the USSR through trade and personal purchases by Russian officers, and some eventually found their way to European markets (Saunders 2003).[5]

The increasing international demand for Afghan war rugs has given birth to a variety of *aksi* (prayer mats, rugs, and carpets), the value of which is linked to their site of manufacture. From this perspective, conflict rugs manufactured by Afghan women in Afghanistan are categorized as being more authentic than those made by Afghan refugees in Iran, for instance. For Lee, "Afghan War rugs . . . provide a potent insight, both beautiful and terrifying, into one of the 20th century's great cultural and historical catastrophes" (Lee, quoted in Saunders 2003: 206).

Amid this growing market for memory (or souvenir) consumption, the external buyer creates a specific demand for local war narratives, which eventually turn objects into overloaded vessels of war iconography. Decorated items that may once have carried a fine and understated mélange of traditional patterns and warfare adornments can become oversized illustrations of war-associated themes. This resonates with Alfred Gell's concept of the "spec-

---

5. Thus the object eventually returns to its place of origin, albeit in another form and texture. "The Soviet war matériel such as AK-47 assault rifles, Hind M-24 helicopters, HIP-8 troop carrying helicopters, BMD-2 armoured personnel carriers and a miscellany of rockets, grenades, handguns and aeroplanes" (Saunders 2003: 202) finds its way back as illustrated motifs on a locally woven carpet.

tator as agent" who is essentially a consumer: his or her "demand for art is the factor ultimately responsible for its existence, just as the existence of any commodity on the market is an index of consumer demand for it" (Gell 1998: 34).

A UXO and mine-action expert told me that Afghan war rugs were once strikingly beautiful because of the subtlety with which images of Russian tanks, planes, and bombs were integrated alongside dominant traditional motifs. But as these rugs became the object of growing demand, fueled by foreign workers, the nuanced depiction of a nation engulfed in a long-drawn-out conflict became coarsened—and even caricatured—as the tools of high-technology warfare took center stage. This trend can be interpreted both literally (in historical terms) and metaphorically (in aesthetic ones) because it shows the direct effect of external influences on local lives. An American photojournalist who has spent time working in Afghanistan told me that "it is hard to find some of the original good ones. Now they seem kind of overdone or not as unique." This comment interestingly suggests that rugs, other than those catering to the tourist market, were becoming more and more difficult to encounter.

Authenticity can be a puzzling concept, especially when some local crafts are being shaped by external demand. For foreign buyers, authenticity may reside in the fine balance between what they perceive as essentially traditional and the subtle hint of external influence or modernity. For others, authenticity means that which has been made by the persons living in the area where the depicted events have unfolded. For a local provider like Sing, the fabric weaver from Plói Laom, authenticity may be an irrelevant concept that matters less to her than the need to satisfy demand and her ability to expand her knowledge and iconographic skills. Yet in providing objects for the wider war-memorabilia market, the act of weaving enables her (and her daughters) to make or create authenticity for foreigners (as well as for herself) as these images and their stories genuinely become her own. This point can be summarized as follows:

> Local memory object > foreign souvenir object >
> localized foreign memory

The biographies of such memory objects show that their prolonged journey through time, refashioning hands, buyers, and consumers, indeed turns them into unusual objects that are continually in the making.

Locally made artistic products offer a remarkable medium for revealing the rich diversity through which ethnic-minority communities envision, process, and communicate their past. For Tim Ingold, "'Art' disengages consciousness from current lived experience so as to treat that experience as an object of reflection" (Ingold 2000: 111). In the same way, ethnic-minority sculptors, carvers, painters, and weavers may want to appropriate the past by using their creations as sites of memory, or *lieux de mémoire* to borrow Pierre Nora's coined expression, where the three dimensions of time can inevitably lead to new stories and interpretations (Nora 1989: 7).[6] The skills, emotions, and experience (or lack thereof) of the craftsperson can attribute new meanings and functions to the inherited past, as shown by the wood-carver who encapsulates personal and collective memories of the war, the funerary painter who tells the past and future of the dead, the fabric weaver who interlaces threads of personal or vicarious experience, and the female carver who repeats old tales and sometimes imagines new ones.

Barbara Mills argued that the term "memory work" refers to the "many social practices that create memories, including recalling, reshaping, forgetting, inventing, coordinating, and transmitting" (Mills and Walker 2008: 6–14). In the case of Leu and other ethnic-minority villages in Ratanakiri, the skills of the craftsman and the act of making may become key to mediating the relationships between the village youth and elders. The following chapter explores this line of thought and investigates the ways in which members of the postconflict generation attempt to carve their own historical space, lived experience, and identity in a rapidly changing world.

---

6. "Our interest in *lieux de mémoire* where memory crystallizes and secretes itself has occurred at a particular historical moment, a turning point where consciousness of a break with the past is bound up with the sense that memory has been torn—but torn in such a way as to pose the problem of the embodiment of memory in certain sites where a sense of historical continuity persists. There are *lieux de mémoire*, sites of memory, because there are no longer *milieux de mémoire*, real environments of memory" (Nora 1989: 7).

Chapter 6

Leu, Present and Future

In what was once a remote region of northeastern Cambodia, today's increased flows of people, communication, and goods have affected the physical and cultural landscapes of Ratanakiri to an unprecedented level. The localized effects of globalization have penetrated further inland, have now reached distant communities, have pervaded household spaces, and have even seeped into sacred places, often leaving external observers with a feeling of isomorphism. In view of these dramatic transformations, how are the Jarai living in Leu adjusting to the multiple changes that are taking place outside and inside their village boundaries? How do people perceive present challenges, and what do they foresee for their individual and collective future? What do young villagers dream about, and where do they locate themselves historically and socially vis-à-vis their elders?

This chapter discusses current seeds of changes and investigates how they affect every aspect of people's daily lives. It focuses particularly on Leu's younger generation, people aged thirty-five or less, who have no experience or only very vague memories of the past conflicts. It examines the space young persons construct for themselves inside the social and cultural body of the village and thus sheds light on where young people feel they fit. This will help us frame conceptually their attitudes toward perpetuating traditional practices, on the one hand, and embracing the world of consumerism, on the other. I use the terms "tradition" and "traditional" within a restrictive time frame of a hundred years because my informants explained that they could not stretch further back in time.

This chapter draws on data I collected regarding people's choices of religious beliefs and lifestyles, individual or group spatial movements, and the ways young people voice their dream life in Leu and beyond. It is divided into two main sections. The first examines Christian conversion, an important feature of northeastern Cambodia since the exposure of ethnic-minority villages to extensive waves of Christian missionaries, starting in the early 1990s (Baird 2009), and how its multiple forms of spiritual, cultural, and social consumption have gradually led to the fragmentation of the village's social fabric. The second considers wider issues of modernity and materiality, whereby the ownership, use, and manipulation of commodities enable people to capture themselves and thereby project themselves into alternative social and aesthetic milieus. I will conclude with a final ethnographic vignette concerning some of my youngest informants. As they ponder their future, they stand at a crossroads between their elders' trodden path and alternative directions that may offer them the prospect of a more individual identity.

From Animism to Christianity

Today's increasing flux of people, trade, ideas, and lifestyles has substantially affected the life of Ratanakiri's ethnic-minority communities, especially in the vicinity of the provincial town of Banlung (Guérin et al. 2003; Bourdier 2006; Paterson, n.d.). In a Jorai village near Leu, one old village chief commented, "Our religion is disappearing, and the cemeteries that once were full of beautiful sculptures now lie barren!" According to the old man, a person who does not perpetuate the traditions of double obsequies, commemoration of ancestors, gong playing, and spirit worshipping is a person who simply "has no values." In Leu village, elders claimed that buffalo sacrifices are increasingly rare, and the village ceremonies that once involved collective participation in music making, dancing, and storytelling have progressively lost their unique attraction as they have been supplanted by television viewing and Christian gatherings.

In his ethnographic study of the Brao in the region, Ian Baird noted that "Protestant Evangelical Christian proselytising has increased considerably in the northeast of Cambodia over the last decade, and many ethnic minority groups have recently converted to Christianity" (Baird 2009: 11). In researching Protestant conversion in Vietnam's Central Highlands, meanwhile, Oscar Salemink observed that since 1980, a massive wave of conversion to evangelical Christianity had taken place as an act of resistance against the current government. He argued that during this conversion process, "religious efforts [were] aiming to convert highlanders to a particular way of thinking and a particular lifestyle" (Salemink 2004: 3). Although most of my informants have spent time living with their relatives in Vietnam, Christian conversion in the village of Leu is less a matter of political resistance than a way to access the modern world. Indeed, a number of village elders blamed the missionaries for being a major cause of the erosion of long-kept traditions, and they often equated Christian conversions with the locals' abandonment, and sometimes betrayal, of established ritual practices. From an external point of view, such differing practices have in fact created a divide between the elder and the younger segments of the population, which culminates in tensions when each side strives to simultaneously expand, protect, and maintain its sphere of influence inside the village boundaries and beyond.

Converting to Christianity in Leu

Wai, a twenty-eight-year-old villager who had converted to Christianity three years earlier, stressed how his life had changed completely since he had begun following the teachings of Jesus. Asked what exactly had changed, Wai responded, "It's like having a new life!" Other Christian converts considered Wai one of the brightest and most literate of their number. He told me that he had learned the Khmer and Jorai scriptures through studying with Christian missionaries and felt that without his conversion he would not have been able to reach this level of education.

Wai now teaches a small group of people how to read and write Khmer, as well as the basics of arithmetic. All these teaching sessions begin at eight p.m. and last for a couple of hours.[1] Men, women, and children (mostly converted) come together in one of the largest open-plan houses, where the teaching is done in a communal and friendly manner. Wai's thirst for knowledge is not easily quenched, and he interpreted my presence in the village as an opportunity to try to learn English in order to "be able to communicate with foreigners." When I inquired what he wanted to learn to say in English, he responded, "Everything!" After some of the lessons I gave him, together with a group of keen but less persevering students, I discovered that he had been regularly practicing on his own despite long days of work in his *hwa* (fruit and vegetable orchard).

When I met his wife for the first time, Wai told me "not to pay attention" to her and described her as "unintelligent" (*akŏ aku*). By using the term "unintelligent," he wanted to emphasize that she was not interested in education but was nonetheless a good wife. Becoming a Christian has opened up new horizons for Wai, affording him knowledge and opportunities that he would not otherwise have been able to access. On one occasion, a secular nongovernmental organization (NGO) was looking to sponsor a Jorai student for a three-year full-time higher-education program in the capital city of Phnom Penh. Seeing Wai as a potential candidate, I asked him whether he would be willing to leave his wife and four-month-old daughter for such an extended period. After considering this idea for a few seconds, Wai looked resolute and told me that he would be ready to leave if he was given the chance. Wai's quest for personal fulfillment through knowledge, which his conversion to Christianity has encouraged, if not catalyzed, means that he has grown somewhat apart from his wife. Drawing on his discourse and bodily attitude toward her, we can infer that by accessing this new religious

---

1. Christian converts in Leu have regular meetings throughout the year and they keep their gatherings scheduled at night. Accurate time is a relatively new concept (as well as accurate distance to some extent) that helps them organize their fellowship better across the villages often using their mobile phones. According to Cupet "The savages have no concept of time and year whatsoever. They use the phases of the moon. None of them know their age. Happy people!" (Cupet 1900: 345–46). Jacques Dournes supports this statement explaining that the moon is the major time marqueur that is key for their daily subsistence activities. The moon indeed enables them to distinguish the dry season from the monsoon season, or the beginning of an agrian cycle and the end (Dournes 1969: 23). For Dournes beyond the third or fourth year, they will not keep track of the age of their children "about their 10 year old son, they may as well say that he is 8 or 12" (ibid.).

and social space, Wai has left another behind in which his wife and other kin still remain confined. As will be further illustrated through other individual experiences, this case of conversion playing a role in the widening of social divisions is far from unique in Leu.

Siu, the talented wood-carver, has been a Christian since 1998. He told me that when he converted, he was living with relatives in Vietnam when some missionaries came to tell the villagers about the "teaching of Jesus." Siu explained the reasons underlying his conversion as follows: "Practicing animism is too difficult since people have to make sacrifices all the time when preparing the *hwa*, when planting, when harvesting. . . . Sacrifices always involve chickens, rice, alcohol, and sometimes pigs. . . . It is a tiresome and very costly belief! Moreover, drinking encourages domestic violence and spending, whereas Christian beliefs nurture good behavior, which prevents oneself from being angry and violent. . . . *Preah* [God, in Khmer] has created us, not the reverse, and he encourages us to be grateful, compassionate, and generous and to help one another." Siu described his past self as "often angry, breaking plates at home and always getting drunk on festive occasions with the rest of the villagers!" He went on to say that since his conversion, he had completely stopped drinking, and he believed that the religion he had embraced had made him a new man.

In Siu's case, believing in Jesus is a way to make amends for past misbehavior, and his conversion has given him an unforeseen opportunity to start anew. Despite having embraced Christianity to the point of refraining from drinking completely (for which he is often teased by nonconverted peers), Siu tries to abide by the rules long imposed by village customs. For example, when he is sculpting a funerary effigy, he usually takes into consideration other people's concerns that sculptures associated with death might pollute the village. He explained that in such cases he hides them in the forest where he knows no one will touch them. However, he also admitted that he sometimes brings them discreetly inside the village to finish carving them. On one such occasion, Siu concealed a sculpted plane inside his bag in order to complete the work in the shelter of his kitchen. When I asked him what the village elders might say if they found out, Siu smiled and said, "Oh, it doesn't matter, I don't really care. People can think what they want!" Although Siu never brings in large effigies that are used for traditional cemeteries, he feels that he can sometimes infringe the local customs by introducing smaller ones inside the enclosed space of the village. For Siu, all the taboos concerning the protected space of and around Leu are "nonsense," and this is why he sometimes feels like violating established customs.

The appearance of Siu's house reflects some of the ambivalence he feels toward traditional practices. The main entrance is flanked by two sculpted peacocks, a pair of funerary effigies par excellence. Siu told me that when he first placed the sculptures on the staircase ten years earlier, around the time of his conversion, fellow villagers complained that such effigies were harbingers of death for anyone living in that house. In such situations, where explicit use of objects and individual behaviors inscribe a spatial dimension (both physically and symbolically) to create a virtual enclave, the entire village then becomes a contested space. Jacques Dournes observed that the presence of such sculptures outside the protected space of the cemetery is perceived as a potent source of pollution; the expectation is that the person responsible for the breaking of this taboo will be struck down by lightning (Dournes 1968). Some time after Siu decorated his house, his four-month-old daughter died of diarrhea, and ever since he and his wife have always hoped to become parents again. It is possible that people interpreted the infant's death as a direct consequence of the infringed taboo.

According to Siu, there were three families in Leu who had converted to Christianity. In the past couple of years, these families had begun building links to other Jorai Christian converts living elsewhere in Andong Meas, as well as districts farther afield, through regular monthly gatherings. Siu described these gatherings as being organized rotationally, providing opportunities for converts in each village to host their friends in turn. I participated in three of these gatherings, each of which was regarded by those attending as quite successful. The monthly meetings typically involve around thirty people, the majority of whom are young literate women who travel relatively long distances with their young children. The atmosphere is extremely convivial, but, from an outsider's perspective, it appears that the sense of cheerful bonding carries with it an exclusivity that further widens the space between the converted and the nonconverted.

When I talked to female participants and asked them what they sought to achieve through the meetings, they told me that they liked seeing one another and spending time together. Most of them said that they were having "fun," and that it was a great opportunity to reunite with friends, learn (new teachings), sing, and share meals. Such gatherings certainly aim to re-create a sense of kinship, and in truth the converts I worked with felt that beyond biological links they were connected to one another by means of sharing the same faith and pooling resources for food and accommodation. In this sense, the group illustrates the Christian metaphor of the "sharing of the bread," which promotes the culture of congregation and sharing.

Activities related to Christianity are spatially confined because only two houses within the village (where converted families live) are designated Christian meeting places. When the monthly gatherings take place in Leu, nonconverted villagers tend either to ignore the activities or to peep in occasionally to see who is taking part. In the latter case, the curious observers are either children who are keen on hearing the songs or young and older women who, because their curiosity has been aroused, have spared a few minutes to listen before retreating to their homes. It is rare for nonconverted males to join the Christian groups (even briefly) because they prefer to stay away and spend their time discussing, smoking, and drinking with their neighbors. In this case, individual religious beliefs and bodily practices are spatially framed within self-imposed terrestrial boundaries, thus carving out a different physical and identity grouping within the communal area.

Although most of the Christian converts I worked with belong to the postconflict generation, some village elders claimed that they too had tried switching faiths. A village elder from Plói Tang told me that he had actually converted several times, switching back and forth between worshipping spirits and following Christian preachers before ultimately reverting to the former. When I asked about his last, albeit probably not final, religious affiliation, he admitted that "it is difficult to follow one faith only because the other has other things to offer." As I will discuss later, conversion to Christianity entails renouncing all former religious practices and hence making it an exclusive religion. Because of their opposing natures in such matters as faith, ritual actions, sacred locations, god and deities, languages, and texts and objects, the would-be convert who is seeking spiritual fulfillment is under pressure to choose one over the other.

Luyin Blen told me that he had converted to Christianity a long time ago in order to "be less poor." He explained, "Animism entails too many sacrifices to the spirits for too few visible effects and too much [animal] waste. Such a religious practice in turn leads to relentless drinking and even more livestock being sacrificed since people become even hungrier when under the influence of alcohol. Medicines, conversely, have more measurable effects. As a poor man, it is essential for my family's survival that I save money, animals, and time."

Luyin Blen described how, when his first wife experienced chronic abdominal pains, the local shaman (*pöjau*) recommended that he sacrifice a cow to appease the spirits who were the cause of her suffering. After the ritual, his wife's illness persisted, and the *pöjau* interpreted this persistence as a clear sign that the spirits needed more sacrifices. Because Luyin Blen was worried by the idea of parting with another cow (meaning most of his personal fortune), one person suggested that he take his wife to the district surgery instead. At the surgery, Luyin Blen's wife was diagnosed with kidney stones, and after medical treatment the pain eventually disappeared. Luyin Blen claimed that since that time he had stopped sacrificing animals to the spirits, frustrated by the fact that he had lost a cow for no return, which, according to him, "was a real waste!"

It was at the time of the Khmer Rouge (KR) that he was first obliged to abandon spirit worshipping because the KR taught him how to live the revolutionary life without wasting resources. He said that since his return to the village and the diagnosed illness of his first wife, he had participated in both village celebrations and Christian gatherings; attending the former out of a sense of social obligation. Village funerals are an opportunity for people to invite members of neighboring communities to attend the rituals and share their food and rice wine. In February 2008, a series of deaths in the area forced a few villages to organize large funerals for their dead, and they thus called village elders like Luyin Blen to participate. He once complained that he had to attend "yet another funeral. . . . People have invited me and I have to go, . . . but I will wait here and set off at the end of the day because I have only just returned from another one." When I asked him whether he somehow remained faithful to the village's religious practices, he responded, "I am in the middle. . . . I never perform any rituals, but I am not a follower of Jesus either. . . . However, if my child happened to die, I would probably do something because I would feel for my child. It would be difficult not to do anything." In visualizing this very tragic event, Luyin Blen acknowledged that animism could provide his child with what is perceived as the care that the departed one deserves, so as to not leave the dead person abandoned after the first burial. This feeling of anxiety is identical to the one that affected—and still affects—local war survivors who have lost relatives in the various conflicts. It explains the collective decision when the war was over to organize a large propitiating ritual in the name of all the unburied dead. In admitting that he would choose the religious space of his ancestors if he was confronted with the tragedy of losing his child, Luyin Blen echoed the words of the Fox Indians quoted by Claude Lévi-Strauss: "Death is a hard thing. Sorrow is especially hard" (Lévi-Strauss 1966: 31).

During my latest visit to Leu in September 2014, I discovered that Luyen Blen had been suffering from partial paralysis for the past few weeks. I was told that he had been struck by an illness that caused half of his body to be motionless. Luyen Blen spoke with difficulty and told me that his leg was "dead." One of the village elders explained that he had offended the spirit of his late wife by not offering her the proper funerals. Luyen Blen's wife had drowned in the river the year before, and it was only a couple of days after the accident that the villagers found her body. In his haste to bury her, Luyen Blen failed to perform the central ritual of the buffalo sacrifice in order to communicate with the spirits and help the soul of his wife depart peacefully.

After her death, Luyin Blen married again and further delayed his funerary duties. A month before my visit, the mother of his new wife passed away, which led him to organize proper funerals for her. After the interment of his mother-in-law, Luyen Blen woke up one morning unable to move half of his body. Village elders, as well as younger people in Leu, including Siu, believed that this sudden illness was a sign of his late wife's revenge for not fulfilling his duties. Even Luyen Blen himself deeply regretted this mistake and said that he would have to make amends by sacrificing a buffalo. In this context of remarriage and in a chronological logic, the idea of failing to perform the funerals of his first wife appears to many less like a serious infringement than performing the rituals for someone else first, in this case the mother of the new wife. Luyen Blen believed that the spirit of his wife had felt neglected and had become jealous. In an ethnography of the ghosts of the Vietnam War, Mai Lan Gustafsson explored the wrathful ghosts who torment their kin. She noted, "It is also exactly what motivated the angry ghosts: they forced, through the infliction of pain and suffering, their victims to remember them" (Gustafsson 2009: 10). Despite Luyen Blen's open-minded views on religion, this accident was a clear warning that he could not afford to act negligently and without caution vis-à-vis the world of the spirits.

Local Views of the Nonconverted

When I was discussing the village's religious makeup with my non-Christian informants, people emphasized the divide either by openly criticizing the converts or by simply ignoring them. In regard to Luyin Blen's participation in both religious spaces, my informants commented, "Oh, he drinks like any one of us!" hence incorporating the village elder into their own traditional sphere. By contrast, when I asked Siu the same question, he responded that Luyin Blen was a Christian, thus locating him instead inside Leu's confined Christian space.

Luyin Blen was aware of being in a singular situation, given the flexibility with which he attended (and was welcome in) both Christian gatherings and traditional funerals. Reflecting on his ability to move between rival spaces of religiosity, the village elder described his status as being "in the middle." He once indicated to me that he had chosen to practice a sort of "mix and match" of animism and Christianity, which on a social level seemed to fit his needs. He insisted, however, that he would never tell other people what to do in this regard since "it is up to them to decide what they wish. Others get involved in arguments, rebuking Christian villagers, but they should not treat them like that. It is up to the individual" (*tam smach tcheut* in Khmer).

Such antagonisms are quite frequent and can take multiple forms, ranging from scornful remarks to silent bodily expressions of disapproval. Wai and other Christian converts complained that some villagers had adopted a deliberately aggressive attitude toward them: "They are angry with us and tell us off. They often harass us until they get bored, at which point they eventually stop. We only need to remain silent. . . . We get used to them, so we should not fight back." When I raised this issue with Pou Ksor, one of the village elders (and nonconverted), he responded,

> There are five families in the village that have converted,[2] and other Jorai do not tell them off for this. It would be inappropriate. . . . This sort of reaction would come from the Khmer Krom. . . . Our ancestors have taught us how to do things, then new people come in and change it all! But it does not come through, . . . it doesn't match our old values, it is replacing them, which is in-

---

2. Siu mentioned only three families in Leu.

appropriate. . . . Villagers here are just following the tradition. The new generation will forget it all. . . . Old values will all soon be lost . . . like the Jorai language. . . . It is up to us to decide what we choose to believe in, but we have never rebuked these young converts.

Although nonconverted villagers blamed their Christian peers for their change of religious practices, no social sanctions seem to have been used against them comparable to the ones used in Balinese communities to keep conversion at bay.[3] In fact, although a few village elders like Pou Ksor strongly disapproved of their abandoning local traditions, there was no indication that Leu Christian converts would be marginalized or even banned from burying their dead in the village cemetery. Instead, most villagers believed that their Christian peers would eventually change their mind and some day "return to the rice-wine jars."

One of the main concerns voiced by Pou Ksor was that the new system of beliefs rejects all prevailing rituals and usurps established religious spaces. Pou Ksor is related to Siu through marriage and described himself as his "extended uncle." He claimed that after his conversion, Siu stopped attending and performing the village traditional rituals. Indeed, on the occasion of his father's death, Siu failed to carry out the rituals that were due to his dead father. As a result, Pou Ksor said that he had to take over the organization and costs of the funerals, the hundred-days ceremony, and the abandonment of the grave, claiming that "otherwise nobody would have done it." The village elder commented that his underlying motivation came from his moral duty vis-à-vis the rest of his kin and affines "so that the entire family would not be suffering in the future as a result of [Siu's] negligence." Pou Ksor's sense of moral obligation illustrates the idea of reciprocal acts through which the dead person will in turn make preparations for the anticipated death of his or her descendants.

Pou Ksor reinforced his argument by asserting that the Khmer expression *tfeu phdeh phdah* (to behave in a foolish manner) is synonymous with "taking risk," and he said that this foolish or risk-taking behavior was exemplified by "someone who does not perform rituals to honor the gods and spirits because they do not think it is important." The village elder's point here is clearly that negligence on the part of the younger generation

---

3. Dr. Leo Howe, personal communication, June 2010.

concerning their duties toward the ancestors and the spirits could make the person—and by extension his or her kin—more vulnerable.

Pou Ksor acknowledged that traditional ritual practices are costly and require a lot of work, however. He recalled that in 2000 a series of deaths within his family (including that of his own mother) caused him to lose part of his fortune.[4] The loss resulted from the performance of successive rituals at a final cost of eight buffaloes and five cows. Pou Ksor nonetheless remained firm in his beliefs. Despite the financial costs, he believed that he carried a personal moral obligation as a family member toward his kin. In his view, Christian conversion had caused injury to the dead (*khoyk phleuv khmaoyk* in Khmer),[5] which he and other nonconverted members of the family perceived as an abandonment or negation of the reciprocal duties linking the living and the deceased. In this instance, we can infer that the Christian path taken by someone like Siu may be perceived as a lonely path that breaks away from the collective attachment to the ancestors, the spirits, and established ritual actions.

In researching the Australian Aboriginal landscape, Nancy Munn studied the ways Aborigines deliberately take alternative paths to avoid being close to ritual sites and activities. She argued that by taking terrestrial detours, the Aborigines create a "negative space" whereby the source of taboo is removed from the perimeter of their senses and bodily contact (Munn 1996: 462–65). In a similar vein, Pou Ksor regarded Siu's behavior as an attempt to extract himself from the sphere of traditional religiosity, creating a negative space as a result of his refusal to carry out the duties incumbent on a son at the time of his father's death. On one occasion, Siu took me to observe a second burial ceremony at the district town. I found out after half an hour that he had stayed away from the crowd, patiently waiting for me on the other side of the house fences. Siu told me later that he did not want to be seen by other villagers because he knew that they would try to force him to join the party and drink. In staying away from the site, Siu created a spatial boundary to protect himself from the others' influences. In this case,

---

4. Death and birth, as mentioned in chapter 2, are usually located in time via events, e.g., season or social activities, but in this case, the series of family-related deaths was identified with the year 2000, like war occurrences, perhaps because of its traumatic emotional and financial characteristics.

5. Or, literally, "damaging the dead's path."

faith in his religious beliefs was bodily enacted via the creation of a buffer, which ultimately aimed to prevent unwanted pollution (Douglas 2002).

Alongside Christianity, Luyin Blen mentioned the growing influence of Theravada Buddhism as a source of new ritual practices. He noted that "there are already lots of changes in our traditional rituals since some have already been shortened [*kat chaol khlah hauy* in Khmer]. . . . Some families would even exhume their dead after five years to cremate the remains and place the ashes in a pagoda." There is currently a limited amount of literature on the conversion of the Jorai in northeastern Cambodia to Christianity, but there is even less regarding the adoption of Buddhist practices. Luyin Blen and other villagers indicated, however, that this was an additional source of religious transformations that had already contributed to the erosion of traditional practices in Andong Meas district.

Amid these changes, the main anxiety of the nonconverted remains the exclusive character of Christianity. At the same time, Pou Ksor, for instance, suggested the possibility of striking a balance between tradition and modernity, with one religion complementing the other. A form of syncretism is indeed visible in some Jorai cemeteries in the district; a few traditional graves feature the name and dates of birth and death on a Christian cross underneath the customary wooden roof.

The response of some younger people, meanwhile, to this competition between old and new religions was one of ambivalence and experimentation. At times of traditional funerals and buffalo sacrifices, for instance, young male adults are particularly active digging the grave or immolating the buffalo, but according to Pou Ksor, these persons "can learn, but they cannot behave as such." For the village elder, although the traditional rites were followed, they remained meaningless because they were "empty" of any spiritual significance for the actor (Humphrey and Laidlaw 1994). Pou Ksor surmised that most of the time, these young people followed others to the ceremonies for the sake of the entertainment, food, and drink. The same individuals then participated in the monthly Christian gatherings, learning how to sing Christian songs.

When I asked younger people in Leu about their attitude toward religion, their responses often suggested an openness to different options and a concern not to be excluded from any of them. For them, the traditional practices offered food, alcohol, and gong playing in the company of relatives, friends, and neighbors. At the same time, the Christian gatherings brought together relatives and friends and provided the opportunity to share meals, play music (guitar), read the Bible, and sing. Although the two spheres of religiosity are exclusive and offer different social and spiritual options to young adults searching for their identity, ultimately they both, to some degree, revolve around consumption.

Perspectives of Christian Missionaries

Nineteenth- and twentieth-century French Christian missionaries, explorers, and foreign travelers produced a rich literature describing Christian missions to convert the local populations. Some of the missionaries' work was evidently facilitated by resonances between biblical stories and the local population's legends (for example, the deluge) (Maître 1912). Guérin, however, argued that the main appeal of following a Christian God was the exclusivity and nonsacrificial attributes that had the power to set them "free from the fears and worries that characterise the pagans' life" (Guérin et al. 2003: 61; see also Simonnet 1977 and Patary 2013). Although this exclusive aspect of Christianity may have helped some missionaries attract dedicated converts, the Christian insistence on the existence of a single god in some instances proved hard to convey. Norman Lewis's notes from his travels across Vietnam in the 1950s capture the conundrum nicely in a description of the efforts of an American pastor to convert the Raglai in central Vietnam:

> I asked if he had ever found the tribes intolerant of his preaching, and the pastor said, no, on the contrary. The trouble was that the natives were only too ready to accept any message but wanted to be allowed to fit in the new revelation among their own idolatries. He just couldn't make them understand that God was a jealous god. That was another term that they didn't have in their language, and he had to spend hours explaining to them. A typical attitude after hearing the gospel was to offer to include the new spirit in their Pantheon along with the spirits of earth, water, thunder and rice. This usually went with the suggestion of a big ceremony, to be provided by the pastor, at which a number of buffaloes and jars would be sacrificed and the new spirit would be invited to be present. (Lewis 1951: 133)

One of my informants, a Christian worker from the Evangelical Fellowship of Cambodia (EFC), confirmed that this tension between the worship of a range of local ancestors and spirits, on the one hand, and the belief in a single god, on the other, continued to affect present-day missionary activities in Ratanakiri and, indeed, the impact the missionaries had on those villages where they did attract some converts:

> The question of ancestor worship is an important one. There is a clash between polytheism and monotheism.... Things are incompatible, and it is difficult to convert people without starting from scratch. The Christian God needs to be powerful enough to be interesting for those who contemplate joining. He is in direct competition with existing deities. The Bible only says: "Thou shall not worship idols," which is different from polytheism. This accentuates the separation as the community is now divided between animists and Christians. The latter are "extracted" from their village. The real question is how can they work or act for the good of the entire community? How can this benefit others instead of creating differences and generating arguments? It is important not to exclude oneself!

This opinion, although quite unusual among the various missionaries I have encountered, resonates with Pou Ksor's previous comments on the exclusivity of the Christian religion. According to my EFC informant, the proselytism currently employed by some Christian missionaries in Ratanakiri province frequently causes disputes and divisions that marginalize individuals from the social body of the community. Ian Baird's study of religious changes in the region makes a similar observation: "Many non-governmental organisation observers are not fundamentally against the highlanders voluntarily becoming Christians, but are concerned that intra-community conflict has the potential to occur when part of the community becomes Christian. For example, the Jorai village of Lom split into two when part of the population converted to Christianity a number of years ago, thus decreasing community solidarity" (Baird 2009: 2).

My EFC informant further said that Christian chapters operate differently throughout the country, each of them using its own approach to preaching. Some are more aggressive in the ways in which they convert people, demanding that they abandon their traditional beliefs completely. My informant commented, "Extreme forms of missionary work can be found in Baptism and Alliance. The Presbyterians, on the other hand, are more relaxed, but there are many chapters: the American, the English, the Irish, etc., which all differ from one another [and which can be active in the same areas]. This offers a possible explanation for the total ban on drinking for the converted villagers in Leu. 'Drinking' is not banned in the Bible, only 'being drunk' is. This form of conversion often means that people are less compassionate about others." Few missionaries I came across during my research agreed, however, that a more inclusive approach to religious conversion might help reduce the risk of social fragmentation.

Many of the missionaries stationed in Ratanakiri province are operating within the framework of NGO development programs. By using such channels of operations, the advocacy of the Gospels can be done in a more discreet manner, alongside efforts to "improve local standards of living." All the NGO missionaries I encountered genuinely believed that their work contributed to enhancing significantly the life of ethnic-minority communities. Some (particularly foreigners) were nonetheless uncomfortable with having an anthropologist working near their project sites. On more than one occasion, my presence was perceived as directly intruding into the mission's operating space.

PROVINCIAL GATHERINGS: WORLD VISION

Christian gatherings occur from time to time in provinces throughout Cambodia. One such event that I was able to attend was a two-day workshop organized by the Christian NGO World Vision in the provincial capital of Banlung. The main purposes of this type of workshop are to convene local chapters, to advocate the Gospels, and to share teachings that local preachers will in turn disseminate when they return to their home villages. This particular occasion brought together two World Vision staff from Phnom Penh, a few foreign missionaries (from the Netherlands and the United States), and Christian converts from the Jorai, Tampuon, Kreung, and Brao ethnic-minority groups, who had traveled long distances, accompanied by their children. Two of my informants from Leu (Siu and Wai), as well as half a dozen others whom I knew from neighboring villages, also came. News of the gathering had been spread by word of mouth.

These kinds of meetings often command high attendance from the local populations, one of the reasons being that the costs of travel are subsidized by the organizers. In addition, those participating in the gathering in Banlung were provided with free meals and lodging. In the case of Siu and Wai, who are dedicated Christians, the financial incentives were very much secondary to a sense of a moral duty to attend, as well as excitement at the opportunity to enhance their knowledge of the Gospels, meet new people, and spend time in the provincial capital. Both of them termed attending such meetings going to "study" (*hrăm*).

By the time of my last research period in January and February 2009, Siu had finally become a father again. Only a week after his child's birth, however, he decided to participate in another provincial Christian gathering, this time in the northwestern province of Battambang. This journey took him two whole days to complete and meant that he was away from his wife and infant for an entire week. Siu's wife said that she was not disappointed by this absence, considering that if it was so important for him to study, then he should not refrain from going on her or the baby's account. In a way that is reminiscent of Wai's situation, Siu's participation in Christian activities creates both a physical and psychological separation from his spouse and other members of the household. The idea of "gendered space" is illustrated here because the wife and child are located within the limited boundaries of the house or village, and the husband is either outside or far away. As I spoke to him while he was traveling, Siu talked with great enthusiasm about how he was making new friends and having a great time traveling and learning with them. Siu felt that by leaving his small household, he was entering into the wider space of Christian kinship, which expanded far beyond the village boundaries.

SELECTING AND TRANSLATING LITURGICAL TEXTS

An important issue, concerns the selection for translation and teaching of specific passages of the Bible. Although local translation of the scenes of the deluge was facilitated by certain ethnic-minority legends, other passages seem to have been chosen precisely because there was no immediate equivalent in the local oral literature. A village elder I met in Plói Leu Pok explained to me that one of the reasons that he was convinced by the teaching of Jesus was that believing in him meant that he could ultimately be free from the "formidable fires of hell." Although most of my informants emphasized the benefits that conversion could provide them in the present and the near future, this village elder was particularly concerned about the afterlife.

As mentioned previously, people in Leu and nearby villages do not readily comment on what happens after someone dies. It is thus possible to infer that one approach used by some missionaries is to exploit such uncertainties by depicting the image of the soul being eternally tormented by the fires of hell. Although these types of future visions may be most relevant to village elders, younger people—like Siu—may feel that they need to atone for past mistakes. In a situation like that of Siu, converting to Christianity may thus appear as a means of addressing the risks of becoming ill fated. My EFC informant commented that one reason missionaries might favor apocalyptic scenes is that the single god is in competition with a multiplicity of existing local deities. This means that it is only by demonstrating the extent of his greater power that people can be convinced of the comparative advantage this new god has to offer them. Emphasizing the graphic violence associated with biblical apocalyptic scenes can become an integral part of a preaching strategy to attract potential converts.

Closely related to the issue of selection from the Gospels is the crucial question of translation into Khmer, Jorai, or other ethnic-minority languages. According to my EFC informant, translations are done either by the Bible Society International (BSI) using scholars with a very good knowledge of both the language and the geographic area or by the Swift Society, which employs professional linguists. My informant claimed that translation works by linguists "tend to be more neutral and systematic in their method," in other words, less subject to personal interpretations. He noted that the Khmer version of the Bible was done by the BSI, while he inferred that the Jorai translation might have been done by the Swift Society.[6]

Two of the people I worked with in Leu had a copy of part of the Bible translated into Jorai. They told me that these copies had been given to them by missionaries based in Vietnam. Although the entire Bible, according to them, had not yet been translated into their language, they felt that they could rely on both Jorai and Khmer versions, an option that had been unavailable fifty years earlier, when such translations had been in their infancy.

---

6. According to Lap, "The American evangelical Protestant missionaries were most likely the people who improved the orthography of Jarai. For instance, most of the books in the Jarai language were written and published by the Summer Institute of Linguistics (SIL), an evangelical Christian organization that worked closely with the government of South Vietnam before and during the Vietnam War in documenting the indigenous languages of the Central Highlands" (Lap 2009: 34).

Norman Lewis's narration of his travels in Southeast Asia brings to life the complex issues of selection, translation, and representation in this very colorful vignette:

> In reply to my enquiry after the progress of his labours the pastor said that they were making some headway against unbelievable difficulties. To take the language problem alone. Like most of these Far-Eastern languages, it was barren in abstractions, which provided the most appalling difficulties when it came to translating the Holy Writ. To give just one example, he cited the text, "God is Love". In Rhadés there was no word for God. In fact these people didn't get the idea at all without a great deal of explanation. Also there was no word for love. So the text came out of translation, "The Great Spirit is not angry." (Lewis 1951: 132)

Similarly, my EFC informant commented that the issue of how one should address God in semantic terms posed challenges to local people's understanding of the intended Christian message. For instance, the Khmer translation of the Bible seeks to reproduce the hierarchical structure that is embedded in all social relationships in Cambodia through its choice of terms of address, particularly in its translation of the words "you" and "thou." As a result, God often appears too distant from the individual, seeming an aloof and unattainable divinity. In the Jorai version, conversely, "you" (*ih* or *kih*) does not reproduce the social hierarchy, and it is possible that in this context, the designation of God may be less problematic. However, the converted people I worked with constantly switched between characterizing God as far and unattainable and as merciful and compassionate.

During the few Christian gatherings I attended, Khmer preachers very often presented God as being an entity to be afraid of. Whether they were preachers traveling all the way from the capital city or local converts like Siu teaching his companions during village monthly gatherings, both recurrently depicted God as a distant figure. A few passages from the Bible that were discussed in such teaching events systematically translated the expression "with awe" as "with fear" or "inspiring fear" (*blao*). One such example is the following: "Everyone was amazed and gave praise to God. They were filled with awe and said, 'We have seen beautiful things today'" (Luke 5:26). In the provincial town of Banlung, the preacher who was then leading the session translated the English version into Khmer using the word "fear" (*klach*) and described how such a miracle had instigated fear in the heart of the people. The same severe image of God was perpetuated through Siu's local teachings because he also used the image of a distant god. My EFC informant contended that a "God who is regarded with awe does not mean that this God is to be severe or uncompassionate." This image prevails, however, as if to perpetuate the idea that such a god is indeed powerful and hence worth the abandonment of the village's traditional ancestors and tutelary spirits.

Religious conversions have been and continue to be a source of social fragmentation whereby village elders feel separated by a physical and spiritual divide from the converted members of the community, who often belong to the younger generation. As I will discuss in the following section, Christian conversion is not the only element that creates such fragmentation, however. On the one hand, regular exposure to consumer goods plays an important role in creating various social dynamics inside Leu. On the other, young villagers often stand in the shade of their parents' war-lived experience, which may turn the search for their own identity into a way to either bridge or widen this divide.

Modernity, Materiality, and Metamorphosis

Like inhabitants of other ethnic-minority villages in Ratanakiri that have only relatively recently been exposed to the world of modern consumerism, Leu villagers have progressively begun to develop desires, needs, and uses for a range of commodities. I use Appadurai's definition of the term "commodities": "things with a particular type of social potential, that they are distinguishable from 'products,' 'objects,' 'goods,' 'artifacts,' and other sorts of things—but only in certain respects and from a certain point of view" (Appadurai 1986: 6).

The accumulation of commodities is limited in a village like Leu, where both food and cash are scarce. Commodities are few, and although they are owned on an individual basis, they are often used by several household members and sometimes others too. In Leu, this limited range of commodities includes mobile phones, motorcycles, and television sets. The subsections that follow examine the ways in which the social value of these and other commodities shapes individual identity and how they provide, or at least promise, experience of a different sort of life outside the village space.

Mobile Phones

As of June 2008, eight of the thirty households in Leu owned a mobile phone.[7] For many male villagers I worked with, owning a mobile phone was an important source of prestige because it illustrated relative wealth and connections beyond the village. Possessing a phone is costly because charging it requires electricity and hence a generator. Out of generosity, the three house owners who have electrical generators usually recharge their peers' phones for free. In addition, one must have credit to make calls on a mobile phone, and very few have enough cash. In most cases, communication by phone is initiated by a caller outside Leu (the farther away the caller is, the greater the prestige). Such calls help build a tangible bridge between the village domain and the people living beyond it.

Luyin Blen was inseparable from his mobile phone, except when he regularly lost it while traveling along the road. He had owned three phones in the space of six months. He used his phone primarily to stay in contact with his daughter, who lives in the United States. He also used it to communicate with members of the provincial and district authorities, who periodically asked him to attend meetings regarding health, education, and local infrastructure development as a representative of the village. The mobile phone thus played a crucial role in connecting him to a wider and important social network outside Leu. Even though he often complained that he attended meetings (*nao louwm*) too often, he nonetheless knew that his geographic and social mobility brought him a certain status within the village. People often asked him to help settle local disputes or negotiate with NGO workers because fellow villagers valued his perceived experience.

Others had a strong attachment to their mobile phones for a different set of reasons. Siu, the wood-carver, enjoyed the fact that some other villagers, especially children, regarded his phone with fascination. Like other phone owners, he used it less to connect with people who lived far away than as a means of entertaining his near neighbors with the phone's array of features (e.g., radio, clock, photographic storing device). Phones, particularly new sophisticated ones, are a means by which their owners can attract people and generate a sense of envy, a powerful and much-sought-after feeling.

---

7. The number tends to fluctuate over time since people (mostly males) often own one temporarily before selling it to get cash in return.

During my research, some of my informants would spend periods of a few days engaged in house construction or work on plantations. After these periods of intense manual labor, most decided to spend their wages on alcohol, cigarettes, and food, but some chose to purchase mobile phones. In this part of Ratanakiri, phones typically cost between 20 and 80 USD (the latter is a substantial amount for the ordinary Leu household). When I asked whether they needed to spend their earnings on such expensive commodities, two of my informants said that it was for the "pleasure of owning something beautiful and quite unique." Furthermore, the fact that a few of the villagers did not know how to use a phone properly (because of a lack of language or technical skills) gave them the sense of owning something exciting and exclusive that they needed to learn to master. Even if they kept the phone for only few weeks before selling it, the mere experience of having owned one was a source of personal enjoyment. Ultimately the money recouped through the sale of the phone often, if not always, found its way back into supporting the household budget through buying food, soap, or medicines. My other informants who did not own a phone simply said that they could not afford one, suggesting that they felt that this particular experience was not open to them.

Motorcycles and Traveling

In Leu, an invitation to go somewhere always sounds like an adventure. Even driving by motorcycle to the nearest village is viewed as an exciting deviation from the daily routine. For children (and young boys in particular), traveling to the nearest town of O'Kop to get food, fuel, or cigarettes is a highlight of a day or an entire week. Children often cling to their fathers as soon as they realize that they are about to set off somewhere, even for a very short time. If the request for a ride is then refused, tears are the inevitable outcome. From time to time, my informants invited me to accompany them on the twenty-minute trip to O'Kop. If I asked them what they needed to do there, they often used the Khmer expression *teuw dau legn*, meaning that they just wanted to go for a fun ride and come back.

Traveling by motorbike to the provincial town of Banlung is regarded as a big adventure. Because it is farther away not only geographically but also socially (few of my Jorai informants have connections, let alone relatives, in the town), the fascination of the big town remains intact, not least because there is a degree of risk associated with it. Illustrating Georg Simmel's sociology of space (see Simmel 1971), the majority of the villagers, through this capacity to travel and be together with others, have effectively expanded their physical, social, and influential boundaries beyond rivers and mountains.

Clothing and Fashion Trends

The adoption of Western clothes, particularly by the younger segment of the population, has contributed to a growing transformation of the body landscape in Leu. These youngsters often wear copies of famous international brands of jeans, shirts, t-shirts, and caps, which have also become an established trend among Khmer youth in Phnom Penh. Imported fashions also manifest themselves in specific hair styles, which in some notable cases are perceived by many as being akin to scientific experiments. When two close friends returned from a few weeks of work with their hair colored in shades of yellow and orange, this triggered lots of sarcastic remarks in the village. The people I worked with commented that they had colored their hair to enhance their physical appearance in order to date young girls in the town, because they were both at an age to marry (fifteen and seventeen, respectively). When I asked them whether this was true, they blushed, shied away from answering the question, and replied that the hair dye was only "to play" (*gnoy*). As Victor Turner noted, "We imagine ourselves experiencing the world through our 'social skin', the surface of the body representing a kind of common frontier of society which becomes the symbolic stage upon which the drama of socialization is enacted" (Turner 1969: 112). In many instances, appropriating foreign clothes and adopting trendy hair styles may turn the body into an experimental site where external influences can be temporarily tested and sometimes permanently adopted.

One example is the local adoption of American soldier dog-tag replicas, a trend observed among the postconflict generation in parts of northeastern Cambodia, southeastern Laos, and Vietnam. In Leu and neighboring villages, each of my young informants (between fourteen and nineteen years old) claimed that the dog-tag replica had been bought either at the local market or at the provincial town of Banlung for 2 USD. Very few knew the original meaning of the necklace, but all of them claimed that they had bought one because it "looks beautiful!"[8] In this case, the adoption of the foreign object (still imbued with a foreign identity) travels through extensive channels of aesthetics and fashion endowments. On one occasion, Siu's cousin, who did not know the historical origin of his necklace, simply described it as "being nice." A village elder then interrupted him and commented sarcastically, "It's an American necklace, and he likes to be like an American. With this necklace he can have his name written on it, as well as his birth date and his blood group, so that when he dies, someone will be able to find him and identify him!"

For Nicholas Saunders, such objects belong to an ambiguous domain because they hold different and sometimes conflicting meanings for those who experienced them in the past and those who interact with them later. He argued persuasively, "Items which would appear as kitsch or ephemera to those who had not experienced the war expressed emotions and memories which words alone could not convey for those who had participated" (Saunders 2003: 129). When it is owned by members of Leu's younger generation, the foreign object that is suffused with warfare significance may thus become a way to reappropriate the past and encode it with new meanings of the present. Since the young people I worked with were born long after the wars of the 1970s, personal experiential meanings that were originally attached to the objects gave way to new interpretations (of fashion and beauty), which were often part of the youth's process of identity making. In this instance, body transformations are a means of finding one's personal identity or experiencing an imaginary one.

Picture Montages and the Projection of a Beautiful Self

Most of the wooden houses in Leu have very few decorative objects inside. In some of the poorest dwellings, walls are made of interwoven bamboo on which a few items of clothing and personal belongings (such as baskets and bags) are hung. A few houses, however, have their walls ornamented with objects that serve only an aesthetic purpose, and these are the ones inhabited by Christian converts. In "decorative objects" I include objects that have

---

8. In the course of my research, I met with a dozen adolescents from various districts of the province who were wearing US dog-tag replicas.

more than a mere functional or practical purpose (e.g., clocks, mirrors, or clothes hangers) and whose value to the house dwellers is vested in their visual attractiveness. Siu's house is the most decorated house in the village, both externally and internally. As previously noted, on the outside, two sculpted peacocks flank the staircase leading to the main entrance. Inside, the visitor finds himself or herself in a square room that has access to the kitchen at one end, as well as two small compartments (the two bedrooms) to the side. The two bedrooms are separated from the main room by curtains.

Siu has plastered half the entire wall surface with a multitude of posters featuring Thai actresses, actors, and singers. He told me that he got the posters when he was buying packaged staple foods at the local market. For Siu, the posters were "beautiful," and he enjoyed imagining that all the attractive women were his "girlfriends." At the top of the main wall leading to the small sleeping quarters hang a few pictures of Siu and his wife and cousins. The pictures are striking in style because they superimpose the individuals on a different social and physical environment. In one photograph, Siu and his wife appear dressed as a Khmer couple in their wedding apparel, striking a pose in front of a lavish Thai-inspired house. In another, the couple are dressed in European style, posing next to brand-new motorcycles. All these picture montages are in fact portraits of Siu and his wife that have been cut and pasted onto well-dressed bodies posing near expensive objects amid a sophisticated landscape. In commenting on such images of themselves, my informants all responded that the pictures were beautiful because they made them look special and wealthy.

According to Setha Low and Denise Lawrence-Zúñiga, Western culture perceives the self to be naturally placed inside the body (Low and Lawrence-Zúñiga 2003). Current photographic technology enables any individual to be playfully placed inside any other body with a view to simulating an imaginary—and often unlikely—self. Although for some of the villagers in Leu, the self may be perceived as an intrinsic part of the organic body, relocating one's face (a metonymic form of the self) inside another body is an alternative way to experience a better-looking self. Thanks to such photographic montages, a new self is thus imagined as more elegant and prosperous using socially encoded forms of dress, virtual landscapes, and, to some extent, virtual bodily practices and discourses.

200   Chapter 6

Television Sets and the Anthropological Study of the Other

One of the most visible (and, at night, audible) commodities associated with social status in Leu is the television set. There are three televisions in Leu, all of which are in the houses of relatively wealthy families. Because of the geographic isolation of the village, none of them are connected to cable, nor do they have satellite dishes. Every night between 7.00 p.m. and 10.00 p.m. the three television sets are switched on, each gathering crowds of ten to twenty people, most of them women and children. Unlike mobile phones and motorcycles, the use of the TV set includes not only the owner and his or her household, but also other people in the village. For the owners, sharing their commodity is also a way to share a source of entertainment, thus in some ways taking over the traditional role of the Jorai storytellers.

In the shopkeeper's house, which was home to one of the three televisions, the DVDs played ranged from poor-quality Thai TV series to relatively less poor-quality American action movies. The Thai TV series tell a story that entertains people for several nights, while the action movies allow the audience to see the entire story unfold in a single evening. The audience's reactions and comments suggest that viewing foreign movies provides them with a window to the outside, even an anthropological medium. The depictions of the lives of foreigners, for example, engender a strong curiosity about life abroad, particularly among some of the female viewers. Because they introduce the outside space within the confines of the village, movies and karaoke clips provide potent opportunities for the villagers to contemplate the possibility of an alternative self. For Leu teenagers, karaoke clips in particular enable the transmission of new Khmer songs and fashion trends (themselves inspired by Thai and other foreign cultures). In this way, a creeping isomorphism slowly infiltrates across distant geographic spaces.

One evening the shopkeeper showed the film *Rambo*, the first installment of an American action franchise starring Sylvester Stallone as a Vietnam War veteran. A conventional Hollywood action production, the movie weaves together such interesting themes as American war veterans' difficult reinsertion into civilian life, psychological and physical traumas relating to war, and social injustice and exclusion, as well as livelihood survival strategies. Although movies do not automatically trigger self-identification of the viewer with the character or hero (especially a foreign film with a Caucasian hero and a story line set in a foreign landscape), this seemed to me a good opportunity to gather reactions from the audience.

In the course of watching the film, the audience gasped a few times as the hero faced particularly challenging situations. One such moment involved Rambo stitching a wound in his arm. This graphic scene explicitly illustrated the determination, resourcefulness, and bravery of the hero and triggered reactions of amazement (and sometimes disbelief) from the audience. The movie had a particularly strong impact on very young viewers; many of the boys returned home afterward voicing their desire to become as strong, valiant, and resourceful as Rambo. On the following day, a few of them played games in which they enacted scenes from the movie. This particular form of entertainment did not last, however.

Another scene that demonstrated the hero's impressive survival skills showed Rambo hunting to feed himself. The hero was shown crouching in the top branches of a fir tree waiting to strike a passing animal with a makeshift spear before carrying it off to a cave where he then cooked it over a low smoking fire. I first imagined that such scenes might strike a chord with the stories that were told by survivors of the US bombing. Unfortunately, on this particular night, war survivors did not watch the entire movie but only moments of it before leaving, apparently out of boredom. Most of the viewers were members of the postwar generation (except for a handful of old ladies who appeared particularly entertained by the gory moments).

I asked a few people whether Rambo's hunting style was redolent of Jorai hunting practices. The responses were incredulous shakes of the head and exclamations of "No, we cannot do this!" Most of the male viewers who practice hunting and fishing regularly were fascinated by the hero's efficiency in killing animals. A twenty-five-year-old hunter who was admiring Rambo's long, sharp knife commented that "before" (conveying a sense of remoteness in time), Jorai people could hunt and live that way. This view was later echoed by two villagers who told me, "Today we cannot do this, it's true. We have lost the skills. But our grandfathers knew how to; they were very good hunters and very strong warriors. They would raid entire villages." An interesting point about the film viewing is that my male informants could not fathom surviving the way the hero does, and even in their minds, such a possible scenario was not comparable with the war experience of their elders.

Chapter 6

Locating the Young Self

When I was gathering information about individuals' personal experiences of the war, the discussions I had with my informants either were conducted one-to-one or occurred in the presence of a small audience of younger people. War survivors commented that in general, members of Leu's young generation were interested in hearing stories of their fathers' lives during the conflicts, sometimes asking such questions as "Why was there a war?" "What did those fighters want?" and "Did they want equipment, people, resources?" My informant Nay, the young bombhunter, who sometimes accompanied me to nearby villages, told me that he liked to listen to these kinds of stories. His father had died a soldier at the time of the Vietnamese-installed regime in Cambodia, and Nay's memories of him were limited. Knowing the focus of my research, Nay often asked me these questions. Despite my attempts to answer as best as I could, Nay, like most members of the postconflict generation, could not find any significant personal meaning to the war that had affected his family. Indeed, the older generation's unique, firsthand experience of the past conflicts seemed a source of distance between the two generations. War experience and memory may act as potent identity makers, but for some members of the younger generation, the absence of such lived experience seems to be a source of uncertainty about where they actually stand vis-à-vis their elders and within the history of their region.

Leu war survivors are generally perceived by young people as experienced and wise. Surviving a conflict can be regarded as a way to gain a form of knowledge that cannot be passed on and can be acquired only by living it. In the same way, the narration of personal warfare experience always remains one's own, like a personal and inaccessible object that is beyond the reach of younger villagers. Consequently, people in Leu are reluctant to talk on behalf of someone who lived through a particular conflict since they feel that the experience is located in the individual and thus forms an intrinsic part of him or her. I was told to "ask him directly," as though recounting that person's experience was somehow an illegitimate form of borrowing, comparable to appropriating the objects of the dead.

In Leu and especially in villages closer to larger towns, some young people seem to have grown bored by such narratives of the past, however. For these young persons who want to carve a place for themselves in history or simply live their own personal adventure, locating oneself can be a daunting challenge because they are subject to both past and new influences. In this regard, the local persistence of bomb hunting is noteworthy as an example of a war-associated activity that is being passed on from one generation to the next. As opposed to other traditional practices, searching for live bombs may open up a distinctive experiential space where young individuals can somehow relive the warfare experience of their fathers. This hypothesis needs testing against further ethnographic research into the underlying motivations of this particular segment of the population. However, the question whether this sharing between generations of the bomb-hunting experience might constitute a rite of passage that reconnects the individual with the heritage of the formidable Jorai warriors certainly merits further exploration.

Nay told me that he had formerly gone hunting for bombs regularly and had often reused their explosive contents to fish in the river, but he said that he was currently busy growing cash crops in his *hwa*, which required him to work and stay up the hills most of the year. Nay, like many of my youngest informants, has tried a range of vocations, from farming to building houses. (This rather mirrors the oscillation in his spiritual life between the traditional rituals in the village and Christian gatherings under the influence of his cousin Siu.) When I asked Nay what he wanted to do in the future, he told me that his dream was to go to Phnom Penh and find work there. He also mentioned some distant relatives who might be able to help, but because the dream somehow appeared spatially and practically distant, Nay would wait until some relative came to the village to give him this opportunity.

In contrast to my male informants, young females living in Leu often projected their dreams within socially defined parameters. Just as their spatial movements were limited to well-known areas, likewise contemplation of their future prospects remained within familiar, feasible, and traditional boundaries. Hlany and Hbit were sisters, twelve and fourteen years old, respectively, and for them, the age of marriage was not far away. They told me that they were waiting for the moment when their parents would marry them locally, and then they would start their own family and work in their *hwa*. Hlany, Hbit, and their inseparable girlfriends nonetheless showed great interest in life abroad, and at times the anthropologist took over from the television set and shared with them her firsthand experience of life beyond Leu. The people I worked with were nonetheless puzzled by the idea that

I had come all the way to the village on my own, thus leaving my husband for a long period of time. In the same way, my young female informants strongly disapproved of my not having started a family and felt sorry to come to the conclusion that I must be a "bad wife."

Although it is probable that some of my informants' choices are forced on them either by the lack of access to new opportunities or by the moral duty to perpetuate a traditional lifestyle, personal attachment to the family, the village, or local practices sometimes remains strong. Through their discourses, attitudes, and the choices they eventually made, some of my informants well illustrated what Dournes wrote about the Jorai sense of continuity:

> The individual is a link in a line of succession. When his linking function has been accomplished—ahead of him, because he has left descendants; behind him, because he has been reunited with his ancestors—he can then lose his individuality as a link, as a number in a series. His "self," however, remains, albeit in a different way. Beyond the apparent changes, there remains a deep-seated continuity in each Jorai being, as in a family, always renewed and yet always the same. It is also an image of the life of Jorai society in history: it evolves and changes while remaining itself. (Dournes 1978: 206)

Siu, for example, who had been one of the first to convert to Christianity, was incredibly knowledgeable about the Jorai legends, as well as the lives of his forefathers. Despite his current stand vis-à-vis the village traditional practices, he had become a repository of the knowledge of the past. It is possible that regardless of his religious interests, which have often taken him outside Leu, his broad knowledge may eventually find its way to the next generation.

This chapter has examined various external influences that have led to current social, cultural, and bodily transformations within the village. Transformation can be interpreted as a mode of consumption whereby the individual makes the informed decision to experiment with various modern trends, whether religious, aesthetic, or merely related to commodities. I have used the lenses of religion and commodities to better comprehend where a person chooses to stand in the face of external and internal pressures and how this choice can have life-changing consequences for him or her and, indeed, for the future of the village. Peter van der Veer persuasively argued that there is more to Christian conversion than the mere adoption of a world religion because it may also entail conversion to "forms of modernity" whereby the religious perceptions of the individual and of the collective are transformed under the growing influence of Western discourses and lifestyles. For the anthropologist, "Christian conversion is a "technology of the self'," to use Foucault's notion, which under modern conditions, produces a new subjecthood that is deeply enmeshed in economic globalization and the emergence of a system of nation-states" (Van der Veer 1996: 19).

In this regard, converting to Christianity and consuming external goods can be interpreted both as experiencing a new sphere of knowledge and as creating new social connections, bringing the outside world inside the village precincts via bodily alterations and physical and imaginary travels. As they negotiate challenges of the present and future, members of Leu's new generation are confronted either with remaining on what is locally perceived as a traditional path or with forging their trail away from the life of the village. In times of anxiety and uncertainty, even the most ambitious young individual who dreams of making his or her mark beyond the village boundaries often resumes the traditional path. After the birth of his son, Siu took some time before naming his child. He said that he wanted to give him a Khmer name because they sound "nicer" than Jorai names. A few months later the child was finally given a name: Drit, a traditional Jorai name, I was told.

Conclusion

The theme of this book is local survival strategies in subsistence societies of Southeast Asia. It explores the symbolism of the material culture generated by thirty years of prolonged conflicts, starting from the US bombing of Cambodia. On the one hand, it discusses the ways Leu villagers perceive and interact with explosive and nonexplosive remnants of war that have rendered familiar environments hazardous; on the other, it examines the variety of responses developed by these subsistence farmers to achieve social and economic sustainability and spiritual well-being.

I have sought to explore the variety of approaches that the Jorai inhabitants of Leu have used to rebuild their life physically and psychologically after years of successive wars. I have argued that the day-to-day livelihoods of the villagers demonstrate how resilience, endurance, and creativity can reduce the vulnerabilities inherent in a life of subsistence activities even in a landscape that is deeply scarred by the violence of the past. In a manner that recalls the self-governing peoples of Zomia, the Jorai of Leu have shown that using their own strategies, they can resist and appropriate diverse manifestations of external power to achieve social and economic sustainability and spiritual well-being. As James Scott put it: "If one were a social Darwinian, one might well see the mobility of hill peoples, their spare dispersed communities, their noninherited rankings, their oral culture, their large portfolio of subsistence and identity strategies, and perhaps even their prophetic inclinations as brilliantly suited to a tumultuous environment. They are better adapted to survival as nonsubjects in a political environment of states than to making states themselves" (Scott 2009: 334–35).

In line with "ways of acting in the environment are also ways of perceiving it" (Ingold 2000: 9), the ways in which the ordinary Leu villager tries to break free from the vicissitudes of nature involve the transformative process of domesticating the forested landscape by imposing his or her human mind and physical imprint. This emancipation is furthered by local categorization that sets clear boundaries between the human and the nonhuman, thereby "absorbing, purifying, and civilizing the hybrids by incorporating them either into society or into nature" (Latour 1993: 131). To this end, an item of clothing will act as an effective signifier that will confirm the Jorai villager's status of social being.

The individual's status, however, is confronted by other types of challenges when he or she meets the "other," whose "strangerhood," to borrow Meyer Fortes's term, may vary by degree of nearness or remoteness (Meyer Fortes 1969: 232). This stranger remains fundamentally "not organically connected through established ties of kinship, locality and occupation, with any single one" (Wolff 1950: 404). But the greater the distance between the villager and this alter ego, the more potent and lasting the impact that the encounter will have on both individual and collective life. Indeed, the emergence of the foreign other from unfamiliar horizons has for the past century heralded tumultuous times, most notably in the case of the US bombing, which forced the villagers to seek refuge in the ambiguous realm of the forest in order to evade the obliterating power of technological warfare.

Since the end of the conflicts, people have reconstructed their livelihoods from the rubble in both a literal and a metaphorical sense. Interacting with a familiar landscape, now rendered hazardous, through the collection and re-collection of material, bodily, and intangible remnants of war can lead to financial and spiritual rewards, although not without courting considerable danger.

Although mechanisms for coping with risk can be developed through recovery of material debris, the symbolic appropriation of war-related objects by means of manufacturing and ritual use provides us with a deeper insight into the array of local survival strategies. After the violence generated by civil and regional conflicts and the horror of the Khmer Rouge regime, the resumption of ritual practices provided scope for people to mix the old and the new, adjusting old rituals so that they could address new sorts of bad death and heal the dead who had never been properly buried. At the same time, individuals who have suffered a partial death by incurring injuries from explosive remnants of war equally need to be partially buried before they can be physically reintegrated into the village's social body. Again, it is by ritualistic means that the discontinuities brought by the war can be bridged so that the villagers can resume their lives and reconnect the living and the dead through reciprocal relationships.

After manifestation of the foreign other, the encounter with the dangerous object can be reenacted through the crafting of weaponry replicas, and I conclude that this appropriation can become a therapeutic means for people to reconcile themselves to their violent past. By reconceptualizing violent death as a life-affirming and regenerating experience (Bloch and Parry 1982), the making, resymbolizing, and use of the bombing-plane replica in ritual practices has become an established feature of Leu's post-conflict landscape.

There is a double narrative at work here whereby the material salvaged from the war debris can be given new shapes and meanings and new value. Similarly, both individual and collective memories can be treated as malleable material, which skillful hands can refashion in the same way in order to give past experiences and narrative accounts new shapes and better meaning. In this regard, the role of the craftsperson provides an interesting window into material culture in this physically and spiritually traumatized landscape. Indeed, the wide range of local artistic practices is illuminating in the way it shows a mosaic of memories from different times and places that are encapsulated in manufactured objects.

According to Alfred Gell, art objects mediate a technology aimed at "accomplishment and power rather than mere beauty." Through the acts of making, resymbolizing, incorporation, and display, war-inspired objects have been used for both ritual and everyday purposes so as to become meaningful and aesthetic features of the local landscape. In the words of Setha Low and Denise Lawrence-Zúñiga, "We use objects to evoke experience thus molding experience into symbols and then melding symbols back into experience" (Low and Lawrence-Zúñiga 2003: 5). However, in the case of those war survivors endowed with a craftsperson's skills, the act of molding can become a self-enhancing process that gives better shape to past and future experience of defeat, loss, and uncertainty.

Some of these objects offer layers of narrative accounts, thus acting as vistas on the ways conflict survivors reflect on their past and the ways members of the younger generation of villagers inherit this past and in turn reflect on it. In this sense, the inspired craftsperson may claim that "the past is never dead. It's not even the past" (Faulkner 1951, in Act I, scene 3), since memories of the present and future may be shaped out of their own material substance. Sculpting, painting, carving, and fabric weaving can become practical means to reorganize the threads of history, thus offering vivid new stories of past, present, and future local lives.

As they gaze into their future, members of Leu's postconflict generation also try to make sense of a violent past that they have inherited and to carve their own historical space in a fast-changing world. In a sense, they stand at a crossroads between "selfing or othering," to borrow Christian Postert's words (2004: 110). The modern state has penetrated the lives of ethnic-minority peoples living in northeastern Cambodia much more decisively than before.

Today new manifestations of power, this time in the guise of religious and material forms of consumption, have penetrated the village space, at times creating tensions, for example, between Christian converts and the defenders of traditional practices. Members of the postconflict generation often perceive such new influences as a way to experiment with various identities while pondering the path they will choose to create their own future. Siu, one of my most valuable informants and a friend, has chosen one that appears to involve deliberately walking away from long-established tradition. At the same time, he is—perhaps without acknowledging it—a vital repository of Jorai cultural and historical knowledge. Although he was aspiring to new social spaces in the company of fellow Christian converts, he told me that he was going to teach his son wood-carving, just as his grandfather had once taught his father and his father had taught him.

REFERENCES

Agamben, Giorgio. 1998. *Homo Sacer: Sovereign Power and Bare Life*. Stanford, CA: Stanford University Press.
Ang, Chouléan. 1986. *Les êtres surnaturels dans la religion populaire Khmère*. Paris: Cedoreck.
Appadurai, Arjun, ed. 1986. *The Social Life of Things: Commodities in Cultural Perspective*. Cambridge: Cambridge University Press.
Aso, Mitch. 2013. "Rubber and Race in Rural Colonial Cambodia (1920s–1954)." *Siksācakr* 12–13: 127–38.
Baird, Ian. 2009. "Identities and Space: The Geographies of Religious Change amongst the Brao in Northeastern Cambodia." *Anthropos* 104: 457–68.
———. 2010. "Different Views of History: Shades of Irredentism along the Laos-Cambodia Border." *Journal of Southeast Asian Studies* 41 (2): 187–213.
———. 2011. "The Construction of 'Indigenous Peoples' in Cambodia." In *Alterities in Asia: Reflections on Identity and Regionalism*, edited by Leong Yew, 155–76. London: Routledge.
Baird, Ian, and Bruce Shoemaker. 2008. *People, Livelihoods and Development in the Xekong River Basin, Laos*. Bangkok: White Lotus.
Beck, Ulrich. 1992. *Risk Society: Towards a New Modernity*. London: Sage Publications.

Becker, Elizabeth. 1986. *When the War Was Over: The Voices of Cambodia's Revolution and Its People*. New York: Simon and Schuster.
Biersack, Aletta. 1991. *Clio in Oceania*. Washington, DC: Smithsonian Institution Press.
Bird-David, Nurit. 1992. "Beyond 'The Original Affluent Society': A Culturalist Reformulation." *Current Anthropology* 33 (1): 25–47.
Bloch, Maurice. 1998. *How We Think They Think: Anthropological Approaches to Cognition, Memory, and Literacy*. Oxford: Westview Press.
Bloch, Maurice, and Jonathan Parry. 1982. *Death and the Regeneration of Life*. Cambridge: Cambridge University Press.
Boholm, Åsa. 1996. "Risk Perception and Social Anthropology: Critique of Cultural Theory." *Ethnos* 61 (1–2): 64–84.
Bottomley, Ruth. 2001. *Spontaneous De-mining Initiatives: Mine Clearance by Villagers in Rural Cambodia; Final Study Report*. Phnom Penh: Handicap International Belgium.
Boucheret, Marianne. 2013. "Les terres à 'caoutchouc' du Cambodge: Histoire d'un eldorado colonial entre les deux guerres mondiales." *Siksācakr* 12–13: 139–49.
Boulbet, Jean. 1975. *Paysans de la forêt*. Paris: École Française d'Extrême-Orient.
Bourdier, Frédéric. 2006. *The Mountain of Precious Stones, Ratanakiri, Cambodia: Essays in Social Anthropology*. Siem Reap: Center for Khmer Studies.
———. 2009. *Ethnographie des populations indigènes du nord-ouest cambodgien. La montagne aux pierres précieuses (Ratanakiri)*. Paris : L'Harmattan.
———. 2014. *Indigenous Groups in Cambodia: An Updated Situation*. Phnom Penh: Asian Indigenous Peoples Pact.
Bourdieu, Pierre. 1977. *Outline of a Theory of Practice*. Cambridge: Cambridge University Press.
Bulletin de l'École Française d'Extrême-Orient. 1904. *Bibliographical Notes* 4, no. 1: 487–89.
Butler, Judy. 1993. *Bodies That Matter: On the Discursive Limits of "Sex."* London: Routledge.
Caplan, Pat. 2000. *Risk Revisited*. London: Pluto Press.
Centre for Advanced Studies (CAS) Interdisciplinary Research on Ethnic Groups in Cambodia. "Final Draft Reports for Discussion at the National Symposium on Ethnic Groups in Cambodia." Presented in Phnom Penh, 18–19 July, 1996.
Chambert-Loir, Henri, and Anthony Reid. 2002. *The Potent Dead: Ancestors, Saints, and Heroes in Contemporary Indonesia*. Honolulu: University of Hawaii Press.
Chandler, David. 1994. *A History of Cambodia*. Bangkok: White Lotus.
———. 1999. *Voices from S-21: Terror and History in Pol Pot's Secret Prison*. Berkeley: University of California Press.
Chomski, Noam, and Edward S. Herman. 1979. *After the Cataclysm: Postwar Indochina and the Reconstruction of Imperial Ideology; The Political Economy of Human Rights*. Vol. 2. Cambridge, MA: South End Press.
Choulean, Ang. 1986. *Les êtres surnaturels dans la religion populaire Khmère*. Paris: Cedoreck.
Collins English Dictionary. 1994. Glasgow: Harper Collins.
Colm, Sara. 1998. "Pol Pot: the Secret 60s, Building the 'People's War' among the Tribal Communities." *Phnom Penh Post*. April 24–May 7.

Condominas, Georges. 1957. *Nous avons mangé la forêt de la pierre-génie Gôo.* Paris: Mercure de France.

———. 1972. "Deux aspects de la civilisation du végétal an Asie du Sud-Est." *Études de géographie tropicale offertes à Pierre Gourou.* Paris: Mouton.

———. 1980. *L'espace social: A propos de l'Asie du Sud-Est.* Paris: Flammarion.

Connerton, Paul. 1989. *How Societies Remember.* Cambridge: Cambridge University Press.

Coville, Elizabeth. 2002. "Remembering our dead: the care of the ancestors in Tana Toraja." In *The Potent Dead: Ancestors, Saints and Heroes in Contemporary Indonesia*, edited by Henri Chambert-Loir and Anthony Reid, 69–87. Honolulu: University of Hawaii Press.

Cupet, Pierre-Paul. 1900. *Mission Pavie Indo-Chine, 1879–1895: Géographie et voyages III; Voyages au Laos et chez les sauvages du Sud-Est de l'Indo-chine.* Paris: Ernest Leroux.

De Koninck, Rodolphe, Frédéric Durand, and Frédéric Fortunel. 2005. *Agriculture, environnement et sociétés sur les hautes terres du Viêt Nam.* Toulouse: Arkuiris-IRASEC.

Delvert, Jean. 1994. *Le paysan cambodgien.* Paris: L'Harmattan.

Dening, Greg. 1988. *History's Anthropology: the Death of William Gooch.* A.S.A.O. Special Publication no. 2. Lanham, MD: University Press of America.

Diffloth, Gérard. 2013. *Kuay in Cambodia: A Vocabulary with Historical Comments.* Phnom Penh: Tuk Tuk Editions.

DiGregorio. Michael. 1995. "Recycling in Hanoi." Southeast Asia Discussion List. http://www.hartford-hwp.com/archives/25b/003.html.

Diguet, Edouard. 1908. *Les montagnards du Tonkin.* Paris: Augustin Challamel.

Douglas, Mary. 1994. *Risk and Blame: Essays in Cultural Theory.* London: Routledge.

———. 2002. *Purity and Danger.* Oxford: Routledge.

Douglas, Mary, and A. Wildavsky. 1983. *Risk and Culture: An Essay on the Selection of Technological and Environmental Dangers.* Berkeley: University of California Press.

Dournes, Jacques. 1968. "La figuration humaine dans l'art funéraire Jarai." *Objets et Mondes* 8 (2): 87–118.

———. 1969. *Bois-bambou: Aspect végétal de l'univers jörai.* Paris: Editions du Centre National de la Recherche Scientifique.

———. 1972. *Coordonnées—Structures jörai familiales et sociales.* Paris: Institut d'ethnologie.

———. 1975. "La mort c'est l'autre: La geste comparée des vivants et des défunts jorai." *Objets et Mondes* 15 (4): 341–48.

———. 1977. *Pötao: Une théorie du pouvoir chez les Indochinois Jörai.* Paris: Flammarion.

———. 1978. *Fôret, femme, folie: Une traversée de l'imaginaire jörai.* Paris: Aubier-Montaigne.

———. 1987. *Florilège jörai.* Paris: Sudestasie.

Dovert, Stéphane 2005. In *Agriculture, environnement et sociétés sur les Hautes terres du Viêt Nam*, edited by Rodolphe De Koninck, Frédéric Durand, Frédéric Fortunel. Toulouse: Arkuiris-IRASEC.

Dunlop, Nic. 2005. *The Lost Executioner: A Story of the Khmer Rouge.* London: Bloomsbury.

Dupaigne, Bernard. 1987. "Les maîtres du feu et du fer: Étude de la métallurgie du fer chez les kouy du nord du Cambodge, dans le contexte historique et ethnographique de l'ensemble khmer." Thesis, Université de Paris X, Paris.

Eriksen, Thomas. 2001. *Small Places, Large Issues: An Introduction to Social and Cultural Anthropology.* London: Pluto Press.

Faulkner, William. 1951. *Requiem for a nun.* New York: Random House.

Ferguson, James. 1994. *The Anti-politics Machine.* Minneapolis: University of Minnesota Press.

Fortes, Meyer. 1969. *Kinship and The Social Order: The Legacy of Lewis Henry Morgan.* Oxford: Routledge.

Geertz, Clifford. 1973. *The Interpretation of Cultures.* New York: Basic Books.

Gell, Alfred. 1996. "Vogel's Net: Traps as Artworks and Artworks as Traps." *Journal of Material Culture* 1: 15–38.

———. 1998. *Art and Agency: An Anthropological Theory.* Oxford: Clarendon Press.

GICHD (Geneva International Centre for Humanitarian Demining). 2005. *A Study of Scrap Metal Collection in Lao PDR.* Geneva: GICHD.

Godelier, Maurice. 1984. *L'idéel et le matériel: Pensée, économies, sociétés.* Paris: Fayard.

Gourou, Pierre. 1970. "La civilisation du végétal." In *Recueil d'articles.* Bruxelles: Société Royale Belge de Géographie. 225–36.

Goy, Bertrand, and Jean-Yves Coué. 2006. *Jaraï: Art de guerre et de mort chez les montagnards d'Indochine.* Paris: Les Indes Savantes.

Guérin, Mathieu, Andrew Hardy, Nguyên Văn Chính, Stan Tan Boon Hwee. 2003. *Des montagnards aux minorités ethniques: Quelle intégration nationale pour les habitants des hautes terres du Viet Nam et du Cambodge.* Paris: L'Harmattan, IRASEC.

Gustafsson, Mai Lan. 2009. *War and Shadows: The Haunting of Vietnam.* Ithaca, NY: Cornell University Press.

Habermas, Jürgen. 1996. "Modernity: An Unfinished Project." In *Habermas and the Unfinished Project of Modernity*, edited by Maurizio Passerin d'Entrèves and Seyla Benhabib, 38–55. Cambridge: Polity.

Halbwachs, Maurice. 1992. *On Collective Memory.* Chicago: University of Chicago Press.

Hardy, Andrew. 2015. *The Barefoot Anthropologist: The Highlands of Champa and Vietnam in the Words of Jacques Dournes.* Paris: EFEO–Silkworm Books.

Harrison, Simon. 2008. "War Mementos and the Souls of Missing Soldiers: Returning Effects of the Battlefield Dead." *Journal of the Royal Anthropological Institute* 14: 774–790.

Hawk, David. 1995. *Minorities in Cambodia.* London: Minority Rights Group.

Hawley, Thomas. 2005. *The Remains of War: Bodies, Politics, and the Search for American Soldiers Unaccounted For in Southeast Asia.* Durham, NC: Duke University Press.

Hertz, Robert. 1960. *Death and the Right Hand.* Translated by Rodney Needham and Claudia Needham. London: Cohen and West.

Hickey, Gerald. 1982. *Free in the Forest: Ethnohistory of the Vietnamese Central Highlands, 1954–1976.* New Haven, CT: Yale University Press.

———. 2002. *Window on a War: An Anthropologist in the Vietnam Conflict.* Lubbock: Texas Tech University Press.

Hinton, Alex. 2005. *Why Did They Kill? Cambodia in the Shadow of Genocide.* Berkeley: University of California Press.

Huckshorn, Kristin, and Tim Larimer. 1996. "U.S. Fails to Monitor Hanoi's Spending." *Honolulu's Advertiser.* April 28, A1–A2.

Human Rights Watch Report. 2011. https://www.hrw.org/world-report/2011/country-chapters/cambodia.

Human Rights Watch Report. 2015. https://www.hrw.org/world-report/2015/country-chapters/cambodia.

Humphrey, Caroline, and James Laidlaw. 1994. *The Archetypal Actions of Ritual: A Theory of Ritual Illustrated by the Jain Rite of Worship.* Oxford: Oxford University Press.

Ingold, Tim. 1980. *Hunters, Pastoralists, and Ranchers: Reindeer Economies and Their Transformations.* Cambridge: Cambridge University Press.

———. 2000. *The Perception of the Environment: Essays in Livelihood, Dwelling and Skill.* London: Routledge.

Ironside, Jeremy. 2013. "Thinking outside the Fence: Exploring Culture/Land Relationships; A Case Study of Ratanakiri Province." PhD thesis, University of Otago, Dunedin, New Zealand.

Jonsson, Hjorleifur. 2010. "Above and Beyond: Zomia and the Ethnographic Challenge of/for Regional History." *History and Anthropology* 21: 191–212.

Kansteiner, Wolf. 2002. "Finding Meaning in Memory: A Methodological Critique of Collective Memory Studies." *History and Theory* 41 (2): 179–97.

Kaplan, Martha. 1995. *Neither Cargo nor Cult: Ritual Politics and the Colonial Imagination in Fiji.* Durham, NC: Duke University Press.

Keane, Webb. 1996. "Materialism, Missionaries, and Modern Subjects in Colonial Indonesia." In *Conversion to Modernities: The Globalization of Christianity*, edited by Peter van der Veer, 137–70. New York: Routledge.

Kiernan, Ben. 1996. *The Pol Pot Regime: Race, Power, and Genocide in Cambodia under the Khmer Rouge, 1975–79.* New Haven, CT: Yale University Press.

Kondo, Dorinne. 1990. *Crafting Selves: Power, Gender, and Discourses of Identity in a Japanese Workplace.* Chicago: University of Chicago Press.

Kopytoff, Igor. 1986. "The Cultural Biography of Things: Commoditization as Process." In *The Social Life of Things: Commodities in Cultural Perspective*, edited by Arjun Appadurai, 64–91. Cambridge: Cambridge University Press.

Kwon, Heonik. 2006. *After the Massacre: Commemoration and Consolation in Ha My and My Lai.* Berkeley: University of California Press.

———. 2008. *Ghosts of War in Vietnam.* Cambridge: Cambridge University Press.

Lafont, Pierre Bernard. 1963. *Prières Jarai.* Paris: École Française d'Extrême-Orient.

Lap, Siu M. 2009. "Developing the First Preliminary Dictionary of North American Jarai." Master's thesis in anthropology, Texas Tech University, Texas.

Latour, Bruno. 1991. *Nous n'avons jamais été modernes: Essai d'anthropologie symétrique.* Paris: La Découverte.

Lee, Gary Yia. 2000. "Bandits or Hebels? Hmong Resistance in the New Lao State." *Indigenous Affairs* 4 (October–December): 6–15.

Le Roux, Pierre, and Bernard Sellato. 2006. *Les messagers divins: Aspects esthétiques et symboliques des oiseaux en Asie du Sud-Est.* Paris: Connaissances et Savoirs.

Lesinski, Jeanne. 1998. *MIAs: A Reference Handbook*. Santa Barbara, CA: ABC-CLIO.
Lévi-Strauss, Claude. 1966. *The Savage Mind*. Chicago: University of Chicago Press.
Lewis, Norman. 1951. *A Dragon Apparent: Travels in Indochina*. London: Jonathan Cape.
Lindstrom, Lamont. 1993. *Cargo Cult: Strange Stories of Desire from Melanesia and Beyond*. Honolulu: University of Hawaii Press.
Low, Setha, and Denise Lawrence-Zúñiga, eds. 2003. *The Anthropology of Space and Place: Locating Culture*. Oxford: Blackwell.
Mabbett, Ian, and David P. Chandler. 1995. *The Khmers*. Oxford: Blackwell.
Maître, Henri. 1912. *Les jungles moï: Mission Henri Maître (1909–1911) Indochine Sud-Centrale*. Paris: Emile Larose.
Malinowski, Bronislaw. 1922. *Argonauts of the Western Pacific: An Account of Native Enterprise and Adventure in the Archipelagoes of Melanesian New Guinea*. London: George Routledge and Sons.
Matras-Troubetzkoy, Jacqueline. 1983. *Un village en forêt: L'essartage chez les Brou du Cambodge*. Paris: SELAF.
Merleau-Ponty, Maurice. 1962. *Phenomenology of Perception*. Translated by Colin Smith. London: Routledge and Kegan Paul.
Meyer, Charles. 1965–66. "Les mystérieuses relations entre les rois du Cambodge et les 'potâo' des Jarai." *Etudes Cambodgiennes*, no. 4 (October–December): 14–26.
——. 1971. *Derrière le sourire khmer*. Paris: Librairie Plon.
Michaud, Jean. 2006. *Historical Dictionary of the Peoples of the Southeast Asian Massif*. Lanham, MD: Scarecrow Press.
Mikaelian, Grégory. 2009. *La royauté d'Oudong: Réformes des institutions et crise du pouvoir dans le royaume khmer du XVIIème siècle*. Paris: PUPS.
Milhaupt, Terry. 2014. *Kimono: A Modern History*. London: Reaktion Books.
Mills, Barbara J., and William H. Walker eds. 2008. *Memory Work: Archaeologies of Material Practices*. Santa Fe, NM: School for Advanced Research Press.
Morrison, Gayle. 2007. *Sky Is Falling: An Oral History of the CIA's Evacuation of the Hmong from Laos*. Jefferson, NC: McFarland.
Mourat, Jean. 1883. *Le royaume du Cambodge*. Paris: Ernest Leroux.
Moyes, Richard. 2004. *Tampering: Deliberate Handling and Use of Live Ordnance in Cambodia*. Phnom Penh: Handicap International Belgium, Mines Advisory Group, Norwegian People's Aid.
Munn, Nancy. 1996. "Excluded Spaces: The Figure of the Australian Aboriginal Landscape." *Critical Inquiry*. 22, no. 3 (Spring): 446–65.
Ngo, Van Doanh. 1991. "Notes sur les cérémonies funéraires des Jarai et des Bahnar (Centre Vietnam)." Translated by Henri Chambert-Loir. *Archipel* 42: 39–45.
NGO Forum on Cambodia. 2006. *Indigenous Peoples in Cambodia*. Phnom Penh: NGO Forum on Cambodia.
Nicolle, R. 1940. *Lexique Français-Jaray et Jaray-Français*. Hanoi: Imprimerie G. Taupin & Cie.
Nora, Pierre. 1989. "Between Memory and History: Les Lieux de Mémoire." *Representations* Special Issue: Memory and Counter-Memory, no. 26 (Spring): 7–24.
Owen, Taylor, and Ben Kiernan. 2006. "Bombs over Cambodia." *The Walrus* (October): 62–69.

Patary, Bernard. 2013. "Jean-Claude Miche (1805–1873), missionaire catholique, témoin singulier et acteur ambivalent du fait colonial au Cambodge." *Siksācakr* 12–13: 39–55.
Paterson, Gordon. n.d. "Animist Cosmology and Environmental Initiatives in Northeast Cambodia." Paper presented at the International Symposium of the Institute for International Studies at Meiji University, Japan.
Pavie, Auguste. 1898. *Mission Pavie Indo-Chine, 1874–1895: Etudes diverses I; Recherches sur la littérature du Cambodge, du Laos et du Siam*. Paris: Ernest Leroux.
Pinney, Christopher, and Nicholas Thomas. 2001. *Beyond Aesthetic: Art and the Technology of Enchantment*. Oxford: Berg.
Popkin, Samuel. 1979. *The Rational Peasant: The Political Economy of Rural Society in Vietnam*. Berkeley: University of California Press.
Postert, Christian. 2004. "Completing or Competing? Contexts of Hmong Selfing/Othering in Laos." In *Grammars of Identity/Alterity: A Structural Approach*, edited by Gerd Baumann and Andre Gingrich, 101–111. New York: Berghahn Books.
Reznick, Jeffrey. 2004. "Prostheses and Propaganda: Materiality and the Human Body in the Great War." In *Matters of Conflict: Material Culture, Memory and the First World War*, edited by Nicholas J. Saunders, 51–61. Abingdon, UK: Routledge.
Ricoeur, Paul. 2004. *Memory, History, Forgetting*. Chicago: University of Chicago Press.
Rosaldo, Renato. 1980. *Ilongot Headhunting, 1883–1974: A Study in Society and History*. Stanford, CA: Stanford University Press.
Russell, Elaine. 2013. "Laos—Living with Unexploded Ordnance: Past Memories and Present Realities." In *Interacting with a Violent Past: Reading Post-conflict Landscapes in Cambodia, Laos and Vietnam*, edited by Vatthana Pholsena and Oliver Tappe, 96–134. Singapore: NUS Press.
Sahlins, Marshall. 1985. *Islands of History*. Chicago: University of Chicago Press.
Salemink, Oscar. 2002. *The Ethnography of Vietnam's Central Highlanders: A Historical Contextualisation, 1850–1990*. London: Routledge.
———. 2004. "Enclosing the Highlands: Socialist, Capitalist and Protestant Conversions of Vietnam's Central Highlanders." Paper presented at the University of Oslo, November 15.
Saunders, Nicholas J. 2003. *Trench Art: Materialities and Memories of War*. Oxford: Berg.
Scheper-Hugues, Nancy, and Philippe Bourgois, eds. 2004. *Violence in War and Peace: An Anthology*. Oxford: Blackwell Publishing.
Schwenkel, Christina. 2013. "War Debris in Postwar Society: Managing Risk and Uncertainty in the DMZ." In *Interacting with a Violent Past: Reading Post-conflict Landscapes in Cambodia, Laos and Vietnam*, edited by Vatthana Pholsena and Oliver Tappe, 135–56. Singapore: NUS Press.
Scott, James. 1976. *The Moral Economy of the Peasant: Subsistence and Rebellion in Southeast Asia*. New Haven, CT: Yale University Press.
———. 2009. *The Art of Not Being Governed. An Anarchist History of Upland Southeast Asia*. New Haven, CT: Yale University Press.
Sennett, Richard. 2008. *The Craftsman*. London: Penguin Books.
Simmel, Georg. 1971. *On Individuality and Social Forms*. Chicago: University of Chicago Press.

Simonnet, Christian. 1977. *Les tigres auront plus pitié*. Paris: La salle des martyrs.
Stendhal. 1854. *Le Rouge et le Noir*. Paris: Michel Lévy frères.
Strathern, Marilyn. 1988. *The Gender of the Gift: Problems with Women and Problems with Society in Melanesia*. Berkeley: University of California Press.
———. 2004. *Partial Connections*. Lanham, MD: Rowman and Littlefield.
———. 2005. *Kinship, Law and the Unexpected. Relatives Are Always a Surprise*. Cambridge: Cambridge University Press.
Strathern, Marilyn et al. 1993. *Technologies of Procreation. Kinship in the Age of Assisted Conception*. London: Routledge.
Taussig, Michael. 1993. *Mimesis and Alterity: A Particular History of the Senses*. New York: Routledge.
Thomas, Nicholas. 1995. *Oceanic Art*. London: Thames and Hudson.
Turner, Victor. 1969. *The Ritual Process: Structure and Anti-structure*. London: Routledge and Kegan Paul.
Uk, Krisna. 2007. "Local Perceptions and Responses to Risk—A Comparative Study of Two Cambodian Villages." In *Lao PDR Risk Management and Mitigation Model*, edited by GICHD, 47–78. Geneva: GICHD.
Valeri, Valerio. 2000. *The Forest of Taboos: Morality, Hunting, and Identity among the Huaulu of the Moluccas*. Madison: University of Wisconsin Press.
Van der Veer, Peter, ed. 1996. *Conversion to Modernities: The Globalization of Christianity*. New York: Routledge.
Van Gennep, Arnold. 1960. *The Rites of Passage*. Chicago: University of Chicago Press.
Vargyas, Gábor. 2013. "Soldier's Dog-Tag in a Shamanistic Headdress—A Semiotic Guerrilla Warfare?" Paper presented at the 11th Conference of the International Society for Shamanistic Research. September 6, 2013. Guizhou, China.
Vickery, Michael. 1986. *Kampuchea: Politics, Economics and Society*. London: Pinter.
Vom Bruck, Gabriele, and Barbara Bodenhorn, eds. 2006. *An Anthropology of Names and Naming*. Cambridge: Cambridge University Press.
Weiner, Annette B., and Jane Schneider, eds. 1989. *Cloth and Human Experience*. Washington, DC: Smithsonian Institution.
White, Joanna. 1995. *The Indigenous Highlanders of the Northeast: An Uncertain Future*. Phnom Penh: Centre for Advanced Studies.
Woodburn, James. 1982. "Egalitarian Societies." *Man* 17, no. 3: 431–51.
Wolff, Kurt H. 1950. *The Sociology of Georg Simmel*. New York: Free Press.
Worsley, Peter. 1957. *The Trumpet Shall Sound: A Study of "Cargo" Cults in Melanesia*. London: MacGibbon and Kee.

Index

aagn gnogn (pipe), 150–51
aagn prieuw (pipe), 150–51
abandonment of grave (*pojah*), 122–23
abductions, 99
Aborigines, 186
accident, 69, 70, 89–90, 91–94, 130–35
acculturation, 27–30, 41–43
acephalous societies, xxi–xxiii
adjusting rituals, 111–23, 112*f*
administration (*angkar*), 70–71
administrators, 21, 37–38. *See also* Leclère, Adhémard; Odend'hal, Prosper
adolescents, 90, 197–98, 200
adults, anthropologist viewed by, 31. *See also* men; women
Afghan war rugs, 172–73
afterlife, 114–15, 121–22, 127, 191–92
Agamben, Giorgio, 108
agency, 81, 85, 98–99, 105
agent, 172–73
agriculture, xxii, 51–52, 78, 85

aide-mémoire, 39–40
Air Force, US, xxiii, 64. *See also* bombardments
ancestors, 16, 21–23, 120, 125
Andong Meas district, 4, 38n3, 78–80, 89–90, 95, 187. *See also* Plói Leu, Cambodia
angkar (administration), 70–71
angkarech (bodyguard), 42–43, 45, 47. *See also* Phuon, Phi; Yeng, Pou
animals, 11, 12, 14, 140, 201. *See also* sacrifices
animism, 8–9, 48–49, 176–94. *See also* sacrifices
anthropologists, xxiv–xxv, 203–4, 205; adults viewing, 31; French, xxvi, 37; missionaries uncomfortable with, 190
anthropology, 80–81, 200–201
antipersonnel land mines (APM), 69, 70, 71
Anti-politics Machine, The (Foucault), 82
Appadurai, Arjun, 172–74, 194
arăt (hair on chest), 14
areak. *See* spirits

art, 135–44, 171–74. *See also* carving; sculptures
Art and Agency (Gell), 98
assimilation, 27–30, 41–43
associations (*correspondances*), 3
atâo. See ghosts
Augustine (saint), 170–71
aunt (*ming*), 25
authenticity, 171–74
ayat. See enemy

Bâ, Amadou, 145
bad death (*glai*), 7, 16, 105, 123–25. *See also* forest
Bahnar, 21, 101
Baird, Ian, xv–xvi, xvii, 29, 36, 177, 189
bamboo, 125. *See also* pipe
Banlung, Cambodia, 88, 104, 176, 190–91, 193–94, 196–97
Banteay Meanchey, xiii
base people. *See* highlanders
bathing, 10
Battambang, xiii, 191
beautiful self, 198–99
Beck, Ulrich, 80, 81, 82, 105
Becker, Elizabeth, 30, 44–45
belongings, 97–98, 113–18, 127
Bessac, Susanne, 163
bestiality, 13–14
Beuragn, Keulagn, 154–58, 154f, 156f
Bible, 191–94
Bible Society International (BSI), 192
biography, 95–96, 172–74
Bird-David, Nurit, 3, 58
birth, 17, 205
black dog, 14–15
blacksmith, xxii, 87, 88. *See also* Tham
blah ngǎ. See war
Blen, Luyin, 4, 15, 18, 33, 50, 181–83; on ancestors, 125; on bombs, 69, 91, 93–94; on Buddhism, 187; land mines for, 69; on mobile phone, 195; on planes, 54, 55; on rice-wine jars, 48; on ritual, 135; on script, 27; Siu on, 184; on survivors, 69; on Veam, 118–19; years used by, 65–66
Blim, 92
Bloch, Maurice, 126
bodies, 11–12, 70, 71–72, 100–108, 113–18, 199
bodyguard (*angkarech*), 42–43, 45, 47. *See also* Phuon, Phi; Yeng, Pou

boh pó čah (bombs), 60, 68–69, 91, 93–94, 99. *See also* accident
Bok, Cambodia, 8–9, 90–91
Bokeo district, 38, 88
bombardments, xiv–xv, 34, 43, 52–63, 158, 201. *See also* explosive remnants of war; plane; scrap metal; conspiracy theories generated by, 64; dead influenced by, 126; KR helped by, 51; map, 83f; tonnage, 64–65
bomb hunter, 18, 87, 90, 91–94, 92
bomb hunting, 84, 89–91, 203
bombs (*boh pó čah* or *luk tek*), 60, 68–69, 91, 93–94, 99. *See also* accident
böngat. See soul
bong pa-on chun chiet (ethnic brothers and sisters), xvii
Borneo, 113
Boulbet, Jean, 2–3
boundaries, 1, 3, 7–9, 10–11, 12, 32
Bourdier, Frédéric, 16. *See also* Phuon, Phi
Bourdieu, Pierre, 87
boys, 13–14, 15, 201. *See also* son; funerary monument for, 154–58, 154f, 156f; grave of, 137
Brao, xvii, 28, 117
breaking of objects (*póčah*), 117–18, 125
British, 54
"British Propaganda and How It Helped the Final Victory" (Fyfe), 54
brothers, 14
Bru, 96
Buddhism, 187
buffalo, 133–35, 138–41, 183
buffer zone, 133–35
Butler, Judith, 108

Cambodia, xiii–xv, xx, xxiii–xxiv, 37–41, 47. *See also* Bok, Cambodia; Bokeo district; bombardments; Ho Chi Minh Trail; Kampuchea; Mondulkiri province; Phnom Penh, Cambodia; Plói Leu, Cambodia; Ratanakiri province; army of, 43; Banlung in, 88, 104, 176, 190–91, 193–94, 196–97; Battambang in, xiii, 191; belongings appropriated in, 97–98; ethnic minorities in, xix, 27–30; government of, 81; Jorai in, xii, xviii–xix; Lom in, 189; Mek in, 159–60; nation-building programme of, xvii;

Index

O'Chheukrom in, 94; O You Dav in, 153–58, 154f, 156f; Peuho in, 153–58, 154f, 156f; Plói Laom in, 165–74, 167f; Plói Leu Krong in, 139–40; Plói Phdol Krom in, 90, 92; Preah Vihear in, 69; Tang in, 97–98; Thailand imported from by, 78; Vietnam and, 78; Vietnamese invading, 51–52; Vietnam War drawing in, 43; Yeak Laom district in, 165–74, 167f
Cambodia Mine/ERW Victim Information System, 90
Cambodian Communist Party, 30
Cambodian Mine Action and Victim Assistance Authority, xiii–xiv, 52
Cambodian People's Party (CPP), 52n14
Cambridge Museum of Archaeology and Anthropology, 151–53, 152f
Caplan, Pat, 85
cargo-cult phenomenon, 141
Carruthers, Mary, 170–71
carver. *See* Siu
carving, 146–53, 152f, 161–65, 162f
caterpillar (*hlăt*), 151, 152–53, 152f
Catholic mission, 21–22
cemetery (*pösat*), 120, 135–38, 147–48. *See also* elephants
Central Highlands, xix, xxii, 22, 62
Central Intelligence Agency (CIA), 56
central Khmer (*Khmer Kandal*). *See* Khmers
ceremonies, 119, 176–77. *See also* funerals; rituals; sacrifices
Chams, 21
Chao Fa movement, 56
charity, 8
charter, 35–37
chemicals, 60
chief, 176
children, xxv, 13–14, 115–16, 182–83. *See also* boys; girls; age of, 178n1; anthropologist's encounter with, 31; clothes worn by, 10–11; forest for, 5, 6; funerary monument for, 154–58, 154f, 156f; ghosts faced by, 31; household contributed to by, 77; nakedness of, 10–11; necklaces keeping safe, 97; risk and, 85, 89; stranger feared by, 30, 31, 32; strong, 47
China, 86, 87, 88
Chocó, 141
chonchiet (nationality), xvi–xvii

chonchiet Jorai, xvii
chonchiet Kmay. *See* Khmers
Christianity, 176–94, 198–99
circumpolar North, 140
civilisation du végétal, 2
clothing (*hnim*), 9–15, 28, 197–98
coal (*Plagn Tchu*), 32
cognitive memory, 170–71
collectivization plans, 46, 48
Collins English Dictionary, 80
Colm, Sara, 42
colonial period, 37–41
commodities, 194–201
Communists, 41–43, 56–57. *See also* Khmer Rouge
communities, 76–77, 105, 189–90
Condominas, Georges, 2, 80
Congress, US, 64
Connerton, Paul, 170
conspiracy theories, 64
consumers, 81, 169–74
continuity, 118–22, 204
conversions, 177–94, 198–99
Cook, James, 55–56
coping mechanisms, 76–85
correspondances (associations), 3
Coué, Jean-Yves, xxvi
counter-fear, 9
coup d'état, 43, 52
Coville, Elizabeth, 115, 128, 142
craftsmanship, 150
craftsmen, xxiv, 159–60
craftswomen, xxiv, 161–65, 162f. *See also* Sing
Cuenot, Etienne, 22
cultural disruptions, 59–63
cup, 67
Cupet, Pierre-Paul, 178n1

Dayak, 113
dead, 11–12. *See also* funeral; ghosts; belongings of, 97–98; body, 113–18; bombing influencing, 126; caring for, 125–30; as complete, 113–18; Dournes on, 123; face of, 113; foreign, 97–98; forest association of, 121, 125, 131; Hertz on, 126; man seeing, 113; objects of, 113–18, 135–44; rituals influencing unburied, 128–30; servants of, 143; as unburied, 125–30; villagers on, 131

deaths, 11–12, 111–23, 112f, 124–35, 142–43, 179–80. *See also* bad death; funeral; of children, 182–83; dreaming as, 18; of ethnic minorities, 50; fear of, 23; Ksor influenced by, 186; malnutrition caused by, 50; of settlers, 41; of village elder, 139–40
decorative objects, 198–99
decree, 46, 48–51
Delvert, Jean, xii
demining, 81–84, 83f, 94, 99
Democratic Kampuchea. *See* Kampuchea
detention center, 133
development sector, 81–84, 83f
"Dictionary of North American Jarai," 127
DiGregorio, Michael, xxii–xxiii, 89
Dinh Diêm, 28–29
disabled, 7, 13–14, 71–72, 133, 135. *See also* accident
discontinuity, 93
disruptions, 59–63
distributed personhood, 70–71, 98–99
districts, xxiv. *See also* Andong Meas district
doctor, 131–32
documents, 64
dog, 14–15
dog tags, 96, 97, 197–98
Douglas, Mary, 81
Dourisboure, Pierre, 21–22
Dournes, Jacques, xii, xviii, xix, 3, 6, 19; on afterworld, 122; on breaking of objects, 117; cemetery and, 120; on clothing, 11; on continuity, 204; on dead, 123; on discontinuity, 93; on effigies, 143; on fabric weaving, 169; on moon, 178n1; on person, 24–25; on plants, 7–8; on risk, 84; on sculptures, 180; on stranger, 30–31
Dovert, Stéphane, 9, 19, 23, 24–25, 29, 120
dreams (*pleboh*), xxi, 18, 127–28, 159–65, 162f, 203–4
dressing, 9–15
driang (violent deaths), 124–35
drinking ban, 190
Drit, 205, 209
driver, 70, 133
Dzo (deacon), 22

economics, 86–94
effigies (*rup*), 8, 123, 136, 141–44, 148; of helicopter, 149–50; Siu bringing, 179–80

elephants, 48, 147
embarrassment, 63–68
empty sacrifice (*sein teute*), 126, 128
enemy (*ayat*), 30–31
entrepreneurs, French, 38
environment (*parethan*), 3, 4, 7, 16
ethnic brothers and sisters (*bong pa-on chun chiet*), xvii
ethnic minorities, xv–xix, 21, 24–30, 38, 41–52, 67. *See also* Hmong; Jorai ethnic minority
ethnic-minority villages, xx–xxi, xxiv, 8–9, 16–17, 38n3. *See also* Plói Leu, Cambodia
ethnonyms, xviii, xxv–xxvi
Evangelical Fellowship of Cambodia (EFC), 188–90, 192, 193, 194
event, 52–63, 73
evil forest, 7–9, 15. *See also* yang
experience, 170–71, 202
explosion, 70, 71
explosive remnants of war (ERW), xiii–xiv, xxii–xxiii, 52, 81–84, 83f, 94–95. *See also* accident; bomb hunter; bomb hunting; land mines; distributed personhood, 98–99; IEDs as, 69; Leu and, 58–59, 86–87; as past persistence, 99; survivors maimed by, 69; villagers on, 58–59
extortion, 25–26

families, 15, 22, 28, 49–50, 91. *See also* kin
farming. *See* agriculture
fashion trends, 197–98
fathers, 134–35, 202–3
fear (*klach*), 193–94
females, xx, 203–4. *See also* girls; women; carving of, 161–65, 162f; on gatherings, 180–81; informants, 203–4; village elder, 111–23, 112f; villagers, 4, 31–32
Ferguson, James, 82
figurines, 141
fines, 25–26, 142
firearm (*phao*), 22–23
fishing, ERW for, 81
flu epidemic, 159–60
food, in household, 77–78
foreigner (*ga gagn*), 30–32, 41, 73, 97–98, 100–108
forest (*glai*), 4–9, 44–45, 58, 121, 125, 131; as evil, 15; insane reuniting with, 12–14
formidable object, 95–96, 141–44

Fortes, Meyer, 31, 207
Foucault, Michel, 82, 205
Fox Indians, 183
fractal personhood, 99
French, xxii, xxvi, 21–22, 37–41, 44–45; gold mining of, 38n3; missionaries, 101
French-Jarai lexicon, xxv–xxvi
Front Uni National pour un Cambodge Indépendant, Neutre, Pacifique, Et Coopératif (FUNCINPEC), 52n14
funerals, 48–49, 62, 111–23, 112*f*, 125, 140–41. *See also* effigies; sculptures; Blen on, 182–83; during KR period, 126; Ksor on, 185; Siu avoiding, 186–87; for violent death, 131–35
funerary monument (*pósat atâo*), 153–58, 154*f*, 156*f*
Fyfe, Henry, 54

ga gagn (foreigner), 30–32, 41, 73, 97–98, 100–108
ga gnao (stranger), xxiv–xxv, 23–25, 30–32, 100, 108, 207. *See also* foreigner
gasoline inflation, 79
gatherings, 180–81, 187–88, 190–91
gecko (*pŏķe*), 151, 152–53, 152*f*
Geertz, Clifford, 32–33
Gell, Alfred, 70–71, 98–99, 143, 172–73, 208
gendered space, 191
ghosts (*atâo*), 5, 31, 106–7, 108, 113, 118–19; kin tormented by, 183; soul visible through, 127–28
gifts, 35–37
girls, 10, 180, 197, 199
glai 7, 16, 105, 123–25. *See also* forest
global crisis, 78–80
God (*Ŏi Adei*), 15, 188, 189, 193–94
Godelier, Maurice, 32
gods (*preah*), 53–57, 59–61, 149
gold mining, 38n3
gourds, 161–65, 162*f*
Gourou, Pierre, 2
governmentality, 81
Goy, Bertrand, xxvi
grandfathers, 18, 201
grandmother, 114
grave, 113–18, 122–23, 127, 136–38
Green Berets. *See* Special Forces, US

Gregorian calendar, 65–66, 69
Guérin, Mathieu, 16, 17, 24, 28, 29, 33; on Christianity, 188; on ethnic minority deaths, 50; on total war, 49–50
guerrillas, 42–45
guides, 42, 171
Gustafsson, Mai Lan, 183

habitus, 87
hair, 14, 197
Ha My, Vietnam, 126–27, 129
Hardy, Andrew, xx
Harrison, Simon, 12, 106
Hawaiians, 55–56
Hawley, Thomas, 102
H'Bia, 15
Hbit, 203–4
headless societies. *See* acephalous societies
healers, 48. *See also* Kluen; shaman
Hebrei, 114
helicopters, 56, 136, 137, 149–50
Hertz, Robert, 114–16, 126
Hickey, Gerald, 49
highlanders, 24, 29–30, 43, 49, 50–51, 207. *See also* Ratanakiri province
highland minorities. *See* ethnic minorities
Historical Dictionary of the Peoples of the Southeast Asian Massif (Michaud), xxvi
history. *See also* event; aide-mémoire, 39–40; bombing as, 52–63; narratives, 63–73; objects, 99; of others, 73; overview, 35–52; perceptual, 73; Rosaldo on, 72
Hlany, 203–4
hlăt (caterpillar), 151, 152–53, 152*f*
Hmong, 56, 163–64
hnim (clothing), 9–15, 28, 197–98
Ho Chi Minh Trail, xi, 43, 52–63, 68–69, 94
home, 105–7
L'homme des Jarai. *See* Dournes, Jacques
homo faber (working man), 5–6, 94
household, xxii–xxiii, 77–80, 85, 87–88, 89. *See also* families
houses (*sang*), 5, 7, 78, 180, 198–99; of husband, 121; of master of element, 20; wife moving into, 121
Huard, Paul, 138–39
Huey gunship, 137

humans; animals separated from, 11, 12, 14; black dog creating, 15; death worth of, 122; forest set apart from, 4–7; nature's relationships with, 1, 2–3, 16; woman creating, 15
Humphrey, Caroline, 130
hunt, of buffalo, 139–40
hunter (*mötah*), 5, 12–13, 140. *See also* bomb hunter
hunter-gatherers, 3, 58
hunting, 102–8, 201. *See also* bomb hunting
husband, 121, 124, 204
hwa (orchard), 32, 203
hybridism, 12–13, 19–20

identity, 32, 115, 198
ideology, 42, 44–46, 48–51
illiteracy, 26–27, 54
illness, 159–60
Ilongots, 72–73
images, death associated with, 142–43, 179–80
immediate-return system, 3
improvised explosive devices (IEDs), 69
Indians, 141, 183
indigenous peoples, xv–xvi
individual, 81, 85
Indochina, 21, 37
inflation, 78–80
informants, xxiii–xxiv, xxvi, 12–15, 18–19, 103–4, 131–32. *See also* Blen, Luyin; Lagn, Ban; Nay; Siu; on dreams, 127–28; EFC, 188–90, 192, 193, 194; on effigy, 141–42; female, 203–4
Ingold, Tim, 1, 90–91, 140, 174
insane (*möhlŭn* or *ving*), 10, 12–14
insurgents, 42–45, 56
integration, 27–30, 41–43

Japanese, 8, 22, 41, 164
Jarai-French lexicon, xxv–xxvi
Jorai ethnic minority. *See also* Plói Leu, Cambodia; as anarchic, xix; belief system of, xix; in Cambodia, xii, xviii–xix; *chonchiet*, xvii; forest loathed by, 6; language, xxiii, xxv; literature on, xix–xx; orthography, xxv–xxvi; overview, xiv–xv, xxvi–xxix; political repression influencing, xviii; in Vietnam, xii, xviii–xix; as warlike, xviii

Jorai Kampuchea, xviii–xix
Jorai Vietnam, xviii–xix

Kachok, 22
Kampuchea, 29, 45–46, 51–52
Kansteiner, Wolf, 170
karma, disabled influenced by, 133
Khloy, Thol, 50, 57
Khmerization, 27–30, 41–43
Khmer Kandal (central Khmer). *See* Khmers
Khmer Krom, 27
Khmer Leu, xvii, 27–28
Khmer Rouge (KR), 18, 43–52, 57, 67, 69, 182. *See also* Pot, Pol; administration, 70–71; funeral during, 126; land mines, 98; rituals banned by, 59–60; soldiers, 66–68, 70, 98
Khmers (*chonchiet Kmay*), xvi, xxiii, xxv, xxvi, 25–30, 41–43; king, 35–37; land prospectors, 165; preachers, 193–94; tourist guides, 171
Kiernan, Ben, 50
kimono, 164
kin, xviii–xix, xx, 12, 80, 111–13, 183
king (*samdech*), 35–37, 68
king of fire (*pötao apui*), 20–21, 35–37
king of water (*pötao ia*), 35–37
kinsman (*maabi*), 31
Kissinger, Henry, 64
klach (fear), 193–94
klay. *See* sacrifice post
Kluen, 17, 19, 80, 132
knife, 88, 131–32
knowledge, 4–9, 204
koma klahang (strong children), 47
Kondo, Dorinne, 150
Kontum, Vietnam, 104
Kopytoff, Igor, 172–74
Kravet, 22
Kreung, 22, 38, 48, 117
Ksor, Pou, 22, 61, 69; on accident, 132–33; on conversion, 184–86; deaths influencing, 186; forearm of, 71; on funerals, 185; on MIA, 104, 105, 107–8; on risk, 185–86; on rituals, 185–86, 187; on sacrifices, 111, 129–30, 132–33; on Siu, 66, 185–86; syncretism suggested by, 187; on total war, 49; on unburied dead, 129–30; on young people, 187
Kwon, Heonik, xxiv, 106; on bad death, 125; on ghosts, 107, 108; on massacres, 126–27, 129

Lafont, Pierre-Bernard, 111, 114, 122, 138
Lagn, Ban, 57, 128
la hot (medical plant leaf), 151, 152–53, 152*f*
Laidlaw, James, 130
la khda (leaf), 151, 152–53, 152*f*
land, 9, 38, 100, 120, 165
land mines, xiii–xiv, 7, 69, 70, 71, 98. *See also* accident; demining; disabled
landscape, 59, 69, 87
languages, xxiii, xxv, xxvi, 63–68, 193. *See also* translations
Lao, xvii, 19
Laos, xiii–xiv, 67, 87, 88. *See also* Ho Chi Minh Trail; belongings appropriated in, 97; Cambodia as part of, 38; geomorphological variations, xvii; helicopters flown to, 56; as refuge, 49; reuse in, 95; shaman in, 105; US flying to, 56
Lao Soung, xvii
Lap, Siu, xxv–xxvi, 5
Lawrence-Zúñiga, Denise, 199, 209
leaf (*la khda* or *la hot*), 151, 152–53, 152*f*
leaflets, 54
Leclère, Adhémard, 36, 37
Lee, Jack, 172
leg, 71
Leu, Cambodia. *See* Plói Leu, Cambodia
Leu Krong, Cambodia, xxi, xxii
Leu Pok, Cambodia, xx
Lévi-Strauss, Claude, 183
Lewis, Norman, 21, 33, 188, 193
liberated zones, 45
lieux de mémoire (sites of memory), 174
life, continuity ensured in, 118–22. *See also* afterlife
lifestyles, 24
liminality, 125
linguists, 192
literacy, 54–55
literature, on Jorai, xix–xx
liturgical texts, 191–94
livelihood, xxi–xxiii, 78–80, 85, 89
Locard, Henri, 38. *See also* Phuon, Phi
loincloth (*tuai blah*, *peung*, or *suu troany*), 10, 28
Lom, Cambodia, 189
longhouses, 78
Lono, 55–56
Low, Setha, 199, 209

Luagn, Sol, 18
luk tek (bombs), 60, 68–69, 91, 93–94, 99. *See also* accident

maabi (kinsman), 31
makers, 169–74
males, xx, 31–32, 85, 90, 159–60, 181. *See also* boys; men
Malinowski, Bronislaw, xxv
malnutrition, 50–51
man-machine, 71
manufacturing, 165–74, 167*f*
marines, 126–27
marriage, 15, 28, 197, 203–4
massacres, 126–27, 129
Master (*potao*), 15
master of element (*pötao*), 13, 19–21
master of fire (*pötao apui*), 20–21, 35–37
materiality, 98–99, 194–204
medical plant leaf (*la hot*), 151, 152–53, 152*f*
Mek, Cambodia, 159–60
Melanesian societies, 141
memories, 162*f*, 165–74, 167*f*; ethics of, 149; funerary monument as site of, 153–58, 154*f*, 156*f*; of war, 69; work, 174
men, 6, 10, 14, 28, 113, 117. *See also* father; hunter; husband; working man
Merleau-Ponty, Maurice, 71
meta-ethnic groups, xvii
metal, 86, 87–88, 94–95, 97, 103. *See also* salvage
metamorphosis, 194–204
Meyer, Charles, xviii, 35–36
Michaud, Jean, xix, xxi–xxii, xxvi, 159
Milhaupt, Terry, 164
Mills, Barbara, 174
mine-action sector, 81–84, 83*f*
ming (aunt), 25
missing-in-action (MIA), 102–8
missionaries, xxii, xxv–xxvi, 21–22, 37, 101, 188–94
mission civilisatrice, 29
Mlu-Mlia River, 114
mnemonic functions, 146–49
mobile phones, 195–96
modernity, 194–204
móhlŭn (insane), 10, 12–14
monastery, 35–37
Mondulkiri province, 38, 41, 48, 171–74

226   Index

montages, 198–99
montagnard, 29
monument, funeral, 153–58, 154f, 156f
moon, 178n1
moral blame, 81
moral economy, 76–77
Morrison, Gayle, 73
mötah (hunter), 5, 12–13, 140. See also bomb hunter
mothers, 10
motorcycles, 196–97
Mouhot, Henri, 44–45
multiplicity, 70–71
Munn, Nancy, 186
My Lai, Vietnam, 129
myths, 14–15, 27, 133–35

Naabdiya, 31
nakedness, 9–11, 12–14
naming, 9, 40, 55–57
narratives, 63–73, 202–3
nationality (*chonchiet*), xvi–xvii
National Liberation Front (NLF), 53
naturalists, 44–45
nature, 2–21. See also forest
Nay, 70, 90, 202, 203
Nayaka, 3, 58
necklaces, 97. See also dog tags
negative space, 186
neighbors, 23–25
nephews, 35–37
Nicolle, R., xxv
1970s, 41–43
1960s, 41–43
Nixon, Richard, 64
Nol, Lon, 43, 67
nonconverted, 181, 184–88
nongovernmental organizations (NGOs), 190–91
nonstate peoples, 21
nonstate space, xii–xiii
Nora, Pierre, 174
Norodom (king), 36–37
Northeastern Zone, 46, 48, 51
North Vietnam, 53
Norwegian People's Aid, xiii

objects, 94–99, 113–18, 135–44, 157–65, 162f, 198–99. See also carving; craftsmen; craftswomen; sculptures; bamboo as, 125; breaking of, 125; making, xxiv; war-associated, 168–74
O'Chheukrom, Cambodia, 94
Odend'hal, Prosper, 21, 37
Öi Adei (God), 15, 188, 189, 193–94
Operation Breakfast, 64
Operation Dinner, 64
Operation Lunch, 64
Operation Menu, 53, 64
orchard (*hwa*), 32, 203
ornamentation, xxiv, 136–38, 198–99
orthography, xxv–xxvi
otherness, 2, 23–25
others, 2, 21–33, 73, 200–201, 209
outsider. See stranger
O You Dav district, 153–58, 154f, 156f

Pacific, 141
Pao, Vang, 56
parachute, 97–98
paralysis, 183
parethan (environment), 3, 4, 7, 16
Parry, Jonathan, 126
partible, 11–12, 99
parts, 70, 71
past, 63–73, 99, 202–3. See also history
pastor, 188
Paterson, Gordon, 17
Paysans de la forêt (Boulbet), 2–3
peasants, 76–78, 84
People's Republic of Kampuchea (PRK). See Kampuchea
People's Socialist Community. See Sangkum Reastr Niyum
perceptual history, 73
personal memory, 170–71
personhood, 1, 3, 10–12, 70–71, 98–99
persons, 12, 24–25
Petrarca, Francesco, 171
petroleum inflation, 78–80
Peuho, Cambodia, 153–58, 154f, 156f
peung (loincloth), 10
peutrang (power), 140–41
phantom limb, 71
phao (firearm), 22–23
Phnom Penh, Cambodia, 37, 64, 133, 197, 203
Phnong, 41

Phuon, Phi, 42–43, 45, 48–49
physical disruptions, 59–63
picture montages, 198–99
pipe (*tagn vach*, *aagn gnogn*, or *aagn prieuw*), 150–53, 152*f*
Plagn Tchu (coal), 32
plane (*sepol* or *Tchai Pol*), 52, 53–57, 61, 136, 137–42, 148–50; effigy, 148; on pipe, 151, 152–53, 152*f*; as scrap metal, 103; sorties, 64
plantations, 38, 165
plants, from forest, 7–8
pleboh (dreams), xxi, 18, 127–28, 159–65, 162*f*, 203–4
Plói Laom, Cambodia, 165–74, 167*f*
Plói Leu, Cambodia, 111–23, 112*f*, 138–41, 146–53, 152*f*, 194–201. *See also* villagers; activities, xxi–xxiv; bomb hunting in, 90–91; Christianity converted to in, 177–88; decree influencing, 46, 48; ERW and, 58–59, 86–87; ethnonyms, xviii; forest's relationship with, 3, 7; global crisis repercussions on, 78–80; livelihood strategy, xxi–xxiii, 78–80; location, xi–xiii, xx–xxi, 4, 68–69; narratives of, 63, 65–66, 68–73; overview, xx–xxiii, *xxi*; planes encountered by, 56; sides changed by, 61; social structures, xx; war and, 63, 65–66, 68–73, 94–95
Plói Leu Krong, Cambodia, 139–40
Plói Phdol Krom, Cambodia, 90, 92
Plói Tang Chiet, Cambodia, 47
pŏčah (breaking of objects), 117–18, 125
pojah (abandonment of grave), 122–23
pŏjau (shaman), 12, 13, 18–19, 105, 182
pŏke (gecko), 151, 152–53, 152*f*
political economy, 77
Popkin, Samuel, 76
pösat (cemetery), 120, 135–38, 147–48. *See also* elephants
pösat atâo (funerary monument), 153–58, 154*f*, 156*f*
Postert, Christian, xvii, 209
postwar economics, 86–94
Pot, Pol, 42–43, 44–46, 48–51, 67, 70–71. *See also* bodyguard; Phuon, Phi; ethnic minorities displaced under, 28; as king, 68
potao (Master), 15
pötao (master of element), 13, 19–21

pötao apui (master of fire or king of fire), 20, 35–37
pötao ia (king of water), 35–37
power (*peutrang*), 140–41
preachers, 193–94
preah (gods), 53–57, 59–61, 149
Preah Vihar, Cambodia, 69
prĭn tha. *See* village elders
propitiating ceremony. *See* sacrifices
provincial gatherings, 190–91
purges, 45–46, 48–51
purity, 44–46, 48–51

Raglai, 188
raids, 22–23
Rambo, 200–201
Ranariddh (prince), 52n14
Ratanakiri province, xii–xiv, xxiii–xxiv, 43–52, 165–74, 167*f*, 176. *See also* Banlung, Cambodia; Ho Chi Minh Trail; Plói Leu, Cambodia; bombing map of, 83*f*; missionary activities in, 189; phone cost in, 196; plantations in, 38
rebellion, 43
recycling, 94–95
religious practices, ban on, 48–49. *See also* funeral; rituals
remains, 102–8
reparation, 92, 107
Republic of Korea (ROK) marines, 126–27
research, xiii–xiv, xxiii–xxiv
restitutive giving, 12
retrieval, 94–95
reuse, 94–95
Reznick, Jeffrey, 71
Rhade, 21, 193
rice, 79–80
Ricoeur, Paul, 149
risk, 76–77, 81–94, 83*f*, 103–5, 185–86, 197
Risk Revisited (Caplan), 85
rituals, 8, 16–17, 48–49, 128–30, 133, 135. *See also* funeral; sacrifices; adjusting, 111–23, 112*f*; for disabled, 7; KR banning, 59–60; Ksor on, 185–86, 187; MIA, 102, 104; for objects, 98; specialists, 102, 106–7
river, 60
Ro, Hiom, 45
roads, 38, 40

Rosaldo, Renato, 72
rup. *See* effigies

saan (stranger), xxiv–xxv, 23–25, 30–32, 100, 108, 207. *See also* foreigner
sacred, 16
sacrifice post (*klay*), 92, 111, 112*f*, 138–41
sacrifices, 17, 48, 92, 131–35, 138–41, 183; Blen on, 50, 181–82; as empty, 126, 128; Ksor on, 111, 129–30; for planes, 53–54, 55
safety, 76, 80
Sahlins, Marshall, 3, 52, 55–56
Salemink, Oscar, 177
salvage, xxii–xxiii, 87
Sambok, 35–37
samdech. *See* king
Sami, 114
sang. *See* houses
sangkriem. *See* war
sangkriem total (total war), 49–51, 61–63
Sangkum Reastr Niyum, 27–30, 41–52
Saunders, Nicholas, 54, 59, 126, 198
Scandinavia, 114
Schneider, Jane, 11
school, 8–9
Scott, James, xii–xiii, xxi, 21, 27, 28, 76; on highlanders, 207; on script, 54; on taxes, 37–38
scrap metal, 87–88, 94–95, 97, 103. *See also* salvage
scripts, 26–27, 54
sculptures, 135–44, 146–53, 152*f*, 159–60, 179–80
security, 76–77
sein teute (empty sacrifice), 126, 128
self, 198–99, 202–4, 205, 209
self-governing peoples, xxi–xxiii, 2
Sen, Hun, 52n14
sepol. *See* plane
servants of dead, 143
Sesan River, xx–xxi, 10
settlers, 41
shaman (*pöjau*), 12, 13, 18–19, 105, 182
Shawcross, William, 43, 53, 64
Sheehan, Neil, 105
shirt, 98
Short, Philip, 45
Siem Reap, xiii
Sihanouk, Norodom, xvii, 27–30, 41–43, 44, 46
Sikoeun, Suong, 45
Simmel, Georg, 30, 100, 108, 197

Sing, 166–71, 167*f*, 173
sites of memory (*lieux de mémoire*), 174
Siu, 13, 14, 15, 19, 23, 194; aunt helping, 25; on Blen, 183, 184; as Christian, 179–80, 190–91; on conversion, 179–80; cousin of, 198; daughter of, 180; on death, 121; effigies brought by, 179–80; funeral avoided by, 186–87; at gathering, 190–91; house of, 180, 199; knowledge of, 204; Ksor on, 66, 185–86; on master of element, 20; on phone, 195; on planes, 138; on sculpture, 136; sculptures of, 179–80; son of, 205, 209; on Tampuon, 24; wife of, 124–25, 191, 199; as wood carver, 147, 149–53, 152*f*, 209
skirts, 10
slaves, families as, 22
snake, 19
social hierarchy, 193
social life, 94–99, 172–74
social skin, 197
social space, 80
social structures, xx
sociology of space, 197
soldiers, 12, 41, 59, 61, 202–3; belongings of, 97–98; dog tags of, 96, 97, 197–98; KR, 66–68, 70, 98; MIA, 102–8; remains, 102–8; US, 20–21, 96, 97–98, 102–8, 197–98, 200–201; Vietnamese, 106–7
son, 134–35, 205, 209
song, 62
soul (*böngat*), 16–18, 105–7, 113, 116, 120, 127–30; of bomb hunter, 92; as free, 123
southern Pacific, 141
South Vietnam, 28–29, 43
South Vietnamese, 53
Soviet Union, 172–73
space, sociology of, 197
Special Forces, US, 53
spectator, 172–73
spirits (*yang* or *areak*), 5, 8–9, 15–21, 58–61, 91–94, 97. *See also* ghosts; sacrifices; fee paid to, 123; funeral influencing, 119, 125; God included among, 188; plane as, 142; villagers on, 135
Srok Ayonapar, 35–37
Stallone, Sylvester, 200–201
stranger (*toäie*, *ga gnao*, or *saan*), xxiv–xxv, 23–25, 30–32, 100, 108, 207. *See also* foreigner

Index

Strathern, Marilyn, 11, 99
strong children (*koma klahang*), 47
S-21 detention center, 133
subsistence, xxii, 76–77, 85
suicide, 124–25
Sulawesi, 115
superhuman power (*yang*), 31
survival, 76–85, 87. *See also* risk
survivors, 57–59, 58, 61, 69, 201–3
suu troany (loincloth), 10, 28
swidden agriculture, 51–52, 78
Swift Society, 192
sword, 21, 36
syncretism, 187, 188–89

tagn vach (pipe), 150–53, 152*f*
Tallensi, 31
Tampuon, xxiv, 24, 38, 117, 165–74, 167*f*
Tang, Cambodia, 97–98
Taussig, Michael, 141
taxes, 25–26, 37–38, 40
Tchai Pol. See plane
technology of self, 205
television (TV) sets, 200–201
texts, 73, 191–94
Thailand, xiii, 67, 78, 88, 164, 200
Tham, 88, 91
Than, 13–14
Theravada Buddhism, 187
things, 12, 95–96, 141–44, 172–74, 194–201
Thoeun, 141–42
Thomas, Nicholas, 143
tigers, 4, 5
time, 63–68, 129, 178n1
toäie (stranger), xxiv–xxv, 23–25, 30–32, 100, 108, 207. *See also* foreigner
tooth filing, 14
Toraja, 115
torture, 67
total war (*sangkriem total*), 49–52, 61–63
Touch, 103–4
tourism market, 165–74, 167*f*
trader, 18, 103
transition, 125
translations, xxvi, 192–94
travel, 6, 196–97
trench art, 137
trinomial model, xvii
tuai blah (loincloth), 10

Tuol Sleng, 133
Turner, Victor, 197

unburied dead, 125–30
unexploded ordnance (UXO). *See* explosive remnants of war
Union of Soviet Socialist Republics (USSR), 172–73
United Nations Transitional Authority in Cambodia (UNTAC), 148, 157–58
United States (US), 56. *See also* bombardments; ambassador, 102; MIA, 102–8; soldier, 20–21, 96, 97–98, 102–8, 197–98, 200–201; Vietnam War wounding, 102

van der Veer, Peter, 204–5
van Gennep, Arnold, 101, 125
Vargyas, Gábor, 96
Veam, 111–23, 112*f*, 140–41
victim discourse, 81–84, 83*f*
Vietminh guerrillas, 42
Vietnam, xxv–xxvi, 37, 49, 53, 104, 188. *See also* Central Highlands; Ho Chi Minh Trail; belongings appropriated in, 97; Cambodia importing from, 78; Cambodia linked with, 38, 40; ethnic minorities in, xix; Jorai in, xii, xviii–xix; massacre in, 126–27, 129; master of element in, 19; political repression in, xviii; rice and, 79, 80; ritual specialists in, 102; scrap metal sold in, 88; South, 28–29, 43
Vietnamese, 14, 28–29, 53, 56–57, 67; Cambodia invaded by, 51–52; soldiers, 106–7
Vietnam War, xxvi, 43, 102–8, 137, 200–201. *See also* bombardments; Ho Chi Minh Trail
village elders (*prĭn tha*), xxi, xxii, 85, 132, 183, 201. *See also* Blen, Luyin; Kluen; Ksor, Pou; on afterlife, 121–22, 191; on bombardment, 63; on ceremonies, 119, 176–77; on Christianity, 191; on conversion, 181; death of, 139–40; on dog tags, 198; female, 111–23, 112*f*; on forest, 4, 8–9, 58, 121; on funeral, 113, 119, 120; on gods, 61; on longhouses, 78; on parachute, 97–98; on planes, 56, 61, 148–49; on rice-wine jars, 48; on ritual, 133; on school, 8, 9; on shaman, 19; on spirits, 8–9, 92; stranger feared by, 32; on warriors, 22

villagers, xviii–xix, xx–xxiii, 4–9, 31–32, 72–73, 85. *See also* disabled; household; informants; Jorai ethnic minority; risk; shaman; survival; survivors; afterworld representation of, 121–22; bombs perceived by, 93; as corporate-driven, 77; on dead, 131; doctor as, 131–32; on ERW, 58–59; ERW influencing, 82, 84; foreigner known by, 41; illiteracy of, 54; on KR, 51; as nonconverted, 181, 184–88; photo, *xxi*; as risk-averse, 77; scrap metal sold by, 88; social space of, 80; soul of, 17–18; on spirits, 135; total war ran away from by, 49–50
villages, 5, 22–23, 49, 119, 133–35, 176. *See also* ethnic-minority villages; Plói Leu, Cambodia; Laom, 165–74, 167*f*; Tampuon, 24, 159–60, 165–74, 167*f*; Tang, 97–98; total war influencing, 50–52
ving (insane), 10, 12–14
Vinn, 92–93
violent deaths (*driang*), 124–35
von Hindenburg, Paul, 54

Wai, 114, 148, 177–79, 184, 190–91
war (*blah ngã* or *sangkriem*), xxiv, 22, 49–52, 56, 61–73, 201–3. *See also* bombardments; Vietnam War; Afghan rugs of, 172–73; economics after, 86–94; objects associated with, 94–99, 138–44, 157–58, 168–74, 198; sculptures, 135–44, 159–60; trophies, 12, 97, 144
warriors, 21–23

water, 60, 161–65, 162*f*
weaving, 165–71, 167*f*, 172–73
Weiner, Annette, 11
wells, 60
Western culture, 199
White, Joanna, xvi, xvii, 8–9, 28, 40–41, 48; on kin, 80; on KR, 51–52; on planes, 136
wife, 117, 121, 124–25, 178–79, 204; of Blen, 182, 183; of Siu, 191, 199
Wildavsky, Aaron, 81
women, 6, 10, 15, 17, 85. *See also* girls; wife
Woodburn, James, 3
wood carver. *See* Siu
wooden figurines, 141
working man (*homo faber*), 5–6, 94
world origin myths, 14–15
World Trade Center (WTC), 126
World Vision, 190–91
World War I (WWI), 54, 59, 71
World War II (WWII), 41, 141, 164
writing. *See* scripts

yang (superhuman power), 7–9, 15, 31. *See also* spirits
Yeak Laom district, 165–74, 167*f*
years, 65–66, 69
Yeng, Pou, 69, 71
young people, 187–88, 197–98, 202–4
young self, 202–4

Zomia, xii–xiii, 2, 21, 28

CPSIA information can be obtained
at www.ICGtesting.com
Printed in the USA
LVHW091957050419
613140LV00008B/62/P

9 781501 703034